T0340349

Fitch and Motion have produced a creative and exciting volume, combining personal, scholarly and professional insights to offer a much needed critical account of the contemporary impact of public relations. Taking on such complex and diverse issues as social justice, gendered occupations, and political subjectivities, Fitch and Motion bring to light the many ways that public relations is a cultural force in our lives. Highly recommended for students and scholars of cultural studies, media theory, and organizational communication.

Dr Melissa Aronczyk, Associate Professor,
School of Communication & Information,
Rutgers University, USA

Fitch and Motion provide a fascinating journey through some of the most visible forms of contemporary cultural life, from fashion to political struggle, zombies to protest songs, and reveal the ways in which public relations permeates these worlds. In a hopeful narrative of potential change, they show the deep connections between the communicative power of mediated popular culture and the impact it has on the ways we understand the world. This is an important book that takes public relations scholarship further by seeking its presence in unexpected places, among unexpected people, and asking how and why it matters for our future.

Dr Lee Edwards, Associate Professor,
Department of Media and Communications,
London School of Economics and Political Science, UK

Academics have not paid much attention to the role of PR in shaping popular culture. It is one of those territories that has not attracted researchers because it is surely frivolous or because of a pernicious organizational-centred perspective of public relations. However, thanks to this book we can go into this, until now, dark side of public relations and discover a fundamental dimension to better understanding the field and capturing a public relations reality, different from the dominant one we can find in the traditional literature. The holistic approach that the authors have given to the subject turns this book into a fundamental text of a new critical thinking of public relations, where the daily life of the social body is not at odds with scholarship. In sum, a must read for everybody interested in how public relations works beyond its corporate function.

Dr Jordi Xifra, Professor,
Department of Communication,
Pompeu Fabra University, Spain

This book is one of few to locate public relations under the lens of cultural studies, and its intersectional concerns. Fitch and Motion ask: 'How would our lives differ if there were no public relations?' The resulting discussion is both reflexive and nuanced, as the authors explore various international campaigns to promote identity, self-determination and social justice across cultural, political and environmental realms. The book will be of interest to a wide range of disciplines; including media and communications studies, cultural studies, gender studies, critical race studies, discourse studies; as well as advertising, marketing, public relations, and political communication.

Dr Clea Bourne, Senior Lecturer,
Department of Media, Communications and
Cultural Studies, Goldsmiths, University of London, UK

Popular Culture and Social Change

Popular Culture and Social Change: The Hidden Work of Public Relations argues the complicated and contradictory relationship between public relations, popular culture and social change is a neglected theoretical project. Its diverse chapters identify ways in which public relations influences the production of popular culture and how alternative, often community-driven conceptualisations, of public relations work can be harnessed for social change and in pursuit of social justice.

This book opens up critical scholarship on public relations in that it moves beyond corporate understandings and perspectives to explore alternative and eclectic communicative cultures, in part to consider a more optimistic conceptualisation of public relations as a resource for progressive social change. Fitch and Motion began with an interest in identifying the ways in which public relations both draws on and influences the production of popular culture by creating, promoting and amplifying particular narratives and images. The chapters in this book consider how public relations creates popular cultures that are deeply compromised and commercialised, but at the same time can be harnessed to advocate for social change in supporting, reproducing, challenging or resisting the status quo.

Drawing on critical and sociocultural perspectives, this book is an important resource for researchers, educators and students exploring public relations theory, strategic communication and promotional culture. It investigates the entanglement of public relations, popular culture and social change in different social, cultural and political contexts – from fashion and fortune telling to race activism and aesthetic labour – in order to better understand the (often subterranean) societal influence of public relations activity.

Kate Fitch is Senior Lecturer in Communication and Media Studies in the School of Media, Film and Journalism at Monash University in Melbourne, Australia, where she coordinates the public relations specialisation. She previously worked at Murdoch University, where she founded the public relations major and chaired the program for 10 years. Her book, *Professionalizing Public Relations: History, Gender and Education*, offered the first sociological history of Australian public relations in the twentieth century. Her research interests and publications span critical public relations perspectives on gender, history, promotional and contemporary culture.

Judy Motion is Professor of Communication in the Environmental Humanities group at the University of New South Wales, Sydney, Australia. Judy's most recent research focuses on public discourse, sense making and change in relation to environmental issues and controversies. Past research has included discourse and identity in organizational change, power and resistance in the implementation of new technologies and the influence of public relations on policy formation. Her latest book, *Social Media and Public Relations: Fake Friends and Powerful Publics*, co-authored with Robert L. Heath and Shirley Leitch, was awarded the Outstanding Book Award in 2016 by the National Communication Association, USA.

Routledge New Directions in PR & Communication Research
Edited by Kevin Moloney

Current academic thinking about public relations (PR) and related communication is a lively, expanding marketplace of ideas and many scholars believe that it's time for its radical approach to be deepened. **Routledge New Directions in PR & Communication Research** is the forum of choice for this new thinking. Its key strength is its remit, publishing critical and challenging responses to continuities and fractures in contemporary PR thinking and practice, tracking its spread into new geographies and political economies. It questions its contested role in market-orientated, capitalist, liberal democracies around the world, and examines its invasion of all media spaces, old, new, and as yet unenvisaged.

The **New Directions** series has already published and commissioned diverse original work on topics such as:

- PR's influence on Israeli and Palestinian nation-building
- PR's origins in the history of ideas
- a Jungian approach to PR ethics and professionalism
- global perspectives on PR professional practice;
- PR as an everyday language for everyone
- PR as emotional labour
- PR as communication in conflicted societies, and
- PR's relationships to cooperation, justice and paradox.

We actively invite new contributions and offer academics a welcoming place for the publication of their analyses of a universal, persuasive mindset that lives comfortably in old and new media around the world.

Popular Culture and Social Change
The Hidden Work of Public Relations
Kate Fitch and Judy Motion

For more information about this series, please visit: www.routledge.com/Routledge-New-Directions-in-Public-Relations–Communication-Research/book-series/RNDPRCR

Popular Culture and Social Change

The Hidden Work of Public Relations

Kate Fitch and Judy Motion

Routledge
Taylor & Francis Group

LONDON AND NEW YORK

First published 2021
by Routledge
2 Park Square, Milton Park, Abingdon, Oxon OX14 4RN

and by Routledge
52 Vanderbilt Avenue, New York, NY 10017

Routledge is an imprint of the Taylor & Francis Group, an informa business

British Library Cataloguing-in-Publication Data
A catalogue record for this book is available from the British Library

Library of Congress Cataloging-in-Publication Data
Names: Fitch, Kate, author. | Motion, Judy, author.
Title: Popular culture and social change : the hidden work of public
    relations / Kate Fitch and Judy Motion.
Description: New York : Routledge, 2020. | Series: Routledge new
    directions in PR & comm research | Includes bibliographical
    references and index.
Subjects: LCSH: Popular culture. | Public relations. | Social change.
Classification: LCC HM621 .F58 2020 (print) | LCC HM621
    (ebook) | DDC 306—dc23
LC record available at https://lccn.loc.gov/2020018941
LC ebook record available at https://lccn.loc.gov/2020018942

ISBN: 978-1-138-70280-6 (hbk)
ISBN: 978-1-315-20351-5 (ebk)

Typeset in Galliard
by Apex CoVantage, LLC

Kate: For Hannah and Tobyn – stars, both of you – and Damian, for everything

Judy: For my wonderful family – Tony, Maddie and Alice – with all my love

Contents

Acknowledgements

This book was written with the support of many people and our respective universities.

Kate:

I thank Monash University for offering collegiality and support for the writing of this book, which I began while I was still working at Murdoch University. Changing jobs and moving interstate was disruptive and I am grateful to my colleagues in the Monash School of Media, Film and Journalism and to the many public relations scholars across the globe, with whom I have had the privilege to work and share ideas. I thank Jordi Xifra and Chris Tulloch for offering me the opportunity to be a visiting scholar at Universitat Pompeu Fabra in October 2017; my experiences in Barcelona led to Chapter 9 and reminded me why I research. I also thank Erich von Dietze for advice on ethics in relation to Chapter 9. A number of people offered useful feedback on draft chapters: thank you Lee Edwards, Therese Davis, Johanna Fawkes, Hannah Fitch-Rabbitt, Akane Kanai, Nneka Logan, Mariola Tárrega and Zala Volcic. Finally, a big thank you to Judy for suggesting we write this book – what a journey!

Judy:

I would like to thank all of my University of Waikato colleagues who started this public relations research journey with me – in particular, Shirley Leitch, Juliet Roper, C. Kay Weaver, Margalit Toledano, David McKie, Debashish Munshi and Ted Zorn – for their intellectual insights, warm friendships and lots of laughter. A heart-felt thank you to Robert Heath for his superb mentorship and wonderful conversations. I am deeply grateful to Jordi Xifra and David McKie for organising the Barcelona conference and Dejan Verčič, Krishnamurthy Sriramesh and Ana Tkalac Verčič for organising the Bledcom conference. These conferences sustained me and I engaged with so many clever and inspiring scholars at these conferences, including my co-author, Kate Fitch.

Finally, we want to acknowledge the Routledge publishing team, including Jacqueline Curthoys, Jess Harrison, Laura Hussey, Guy Loft and Matthew Ranscombe, for their patience and faith in this book: thank you. We also thank Umamaheswari Chelladurai for overseeing the production of our book.

1 Popularity, popular culture and public relations

Judy Motion and Kate Fitch

Introduction

Popular culture enlivens and enriches our everyday experiences in ways that are transient or lasting, pleasurable or distasteful, cool or uncool. It offers a contemporary cultural space where we learn the narratives, images and activities that are popular and meaningful for society. Behind the scenes, public relations efforts create, promote and amplify these popular culture experiences. It is a mutually beneficial relationship, but generally the efforts of public relations, which are organised around profit, remain invisible or subtle. Perhaps, for this reason, the relationship between public relations and popular culture is a neglected theoretical project. We are interested in identifying the ways in which public relations influences the production of popular culture – from covert, shady attempts to insert commercial or political imperatives into our everyday lives to a range of progressive challenges that seek to undermine the existing moral and social order.

Public relations here is conceived of as a complicated and pluralistic communicative and promotional endeavour. It is a set of practices rather than a narrowly defined occupation. Within a popular culture context, public relations can also operate as a transformational catalyst in its role as a socialisation machine, a normalising, legitimising mechanism and a mode of resistance that can be harnessed for resistance and contestation. It is involved in the production of culture and is simultaneously part of culture, and therefore not neutral (Edwards, 2015). Along with other critical scholars, we are interested in the institutional structures and processes through which knowledge is constructed (Pal & Dutta, 2008). We therefore attempt to rethink cultural and social competencies in public relations in relation to popular culture concerns. Such concerns offer insights into the ways in which popular culture may be mobilised to achieve positive social change. Thus, studying the relationship between popular culture and public relations will make a significant contribution to understanding how social and cultural practices take shape and the potential for transformation.

Popularity and popular culture

An exploration of what 'popular' means and how popularity occurs is a critical starting point for making sense of the relationship between popular culture and public relations. It is generally understood that if something is popular, it is widely liked and readily accessible. Definitions of 'popular' have evolved from notions of social power, political democracy and cultural production to notions of accessibility and likeability (Shiach, 2005). According to Shiach, contemporary definitions of 'popular' include: 'of the general public, suited to the needs, means, tastes or understandings of the general public, having general currency [and] commonly liked or approved' (2005, p. 61). These definitional shifts suggest a de-politicisation of the concept; however, Hall (1980) contends that ideological messages are encoded into popular texts, which we then interpret through the lens of our existing ideologies. Following Hall's line of reasoning, popularisation is inherently politicised and culturally constructed during meaning production and sense-making processes. In summation, 'the popular is political and sometimes pleasurable' (Jenkins, McPherson, & Shattuc, 2002, p. 23).

Popular culture integrates these notions of the popular, particularly around social power and cultural production. It is a multi-faceted, nebulous, catch-all term applied to the mass consumption of contemporary ideas, values and practices circulating within particular cultures. It is expressed through various modes such as entertainment, music, sports, media, fashion, technology and in our everyday lives. Popular culture counters or stands in opposition to high or elite culture. At the centre of its genealogy, popular culture has a focus on 'the everyday, the intimate, the immediate' (Jenkins et al., 2002, p. 3) and a concern with collective and egalitarian imperatives. The significance of insinuating the popular, the ordinary, the things that happen in our everyday lives, according to Stewart (2007) 'lies in the intensities they build and in what thoughts and feelings they make possible' (p. 3). She suggests that ordinary affects are more compelling than ideologies and more complex than symbolic meanings. This aligns with Williams' (1958) contention that culture is 'ordinary'. For civil society groups and activists, popular culture is an ordinary or everyday site for the production of 'new language, meanings and visions of the future' and 'a place to build community networks, and organizational models' (Duncombe, 2002, p. 8).

For public relations, popular culture is both a strategic resource for connecting with society and the product of promotional efforts. Gray argues that approaches to understanding promotional culture are too often reductive, focusing on exploitation, propaganda and superficiality rather than recognising its contributions to artistic endeavours (2010, p. 307). The blurred distinctions between popular culture and promotional culture have opened up opportunities for public relations to commodify and popularise our social, everyday practices while simultaneously normalising celebrity and entertainment cultures. However, these public relations efforts to popularise and commodify culture are not without resistance. Like all cultural sites, popular culture is a site for macro and micro politics. Popular culture is therefore a type of nexus, integrating everyday experiences with political concerns about collective, participatory and egalitarian imperatives and mass commodification and consumption. This nexus forms the focus of our interrogations into the relationships between public relations and popular culture.

Much of the scholarship on public relations in popular culture has explored the various ways in which public relations is represented, primarily in television and film and, more rarely, in novels. However, authors variously point to the 'failure' of such representations to portray the reality of the industry as if there is an external and stable reality (Fitch, 2015). In order to reframe the debate, we are interested in popular culture because of its potential for transgression and resistance. Precisely because popular culture is concerned with the everyday, and entangled with consumption and production, engaging with the intersection of popular culture and public relations allows us to explore the role of public relations in society in terms of producing, extending, and contesting dominant narratives that frame knowledge and understanding.

Popular culture and social change

This book is about how popular culture is mobilised through both professional and community-orientated public relations activities to influence and/or undermine social change. We acknowledge justified criticism of an assumed association with dissent and left-wing causes (see, for example, Moloney & McKie, 2016), but we are interested in a progressive social change that adopts social and environmental justice perspectives. What we mean by this is that our approach emphasises rights, fairness and equity. The public relations practices we examine here may be institutional efforts in defence of social and environmental progress or deployed by civil society to contest policies and practices that contravene social and environmental justice expectations. These forms of social change embrace activism and advocacy to advance issues of equity and justice.

Popular culture has the potential to be a critical, transformative and emancipatory space (Jenkins et al., 2002), in that it offers a sense-making space for citizens to represent and voice concerns in creative and ludic ways. Cultural forms of social critique are promoted to advocate for social, cultural and environmental justice. In particular, instances of cultural and creative resistance shape our concerns about how public relations can engage with popular and contemporary culture to change dominant political and social structures (Duncombe, 2002; Edwards & Hodges, 2011).

Our intent here is to understand how various forms of public relations attempt to outplay one another by rethinking public relations through the lens of cultural production and primarily focusing on how public relations is mobilised. The task of reconceptualising public relations has fallen largely to critical scholars who attempt to reimagine how public relations may act as a force for positive change in society. Public relations interventions in popular culture may offer an ideal opportunity to think through the complexities of various pursuits of social and cultural authority, integrity and justice; to discern multiple ways in which the dominance of sexism, racism and anti-environmentalism may be undermined and to understand how the importance and value of our everyday experiences may be reasserted within popular culture.

Public relations as hidden work

The work of public relations is often hidden, invisible, marginalised or behind the scenes; for example, Cutlip (1994) called public relations 'the unseen power' and Hartley (1992) referred to it as 'hidden work' (Fitch, 2017). Bourne (2016) argues that public relations works in the background to manage public conversations through, for example, media training of executives and framing or 'spinning' unpopular actions in ways designed to increase public acceptance or at least mitigate the damage. Similarly, Edwards notes that the 'behind the scenes' work of public relations, which primarily focuses on targeting journalists, means that there has been limited scholarly investigation into its cultural intermediary role or, subsequently, recognition of its quest for symbolic power, or of the ways in which public relations is intimately involved in meaning making and identity formation (2012, p. 439; see also L'Etang, 2006). Hobbs (2019) has documented the extensive resources lobbyists in the Australian mining and energy sectors draw on to develop emotive and targeted campaigns and manage issues 'under the radar'. We therefore do not always see the ways in which some public relations activity advances neoliberal agendas and the efforts that go into shaping sense and meaning making.

In a recent Australian Royal Commission, the banking sector was heavily criticised for its heavy investment in 'marketing their good social deeds' through glossy social impact, corporate responsibility and sustainability reports as their corporate conduct and governance was held to account (Alberici, 2018). Doing good (in social and environmental terms) did not negate the capacity to do bad. In the Australian banking sector, this included overcharging customers and even charging fees to dead customers. Writing on public relations and environmental risks, Demetrious described 'activities [that] were subterranean and unseen by the so called "publics" that PR sought to influence and control' (2016, p. 101). Some of this activity falls firmly within the domain of public relations, where the banks advance a neoliberal, profit-driven agenda and paradoxically aim to (re)frame their organisations within social and environmental agendas. These agendas co-exist.

We are not seeking to redeem public relations but rather to understand how public relations, as a set of social and cultural practices, is both used and useful for bringing about social change. Public relations, along with media, publicity and promotional industries, plays a significant role in shaping contemporary public culture (Hartley, 1992). We argue that public relations can be activated and/or harnessed for social good, and that this framing of the field is under-studied and under-theorised. We embrace the full range of public relations activity, beyond professional and occupational contexts, and note the techniques of public relations are widely adopted in contemporary promotional culture.

In contrast to the notion of public relations as hidden work, certain kinds of public relations work are highly visible. Publics willingly participate in promotional activity across, for example, celebrity, music, fashion, sport and entertainment sectors. Hartley argues that public relations (he uses the term 'publicity') is a necessary social institution that 'calls the public into being and doing':

> The quest for the public is not, or not only, a quest for a real collective of human bodies or organized populations 'real'; it is a quest for the discourses,

imaginings, and communicative strategies by means of which those populations might be recognized, organized, mobilized, and 'impressed', or even congregate to take collective action in their own name, the name of the public.

(1992, p. 122)

Publics, audiences and fans play a significant role in recognising, reproducing and willingly, even passionately, engaging with public relations activity (Hutchins & Tindall, 2015, 2016). They engage in 'sophisticated interpretative activity' that demonstrates 'playfulness' (Turner, 2013, p. 112). We seek, then, to explore these dynamics and contradictions between visible and invisible work, and how public relations activity might be harnessed by diverse social actors – and not just organisations – for positive social change.

Boundary riding

Popular culture offers an opportunity to learn about and engage with playful and creative forms of public relations in addition to the vital work on social problems and transformation. New modes of theorising public relations that situate it within a popular context require a form of boundary riding that opens up the borders between particular cultural ways of thinking and articulates alternatives. A boundary rider, originally someone who checked fences on sheep and cattle stations, is a term now used by sport commentators who work from the sidelines at Australian Rules Football and place audiences closer to the centre of the action. The act of boundary riding, in this book, is a mode of navigation, enquiry and review – tracing the storytelling that evolves from questioning the boundaries of our thinking about the complicated relationship between public relations and popular culture and its role in social change.

It is necessary to distinguish our notion of boundary riding as a mode of enquiry that allows us to excavate and explore the links between public relations, popular culture and social change from functionalist perspectives that argue public relations offers an important boundary-spanning role, in that practitioners cross internal/external boundaries to allow stakeholder perspectives to inform organisational decision making in order to achieve mutually beneficial outcomes (see, for example, Grunig, 1992). The term boundary spanning is not unique to public relations and has persisted in the business literature since at least the 1970s (Aldrich & Herker, 1977). Even critical scholars such as Holtzhausen (2000) build on this notion to argue that practitioners, alert to the imbalance in power relationships, should be the organisational activist and conscience in representing outside perspectives within.

Our interest is not in a somewhat artificial inside/outside boundary construction between an organisation and its environment. Instead, we are interested in boundary construction generally and, in particular, the role of public relations in that construction. Our boundaries are porous: public relations is not a two-way symmetrical, mutually beneficial practice, as conceptualised and evolved from the original Grunigian paradigm, but rather one where the boundaries between audiences/fans/publics and producers/practitioners/organisations/and others engaged in communicative activity are dynamic and increasingly blurred. We recognise audience agency and the significance of public relations in meaning making and identity construction. Whereas the original boundary rider was concerned with fencing in, it is through our navigation of these socially constructed boundaries that we can begin to decipher and excavate the visible and invisible impacts of public relations work. Our version of boundary riding, then, is concerned with tracing the storytelling of boundaries of thinking and concerned with the complicated reshaping between boundaries and culture as part of a quest to review, challenge, contest and (re)conceptualise public relations.

Book structure

Why are our understandings of the role of public relations in cultural production so narrow and restricted? What could a broader understanding of public relations offer to popular culture and the advancement of social change? These questions establish the conceptual arguments that guide the social, cultural and environmental justice themes explored in the following chapters. This book avoids a narrow understanding of public relations in order to consider its engagement with popular culture and its role in social change. Its goal is to provide rich analyses of public relations and meaning making in diverse cultural contexts ranging from popular culture to cultural resistance.

The book is organised into ten chapters that investigate markedly different aspects of public relations, popular culture and social change. There is no one methodology: many of the chapters are conceptual reflections, some are autoethnographic, and some draw on empirically grounded research.

Chapter 1: popularity, popular culture and public relations

In this opening chapter we introduce readers to contemporary understandings of what it means to be popular and explore how notions of popularity play out in the contexts of popular, promotional and participatory cultures. We engage with the challenge of attempting to encapsulate the myriad ways that trends, fads, fashions and moments capture our attention and become part of broader cultural contexts. As time, spaces and genres are navigated, popularity takes on multiple meanings. Often, popularity is associated with trivia, superficiality and frivolity – in other words, ephemera that is lacking in substance. Our intention here, however, is to mostly sidestep the more mundane aspects of popularity in order to develop a deeper critique of how popularity links to our concerns about global and local sociocultural and politico-economic issues. At the heart of these critiques is a reconceptualisation of the roles that public relations may play in the popularisation of particular popular culture trends.

Chapter 2: public relations in our everyday lives

This chapter applies an auto-ethnographic method to examine how public relations plays out in our everyday lives. It adapts the media trope of 'a day in the life of' to examine a series of anecdotes about mundane activities that take place over a weekend and offers a reflection on how public relations works in the shadows to influence these activities. By applying a Foucauldian 'technologies of the self' framework, it is possible to analyse how public relations strategies may function as part of a socialisation machine or, alternatively, allow for the exercise of individual agency. Awareness of how public relations machinations politicise, commodify or capture leisure through discursive frames and particular power relations is discussed in relation to a series of rights relating to information, identity, cultural sense making and autonomy. Modes of agency in this auto-ethnographical narrative play out as an embodied force, contingent preferences, civility and justice-oriented decision making.

Chapter 3: trending . . . fortune tellers, dream weavers and charlatans

The apparent randomness of popular trends needs to be considered in relation to broader sociocultural conditions and public relations practices that mediate popular culture. The conditions that give rise to trends may be part of a broader social fault line that impact upon professional public relations or they may be deliberately manufactured and driven. Within this chapter, the role of public relations in foresight trends is considered by drawing upon future studies to analyse and critique public relations approaches to a range of future trend forecasting. The chapter examines how a range of trends are discursively promoted and highlights some implications for public relations. A key promotional strategy identified in the chapter is mimesis – imitating already recognised and accepted approaches to popularisation. Mimesis, in public relations trend-setting efforts, functions as a type of sense-making shortcut or a substitute for authenticity and truth. The chapter also discusses a range of tactics, from forecasts and surveys to algorithms, in order to understand the public relations practices at play and analyse the value of these practices. The forecasting work undertaken by public relations is critiqued as part of a broader neoliberal agenda that prioritises consumption and invokes illusions of pleasure and desire rather than a sustainable and equitable society.

Chapter 4: undead PR: theorising public relations and popular culture

Recognising popular culture as a transformative and critical space, this chapter engages with the popular zombie trope, a key cultural motif in the twenty-first century. It identifies the use of zombies in public relations campaigns to highlight the cultural intermediary role of public relations. It also considers how the zombie offers an apt metaphor for exploring the links between public relations and neoliberalism. Precisely because the zombie is located at the threshold between life and death (Luckhurst, 2016), it is a useful device for crossing, navigating and investigating the construction of, boundaries and public relations' double game and entanglement with neoliberalism. It engages playfully with screen representations of zombies and public relations to highlight the constraints of professional rhetoric and construct other realities of the industry, recognising the inherent contradictions between professionalism, corporate social responsibility, ethics and the reality of neoliberalism and the market logic of the public relations industry.

Chapter 5: 'The PR girl': gender and embodiment in public relations

This chapter offers a feminist perspective on the construction of meanings in relation to the public relations occupation, by investigating socially mediated representations of the female practitioner through a corporeal lens. It illuminates a little discussed aspect of the professional identity of public relations: that of the body and the challenges for practitioners in negotiating gendered professional norms in terms of having 'the right look' to ensure occupational fit. The chapter draws on Mears' (2014) concept of aesthetic labour to analyse gendered and raced representations of practitioner bodies. The bodily images encapsulate very real tensions around professionalism (and therefore, gender) in public relations discourses. These tensions play out on the gendered representation of the body and in the disciplining of the female body in line with institutional norms in public relations. This chapter therefore identifies the significance of the virtual, mediated body in promotional work and explores how the gendered embodiment of public relations replicates sexual hierarchies and norms.

Chapter 6: fashionable ephemera, political dressing and things that matter

This chapter deals with the seemingly ephemeral nature of fashion to ask: what conditions, movements and connections form these modes of meaning production and sense making? How do particular instances of fashion signal what matters? What affective work are we called upon to enact and what are the possibilities for social change? Stories about the fashion choices made by leading women, including Michelle Obama, Melania Trump, Meghan Markle and Jacinda Ardern, are discussed and a reconsideration of the public relations efforts that influence the significance of fashion is offered. The chapter argues that the political importance of popular culture in influencing social change is that it acts as a vehicle for affecting hearts and minds – simply wearing the right clothes is not enough – so the promotional efforts need to resonate with and matter to publics and audiences. Mattering, the way that particular values and messages are advanced through aesthetic choices, is the compelling dimension that convinces publics of the significance of issues that are being advanced by leading women. Mattering is a concept that has significant implications for thinking through the role of public relations in social and environmental change – change can only occur when issues matter.

Chapter 7: public relations, race and reconciliation

Focusing on contemporary race politics in Australia, this chapter considers the role public relations might play in reconciliation and social justice, and high-lights the need to locate public relations within social and cultural contexts and the need for an historical understanding of Indigenous people and public rela-tions practices. Given the themes of this book, this chapter explores how public relations, by organisations and in more community-driven conceptualisations of public relations activity, can challenge established power imbalances to promote greater social justice and allow a stronger understanding of public relations' role in social change. Investigating the ways race is entangled with public relations offers an opportunity to deconstruct public relations and its discursive bounda-ries. It advocates a critical pedagogy for future practitioners to reflect on race, whiteness and Indigeneity and to consider the ways public relations might chal-lenge existing knowledge and power structures in order to bring about positive social change and social justice.

Chapter 8: environmental protest songs and justice perspectives

An environmental humanities framework is applied in this chapter to analyse how protest music functions as transformative public relations. A range of environ-mental protest songs is critiqued in line with the concepts of the nature-culture divide, mastery over nature, and multispecies relations, and the justice implica-tions are discussed. The importance of understanding the contextual conditions that may affect how nature is popularised, opening up justice-oriented modes of thinking to reconfigure our relationships with nature and the ways in which agency may be attributed to nonhuman entities are emphasised. What is evi-dent in this chapter is the significance of understanding how certain atmospheres and moods affect and potentially transform cultural discourses. The chapter con-cludes that although protest music may evoke atmospheres, bring issues to public attention, and position them as matters of concern through language and sound, it is less clear whether protest music mobilises action and influences social and environmental policy change. Learning from the performative role of mattering in popular culture, public relations aimed at environmental transformation will not only need to draw attention to issues, it will also need to reconfigure our relationships and interactions with nature.

Chapter 9: *Cassolada*: communication, protest and the 2017 Catalan Indy Ref

This chapter draws on recent scholarship on activism and public relations to consider the significance of protest PR and dissent PR in relation to the protests in Barcelona following the Catalan independence referendum in October 2017. It includes observations and impressions of that period in order to understand how activism and protest may inform theorising about public relations. Focusing on what communication means in this context is disruptive for traditional conceptualisations of public relations and its strong association with the corporate sector (Weaver, 2019). Rallies, strikes, demonstrations, media statements, posters, graffiti, social media posts, interviews and speeches, as forms of protest PR and dissent PR, sought to influence ideas and public discourse around Catalan independence, built on a strategic narrative of social justice, Catalan national identity and Spanish oppression. Communication played a significant role in constructing, amplifying, demonstrating and reinforcing that narrative, and enabled protestors and dissenters to contribute to public and political debate about Catalan independence.

Chapter 10: critical reflections

In this final chapter, we draw together the multiple threads and arguments from the preceding chapters to theorise the links between public relations, popular culture and social change. We argue public relations' role in producing and circulating popular culture is a type of double game in which public relations simultaneously promotes and undermines efforts at social change. However, rather than the mass-produced versions of popular culture, social change seems to emerge and evolve from community spaces and organising. The work undertaken by activists, artists, environmentalists, comedians and musicians not only influences popular culture, but it also transforms our understandings of how public relations may be deployed to meaningfully engage with publics and how publics resist mass culture in favour of local and community cultures. We conclude that the study of public relations in popular culture contexts enables a stronger understanding of critical perspectives of social practices and cultures and how social change may be realised and achieved.

References

Alberici, E. (2018, November 1). Royal commission casts a shadow over banks' corporate good deeds. *ABC*. Retrieved from www.abc.net.au/news/2018-11-02/bank-corporate-social-responsibility-royal-commission/10456964

Aldrich, H., & Herker, D. (1977). Boundary spanning roles and organization structure. *The Academy of Management Review, 2*(2), 217–230.

Cutlip, S. (1994). *The unseen power: Public relations, a history*. Hillsdale, NJ: Lawrence Erlbaum.

Demetrious, K. (2016). Sanitising or reforming PR? Exploring 'trust' and the emergence of critical public relations. In J. L'Etang, D. McKie, N. Snow, & J. Xifra (Eds.),

Routledge handbook of critical public relations (pp. 101–116). Abingdon, England: Routledge.

Duncombe, S. (2002). *The cultural resistance reader*. London, England: Verso.

Edwards, L. (2015). Understanding public relations as a cultural industry. In K. Oakley & J. O'Connor (Eds.), *The Routledge companion to the cultural industries* (pp. 371–381). London, England: Routledge.

Edwards, L., & Hodges, C. (Eds.). (2011). *Public relations, society and culture: Theoretical and empirical explorations*. Abingdon, England: Routledge.

Fitch, K. (2015). Promoting the vampire rights amendment: Public relations, post feminism and *True Blood*. *Public Relations Review, 41*(5), 607–614.

Fitch, K. (2017). Seeing 'the unseen hand': Celebrity, promotion and public relations. *Public Relations Inquiry, 6*(2), 157–169.

Gray, J. (2010). Texts that sell: The culture in promotional culture. In M. Aronyczyk & D. Powers (Eds.), *Blowing up the brand: Critical perspectives on promotional culture* (pp. 307–326). New York, NY: Peter Lang.

Grunig, J. (Ed.). (1992). *Excellence in public relations and communication management*. Hillsdale, NJ: Lawrence Erlbaum Associates.

Hall, S. (1980). Encoding/decoding. In S. Hall, D. Hobson, A. Love, & P. Willis (Eds.), *Culture, media, language* (pp. 128–138). London, England: Hutchinson.

Hartley, J. (1992). *The politics of pictures: The creation of the public in the age of popular media*. London, England: Routledge.

Hobbs, M. (2019). Conflict ecology: Examining the strategies and rationales of lobbyists in the mining and energy industries in Australia. *Public Relations Review, 46*(2), 1–8.

Holtzhausen, D. R. (2000). Postmodern values in public relations. *Journal of Public Relations Research, 12*, 93–114.

Hutchins, A., & Tindall, N. (2015). 'Things that don't go together?' Considering fandom and rethinking public relations. *Prism, 12*(1). Retrieved from https://www.prismjournal.org/v12-no1.html

Hutchins, A., & Tindall, N. (2016). *Public relations and participatory culture: Fandom, social media and community engagement*. Abingdon, England: Routledge.

Jenkins, H., McPherson, T., & Shattuc, J. (2002). *Hop on pop: The politics and pleasure of popular culture*. Durham, NC: Duke University Press.

John, N. A. (2012). Sharing and Web 2.0: The emergence of a keyword. *New Media & Society, 15*(2), 167–182.

L'Etang, J. (2006). Public relations and sport in promotional culture. *Public Relations Review, 32*(4), 386–394.

Luckhurst, R. (2016). *Zombies: A cultural history*. London, England: Reaktion Books.

Mears, A. (2014). Aesthetic labor for the sociologies of work, gender and beauty. *Sociology Compass, 8*(12), 1330–1343.

Moloney, K., & McKie, D. (2016). Changes to be encouraged: Radical turns in PR theorisation and small-step evolutions in PR practice. In J. L'Etang, D. McKie, N. Snow, & J. Xifra (Eds.), *The Routledge handbook of critical public relations* (pp. 151–161). Abingdon, England: Routledge.

Pal, M., & Dutta, M. J. (2008). Public relations in a global context: The relevance of critical modernism as a theoretical lens. *Journal of Public Relations Research, 20*(2), 159–179.

Shiach, M. (2005). The popular. In R. Guins & O. Z. Cruz (Eds.), *Popular culture: A reader* (pp. 55–63). Los Angeles, CA: Sage.

Stewart, K. (2007). *Ordinary affects*. Durham, NC: Duke University Press.

Turner, G. (2013). *Understanding celebrity* (2nd ed.). London, England: Sage.

Warfield, K. (2016). Making the cut: An agential realist examination of selfies and touch. *Social Media + Society*, April–June, 1–10.

Weaver, K. (2019). The slow conflation of public relations and activism: Understanding trajectories in public relations theorising. In A. Adi (Ed.), *Protest public relations: Communicating dissent and activism* (pp. 12–28). Abingdon, England: Routledge.

Williams, R. (2011). Culture is ordinary (1958). In I. Szeman & T. Kaposy (Eds.), *Cultural theory: An anthology* (pp. 53–59). Malden, MA: Wiley Blackwell.

2   Public relations in our everyday lives

Judy Motion

Introduction

Theorising the relationship between public relations, popular culture and social change opens up opportunities to examine the power of public relations in our everyday lives. The public relations industry, according to Weinstein (2013), 'has been centered on identifying and igniting cultural conversation'. Yet, scholarship has largely ignored these cultural interventions in our everyday lives and how possibilities for agency and resistance are influenced. Analysing how individuals enact and experience public relations practices socially aligns with a broader critical agenda to open up the theoretical scope of public relations scholarship and integrate social theory (Ihlen & van Ruler, 2009). An exploratory research question we may ask, then, is 'how would our lives differ if there were no public relations?' Depending on our definition of public relations, it may be that we cannot imagine a world without public relations. Public relations is a ubiquitous, relational form of communication that extends beyond formalised organisational efforts to communicate. It is an everyday activity we all experience and engage in. Alternatively, we may believe that without the profession of public relations, we would be free to live a more meaningful existence. Edwards (2016) offered a nuanced explanation, noting that public relations is 'part of our everyday lives, but its influence is multifaceted, not always only good or bad, and mostly somewhere in-between' (p. 24). We need to consider this notion of an 'in-between' influence when thinking through mundane, everyday sense-making practices and social agency. De Certeau (1984) considered that it is important to pay attention to how we navigate everyday life and how we use culture to appropriate and reappropriate meanings. He was interested in shifting our attention from consumer to the everyday user, so that we may understand how autonomy and agency may be reclaimed by reinserting ordinary meanings into institutional discourse domains. In this chapter, the focus is on the insinuation of the ordinary into public relations and, conversely, how we appropriate routine professional practices and make them our own. Concentrating on citizens' ordinary, everyday experiences of public relations offers a flip side to studies that focus on professional public relations practitioners such as Yeoman's (2016) research on discourses of empathy and the international perspectives presented in the edited collection by

Bridgen and Verčič (2018). Studying the relationships between individual everyday experiences of popular culture and public relations may call into question, modify, negate or suggest new theories of the power of public relations as a 'socialization machine' (Clegg & Haugaard, 2009, p. 402).

As a conceptual starting point, Foucault's work on subjectivity provides a number of lenses for understanding how public relations may function as an everyday socialisation machine. Those who are new to Foucault's work and how it can be applied to public relations may find it helpful to consult Motion and Leitch (2018). Foucault was interested in the stylisation of the self and suggested that everyone's life could become a work of art or, quite literally, the self could be created as a work of art. 'From the idea that the self is not given to us, I think there is only one practical consequence: we have to create ourselves as a work of art' (Foucault, 1997, p. 262). Foucault also investigated the cultivation or ethos of self, that is, the way in which individuals constituted themselves as ethical subjects according to the practice of a moral code. By drawing on these understandings, it is possible to look at how public relations constitutes or intervenes in the relations between the subject and truth, creating the self as an object of particular power/knowledge and truth systems. So, adaptation of Foucault's work to a public relations perspective suggests two contrasting views on the constitution of the self as a subject: the notion that the self is a work in progress and that working with public relations is a worthy, worthwhile task; or, that the self is both subject to and the subject of public relations as a power/knowledge and truth system.

This chapter will critically analyse a range of public relations practices that function as socialising or normalising techniques associated with subjectivity and the development of an ethic of the self, questioning our understanding of the relationship between public relations and popular culture. The dominant focus on organisational public relations has led us as public relations scholars to overlook or ignore the modes by which public relations intrudes into our constructions and practices of self and how that affects social agency. The power effects of public relations in popular culture may be positive, negative, subtle or invasive; we may, for example, be persuaded to care about global warming by Naomi Klein, Brian Cox or Bill Nye the Science Guy, taught how to protest and implement better environmental practices by Greenpeace, adopt a new diet or exercise plan promoted by a celebrity blogger or be tempted by television makeover shows to have anti-ageing treatments in an attempt to recapture our once youthful looks or to reinvent our appearance. How and why do these public relations practices succeed or fail to capture our attention? This chapter seeks to initiate a conversation about the power of public relations as a discursive 'socialization machine' (Clegg & Haugaard, 2009, p. 402) within popular culture that infiltrates the ways we think about and practise ourselves and the possibilities for resistance.

Power: a discourse analytic approach

Power is typically viewed as a negative dimension of public relations practice, yet power may also be positive and productive (Clegg & Haugaard, 2009;

Foucault, 1980). Within this chapter, the aim is to interrogate and theorise how the power of public relations plays out in our everyday lives, drawing on the work of Goffman (1959), Foucault (1979, 1980) and Clegg, Courpasson, and Phillips (2006). Although power was generally understood as a force that acts upon individuals, a type of control, Foucault argued that 'power means relations, a more-or-less organised, hierarchical, co-ordinated cluster of relations' (1980, p. 198). He argued that in order to analyse strategies of power it is necessary to examine how they function at a micro level, to distinguish between a range of power mechanisms by asking what happened and whether one can talk of interests. At a societal level, governmentality is a form of power that integrates the art of government with institutional power to render citizens governable. Power emanating from knowledge production may be derived from established regimes of thought that emanate from institutions or local, subjugated and popular knowledges. An associated concept of governmentality is biopower, which is concerned with politics of the body, how the body becomes an issue of power and control, for example, the call to 'be slim, good looking, tanned' (Foucault, 1980, p. 57). The problem of the body is a political struggle; for example, fat phobia versus fat empowerment brings into play moves and countermoves by adversaries that call into question the modes of investment into bodies that are necessary and adequate for capitalist societies. It is critically important to also distinguish between discipline and disciplinary power techniques. Discipline power is associated with fields such as science or medicine and engenders 'apparatuses of knowledge (*savoir*) and a multiplicity of new domains of understanding' (Foucault, 1980, p. 106) that define normalisation, whereas disciplinary power defines and instantiates domination, control, regulation and corrections. Both discipline and disciplinary power depend on and invoke discourse and may normalise tactics of control in what Foucault refers to as '*a society of normalization*' (1980, p. 107). To struggle against or escape discipline and disciplinary power, Foucault argued that we must turn 'towards the possibility of a new form of right' (1980, p. 108). Although he did not specify what that right might be, it is an important consideration for critical public relations scholars – what are those rights and how may they play out in our everyday lives? The perspective adopted in this chapter conceptualises power as discursively shaped; it operates through a network of sense-making relations (Foucault, 1980). So, for citizens actively participating in public relations, new forms of rights may be discursively conceived and enacted. Rights, here, are concerned with choice and self-determination in relation to particular discursive regimes and the public relations mechanisms that promote them. From this perspective, discourse is the vehicle through which power/knowledge circulates and discourse strategies are the means by which the relations of power/knowledge are created, maintained, resisted and transformed (see also, Clegg et al., 2006; Davenport & Leitch, 2005).

By drawing upon a discourse analytic approach it is possible to explicitly emphasise 'the mutually constitutive links' in power and discourse (Clegg et al., 2006, p. 317). For Foucault, discourse was understood as an institutionally generated 'system of thought' (Rabinow, 1997, p. xi). Foucault explained that 'discourse is not simply that which translates struggles or systems of domination, but it is the thing for which and by which there is struggle, discourse is the power to be seized' (1984, p. 110). A discourse analytic approach may offer insights into power struggles embedded in the representative and constitutive processes that inform our view of the world. Discourses thus constitute the ways in which we understand the world: the concepts, objects and subject positions that inform our views. Within this approach, power is understood to circulate via the production, distribution and consumption of texts designed to facilitate sociocultural change (Fairclough, 1992). Clegg et al. (2006) point out that discourse analytic studies have primarily focused on the textual dimensions of discourse and have ignored the social contexts that they function within. The micro-focus on texts has also led to a neglect of the power relations underpinning the texts and notions of agency (Fairclough, 2005). Agency – the capacity or power to make and act upon choices – has always been a somewhat murky area of Foucauldian-oriented research. The emphasis has been on subjectivity – the practices by which individuals are subjects of and subject to discourse. Within these approaches, individuals are understood to occupy pre-existing subject positions offered by various discourses, which means that agency is negated or limited. Foucault (1988) identified four discourse 'technologies' that allow people to understand and transform themselves: technologies of production, sign systems, power and the self. These technologies interact, enabling us to constitute knowledge and act upon our identities. Technologies of production 'permit us to produce, transform, or manipulate things' (Foucault, 1988, p. 18) and contribute to the constitution of a public identity for the self or subject. The discourse strategies and practices that construct meanings were referred to as technologies of sign systems that 'permit us to use signs, meanings, symbols or significations' (Foucault, 1988, p. 18). Foucault's technologies of power 'determine the conduct of individuals and submit them to certain ends or domination' (1988, p. 18). Such technologies create sets of rules and norms for controlling and regulating identities. Technologies of the self 'permit individuals to effect by their own means or with the help of others a certain number of operations on their own bodies and souls, thoughts, and way of being, so as to transform themselves in order to attain a certain state of happiness, purity, wisdom, perfection, or immobility' (Foucault, 1988, p. 18). Technologies of power are imposed whereas technologies of the self are chosen by subjects to construct, modify or transform identity. Thus, Foucauldian approaches do attend to agency in acknowledging the power to resist, but the power that influences incremental efforts to change is ignored – what Alvesson and Wilmott (1992, p. 461) refer to as 'micro-emancipation'. This term refers to a concern for engagement, the recognition of a conflict of interest and a focus on emancipation (see also Clegg et al., 2006, p. 277). Alongside this concern is a need to integrate our understandings of contested sense making and the process of how meaning takes hold. Investigating the nature of our quiescence to the normalising power of public relations that empowers and disempowers us, the norms and rules that contribute to and shape our lives, is crucial for understanding the role of public relations in society and how it impacts individual agency to drive change.

Research method

In response to Moloney and McKie's (2016) observation that stylistic experiments in critical public relations writing are rare, this chapter seeks to open up alternative ways of theorising public relations. One of the many challenges in designing a research study that examines the role of public relations in our everyday lives is to decide who to sample – who would be appropriate to reflect on the role of public relations in society? Another challenge is to decide upon an approach that could make explicit the politics of representation, issues of agency and intersecting power relations. To address these challenges, I decided to undertake a pilot study – a reflective ethnography of the self (Ellis & Bochner, 2000; Holt, 2003; Reed-Danahay, 1997; Richardson, 2000) – to capture the infiltration of public relations into my life and generate a conceptual map in order to address the question of how public relations plays out in our everyday lives. To use auto-ethnography is to wade into the 'politics of evidence' and think about 'experience, emotions, events, processes, performances, narratives, poetics, the politics of possibility' (Denzin, 2009, p. 142). Auto-ethnography is a valid mechanism for understanding the relationship between the personal and cultural sense making (Reed-Danahay, 1997). Key criticisms of auto-ethnography relate to the focus on self as a sole data source (Holt, 2003) and the notion that it is a type of narcissism. However, in this chapter, the power and influence of public relations is the object of study rather than me. As a guiding framework to ensure the quality and value of this research, I have drawn upon and applied the work of Richardson (2000, pp. 15–16) who suggested a set of criteria for evaluating personal narratives that emphasised the substantive contribution to our understanding of social life. The evaluation criteria required reflexive accounts of the subjectivity of the text; discussion of the impact of the text emotionally, intellectually, theoretically and practically; and expressions of lived experience.

The analytical frame developed was an amalgam of a 'typical' weekend in my life because it meant I would avoid possible bias or distortion from the scholarly and educational practices in my working week related to researching and lecturing about the discipline of public relations. In line with Foucault's observations about how the complex systems of relations that govern our lives are so subtle in distribution, mechanisms, reciprocal controls and adjustments (1980, p. 62), I set out to discern how different pieces of these systems were set in place and discursively enacted by discussing discursive experiences of public relations power within the following section.

Health discourse – a willing vehicle of power

The day begins with a walk – a seemingly public relations free activity – yet the importance of daily exercise is communicated to us through numerous government health campaigns. For example, television campaigns repeatedly urge us to get off the couch. In this instance, exercise-related public relations efforts may be understood as a positive, productive force for change – what Foucault (1988) would refer to as a 'technology of production' – it permits us to produce and transform ourselves. However, public relations may also be used covertly or subtly as a mode for training and modifying individuals – a technology of power. As a favour to my sister, over the weekend I had made myself available for a public relations firm which was promoting asthma awareness. The public relations firm had asked me to speak to the media about my asthma if contacted. When I asked the firm who was the client they were conducting the campaign for, it was not the Asthma Foundation, as I had assumed, but a pharmaceutical company that sold asthma medication. The explicit aim was to conduct an asthma awareness campaign, perhaps part of their corporate social responsibility program (or efforts to legitimise their role in society and protect mega profits). But it also had a secondary purpose: to remind those asthmatics who get seasonal asthma that they needed to renew their medication. Although it may seem that this type of power falls in the 'in-between' category, power that operates in this covert way, in spite of the potentially positive outcomes, is a type of domination. Public relations that is manipulative or disguised is fundamentally dishonest. In order for individuals to exercise agency and make informed decisions, we have a right to know the source and purpose of communication. We can only resist what we know.

Nutritional discourse: The next weekend activity is breakfast – nutrition – and I eat a selection of fresh fruit and prepare porridge from organically grown oats. The fresh fruits I consume for breakfast have been promoted through numerous public relations efforts. Journalists have attended media conferences where scientists promote 'super foods', such as blueberries or kiwifruit, that are written about in numerous food magazines; chefs have used that superfood on television cooking programs; we have sampled the fruits at train stations; and our children bring home pamphlets from school. In Australia, we have the 'five plus a day' campaign exhorting the importance of fruit and vegetables. In the body+soul section of the paper I read while having breakfast, there is an article titled 'powerhouse foods' which tells me that colour is the key in choosing fruit and vegetables. The article then quotes a spokesperson from the Cancer Council's nutrition program who says that 'Australians are lucky to have such a variety of fruits available and now it's time to get motivated to eat them' (Labi, 2016). The article also discusses scientific research programs focusing on the importance of phytonutrients. I learn that some sources of phytonutrients are superior – strawberries are good but raspberries are better, carrots are good but sweet potato is better. 'Phytonutrients' is an interesting but unfamiliar word; clearly a scientific discourse underpins the article. The use of scientific language to promote fruit and vegetables is an example of discipline power, a discursive attempt to integrate promotional, scientific and nutritional discourses. It also builds symbolic capital for the horticultural industry. Language, deployed in this way, is a resource to bring about change. This discursive manoeuvre generates new meanings designed to help the enactment of particular public relations strategies (Hardy, Palmer, & Phillips, 2000, p. 1228). However, little attention has been paid to how the knowledge that underpins promotional communication is 'put into discourse' (Foucault, 1978, p. 11) or what happens to knowledge when it moves across discourse boundaries.

Fruit and vegetables feature within multiple discourses and the meanings they take on in each discourse are governed by the rules pertaining to that particular discourse. When knowledge moves from one discourse to another it is, therefore, potentially transformed in the process. Increasingly discourses are actively managed by what Fairclough (1992) termed 'discourse technologists' employed by organisations which seek to create, transform, transplant and circulate meanings in order to achieve their objectives. These strategies and practices operate through public relations efforts (Motion & Leitch, 1996) to produce acceptance of particular meanings or conceptions of 'truth' (Foucault, 1980). These efforts are complicated by what Heath (1992) termed the 'wrangle in the marketplace' or the struggle for our attention by multiple competing discourses. Will people continue to eat strawberries in spite of their slightly less valuable nutritional benefits or will they now reach for raspberries because they have higher phytonutrients? Or will they buy what tastes good, is in season or what they can afford? The power of public relations in instances like this is nebulous and difficult to gauge. Clegg et al. (2006, p. 256) suggest that 'where there is power, then the appropriate question to ask is: how is this power possible?' In this instance, any power that the nutritional discourse has may be attributed to the epistemic status of science in society. For many, science still occupies a position as a truth-producing discourse. Here, my rights to be informed and exercise choice have been maintained; agency and resistance are possible when it comes to promotional health discourses.

Fashion discourse – an ethical shopper?

Public relations efforts have already attempted to influence how I understand the world – and that is only up to breakfast. After breakfast I head to the mall to buy a few necessities for travelling. In the dressing room of Gorman, an Australian designer label that sells organic cotton clothing, I am trying on clothes that I hope are better for me and for the planet. There are numerous public relations promotional discourses at play here. I first learned about Gorman from an article in *Vogue*; no doubt a media release sparked that article. My desire to buy Australian and New Zealand made products is driven by environmental discourses from organisations such as Greenpeace that urge us to lessen the travel miles of our clothes and the desire for organic cotton is driven by promotion from the organics industry telling us of the benefits. The young woman who emerges from the dressing room next door is blond, striking looking, slim and at least six foot; I think I've seen her modelling in *Vogue*, and she is buying Gorman. There's so much evidence of public relations at play here, it is hard to disentangle it all. First, aesthetics – I note her makeup: natural looking in a made up way – smudgy eyes, a nude coloured lipstick – slightly tousled hair – how and why do I register and name these things? My understanding of the newest colours, trends and products has been garnered from fashion magazine and social media commentaries that probably originated from promotional media kits. These intrusions of public relations into my everyday life are often subtle and seemingly harmless but, without knowing how public relations works, would I or could I make independent choices? Public relations discourses that attempt to act upon our sense of agency and the choices we make in these ways are questionable but widely practised and accepted manifestations of market domination and power in our everyday lives. Makeup, for example, is part of a broader discourse about gender and consumption. Efforts to shop for clothes may also be conceptualised, from a Foucauldian perspective, as a problem of how to transform the self in accordance with one's own conception of beauty or value (Foucault, 1996, p. 458).

Thus, from a public relations perspective, clothes shopping may be considered an attempt to control representations of self or impression management (Goffman, 1959) that imposes on one's life a distinctive individual style. Creating the self as a 'work of art' requires one to 'constitute oneself as the worker of beauty of one's own life' (Foucault, 1996, p. 458). Aesthetics has been defined as a 'concept inherited from idealist philosophy, referring to the principles of taste, especially good taste, and hence beauty' (O'Sullivan, Hartley, Saunders, Montgomery, & Fiske, 1994, p. 6). According to Hein (1993), aesthetics theories actually make critical recommendations rather than generate definitions of art. In this sense, aesthetics is construed as a method of judgement. Aesthetics may be critiqued as an elitist construct which is imposed upon others, to operate as a normalising technique, but we also impose certain judgements on what is appropriate for ourselves. For Bourdieu (1984), the concept of aesthetics signified taste. Bourdieu argued that taste is used as a criterion for cultural judgements. He believed that the social uses and interpretations of aesthetics required a system of judgements based on an acquired cultural code which functioned as a marker of class. According to Foucault (1988), 'the main interest in life and work is to become someone else that you were not in the beginning' (p. 9). Bourdieu stated that '[t]aste classifies, and it classifies the classifier' (1984, p. 6). For Bourdieu, art and cultural consumption are predisposed, consciously and deliberately, or not, to fulfil a social function of legitimating social differences (1984, p. 7). What we choose to buy and wear is part of our symbolic capital – the meanings and value we add by aesthetically commodifying and promoting ourselves, cultivating fashion and styling ourselves. Although we have agency, we need to remember that we are choosing from a limited set – unless we can craft our own clothes! We therefore become subject to a hegemony of appearance (Finkelstein, 1991). Engagement with the fashion industry is an experience and enactment of an 'in-between power' that is both good and bad – good for some of us but bad for the planet. Fashion functions as a type of disciplinary power over the self or what Foucault (1988) referred to as a 'technology of the self'.

Work: The afternoon is spent working on this chapter about public relations – this skewed work-life balance is a reflection of how academia has infiltrated what may be considered private time and also a reflection of my need to complete tasks so that certain views of myself can be enacted. It is also compliance with newly imposed research expectations for academic staff. This is an exercise of power over me but I am also a willing vehicle of power – I like the process of thinking through research problems.

Leisure: Later in the day we go out for dinner. We head out to see whether we can get into any restaurants featured on a television program called Masterchef, which is an Australian public relations vehicle for promoting a supermarket, a knife brand, chefs, restaurants, the presenters and the restaurant industry. The restaurants are all fully booked and we end up in a small favourite pub instead. Later that evening an advertisement for apples features on television – and the website is www.oneadaysuperfoods.com.au. Promotion of fruit and vegetables as 'superfoods' is an interesting public relations strategy, the same strategy I observed earlier in the day with 'phytonutrients'. It provides symbolic capital for growers and retailers and establishes a hierarchy of food values. This experience of public relations may be categorised as positive and productive – it may have a positive impact on my health. There are no doubt numerous other public relations incursions into my day but the fitness, nutrition, fashion and food industry discourses prevailed on that day.

Internet activism – trolling the trolls

The next day starts with a spot of internet activism – or what I refer to as 'trolling the trolls'. Citizens who undertake this type of engagement with social media to achieve public relations outcomes – to inform, promote, popularise or engage – may be understood as citizen or 'ordinary practitioners' (de Certeau, 1984, p. 103) of public relations. A recent scholarly trend that has the potential to open up new ways of theorising and understanding our everyday interactions with social media, and more broadly, popular and promotional communication, is conceptualising activism as a form of public relations (Moloney & McKie, 2016; Motion, Heath, & Leitch, 2016). Two new concepts are recommended by Moloney and McKie to differentiate between various forms of activist public relations: 'dissent PR and protest PR' (2016, p. 157). Dissent PR, they suggest, is the use of public relations messaging techniques to change contemporary and hegemonic discourse, whereas protest PR uses activist techniques to influence policymakers. This useful distinction draws our attention to the entangled nature of public relations and activism. The relationship is combative and confrontational and, often at the same time, correspondingly complementary. It suggests that our everyday acts of resistance may be theorised in terms of public relations, rather than solely activism. We develop our discussion of activist public relations, and these concepts, in Chapter 9.

To offer international readers some context for this experience, in 2017 the Australian government conducted a survey to gauge public opinion about same sex marriage, or what proponents prefer to term marriage equality. The use of a survey to determine equality and justice issues has been highly controversial and the UN deemed it a contravention of human rights (Doherty, 2017). As an advocate for marriage equality, I have been dismayed by some of the comments about the issue on social media, particularly my Facebook page. It seemed to me that debate about the issue had resulted in polarised positions and attempts to reconcile diverse opinions had stalled or failed. This type of 'devil shift' (Sabatier,

Hunter, & McLaughlin, 1987; Sabatier & Jenkins-Smith, 1999; Sabatier & Weible, 2007, p. 194) marks a critical impasse in public controversy and policy planning. The devil shift explains how the negative motives, behaviour and influence of opponents may be exaggerated (Sabatier et al., 1987) and contingent on both the distance in beliefs between opponents. Among the outcomes of the devil shift are polarised coordination efforts between rival coalitions, minimal communication channels between opponents and long-term disagreement about major policies (Weible, Sabatier, & McQueen, 2009). As a mechanism to support family, friends, colleagues and students who may be stressed by the comments, I decided to engage with trolls who were commenting on the issue. I started off by simply writing 'vote yes' on every Facebook entry about the issue of marriage equality. Then my responses escalated to addressing homophobic comments. I decided that my strategy would be to be nice, polite, make only one comment and not engage further. In one conversation thread, a number of commentators said that they had intended to vote yes but were going to vote no now because they had been contacted by the marriage equality group, which they considered an invasion of privacy. I was, of course, suspicious that it was actually just an attempt to rally support for the no side. My response was to comment that if they had intended to vote yes, they were clearly a kind person and it was important to adhere to their values. There was no response to these comments. I grew bolder, talking about the need for Australia to be a country where empathy and compassion prevailed but always adhering to my two rules. The interesting thing was that at no stage was I attacked in the way that others were. This was a significant finding about how to engage with trolls – adhere to my values and be nice regardless of the interactional tone of others. So, a key lesson from this social experiment was that politeness and niceness are an important form of power that may influence the tone of communication and public debates. As scholars, we do not talk about the power of civility in public relations but it is actually a key technique. Civility can take the heat out of conflict, yet we do not theorise how it is deployed in business and how it plays out in our everyday lives. Similarly, kindness is a critical value for public relations, so we need to think about how we apply it in situations that are not only positive but also to defuse conflict. The level of vitriol and viciousness on social media is often hidden from us because we interact with friends and only read topics that appeal. However, when a controversial or political issue emerges, that is when we learn about contrasting viewpoints and levels of polarisation. Popular culture tends to be a space where rules are broken and norms are resisted but acts of civility are also recognised and applauded. Civility may be understood as a mode of polite conduct for 'negotiating interpersonal power' (The Institute for Civility in Government, n.d.) that also functions as a mechanism for maintaining or reclaiming power.

Having sought to resist trolls, the day unfolds with a walk and breakfast followed by more work on this chapter. The afternoon is spent swimming and avoiding sunburn at Bronte Beach in Sydney. Multiple public relations discourses intersected – the need for sun protection and the need to look a certain way (swimming costume, beach umbrella, towel). These promotional discourses all contribute to various understandings of beach culture. In addition, there always lurks a fear of sharks thanks to the movie *Jaws* and media coverage of shark-human interactions – swimming in the ocean pool partly takes care of that lingering anxiety. Although media coverage uses terms such as attacks, I have been educated by Chris Neff (2012) to understand the sea as a 'wild' environment and to use the terms 'interactions' and 'bites' rather than attacks. Here is an attempted public relations discourse transformation – Neff is advocating for shark rights. There are also discourses about the beach landscape itself – safety and aesthetics – that influence beach etiquette. The surf lifeguards are a reminder that this is an iconic Australian landscape. Absences are also marked – the people at the beach are white – Australian accents mingle with European and New Zealand accents. This is a colonised landscape, part of the heritage of a settler nation that has yet to confront the need for reparation and self-sovereignty of Indigenous people. In the evening, I research Bronte Beach and learn that it is not actually named, as I had romantically assumed, after the Bronte sisters, but instead it is more likely to have been named after Lord Horatio Nelson, the Duke of Bronte (Vesper, 2008). How disappointing – although, upon reflection, having visited the Bronte Parsonage in Haworth on a bleak Yorkshire day, I appreciate it would not be the most appropriate name for the beach. Naming places after military figures is a colonising practice – a legacy of the colonising power to erase not only names, but people and cultures. I search online for the Indigenous name for Bronte in the spirit of reconciliation and decolonisation but cannot locate it. In these instances, Plumwood (2002) suggests that we should 'democratise, de-bureaucratise and put up for community cultural engagement, elaboration and contest our processes of naming' (pp. 28–29). In this instance, not only were Indigenous people and culture erased, but I learn that the landscape has also been erased. Bronte beach was twice the size and had a waterfall and stream replaced by concrete and lawn (Vesper, 2008). It is not difficult to imagine the modernising public relations discourse that was deployed to persuade people that this landscape was more suitable. A recent council proposal to upgrade the changing facilities and build a disability ramp was opposed and defeated. A community engagement process to decide upon the proposed changes had taken place but because we are not 'locals' we had no say, even though we are 'regulars', an important reminder that engagement processes are often acts of exclusion. In this instance, modernising would be useful and equitable; the rights of the disabled were overridden by those opposed to change. The power to erase, ignore and exclude forms part of a pattern of public relations practices linked to governance processes that prize consultation over justice, equity and rights.

Discussion and conclusion

Public relations is theorised here as a form of socialisation that seeks to normalise particular power relations and practices. However, identifying the influence of public relations within democratic societies is challenging because decisions are rarely made in neutral or controlled conditions. Instead, competing options jostle for attention and create possibilities for agency and resistance. It is important to note that these influences do not have equal power; pervasive or appealing messaging, for example, influences identification and acceptance, whereas other options may not enter our consideration sets. These competing possibilities vie for attention within contested moral orders about values and priorities; for example, social, cultural and environmental justice concerns are weighted against the pull of neoliberal values such as work commitments and material consumption. Often, seemingly mundane, ordinary choices are actually linked to issues of rights and agency. Many rights that are influenced and impacted by public relations are associated with the politics of representation: for example, the right to make informed choices and access multiple meanings; the right to assert identity; the right to understand and participate in cultural sense making; and the right to inclusion and autonomy. It is critical that public relations work – both scholarship and practice – considers how such rights may be enacted and performed within popular culture and during moments of social change.

The auto-ethnography within this chapter has presented an anecdotal history of various cultural dynamics, discourses and experiences of public relations that shape how power and rights played out in particular decisions. Public relations power operates in two ways: the imposition of socialisation and the exercise of individual agency. Although Foucauldian approaches, in particular the technologies framework, generate valuable insights into how public relations socialises our everyday lives, they have some limitations when considering the exercise of individual agency, in particular a consideration of rights. As an alternative, explanations about modes of agency – how we realise and perform power – are now developed and mapped out in the following discussions about everyday decision making.

In the example presented, decisions about health represented embodied agency, a type of power that we exercise over our own bodies. However, health decisions are also influenced by politics of the body – what Foucault referred to as biopower – that manifest in information from multiple sources with varying levels of expertise and authority. Biopower may be positive and transformational, it may be a manifestation of the wellness industry marketing and commodifying health or just a more sophisticated version of peddling snake oil. In contrast, informed choices and embodied agency emanate from meaningful public relations representations of discipline power – primarily medicine and science. For public relations, consideration of whether power is an imposed (a technology of power) or embodied agency (a technology of the self) opens up questions about the right to choose and the value of proposed social change for various publics.

Decisions about shopping link to technologies of the self, our identity, ethics and aesthetics. Such decisions take place within a broader neoliberal system that fosters and rewards consumption. Foucault (1980) argued that we become 'willing vehicles of power' because it is productive – it offers us something. Seeking beauty is perfectly acceptable – however, it is entangled in discourses about gender, environmental harm and animal cruelty insofar as it relates to the marketisation and manipulation of the self. Our subjectivity, that is the process of being subject to various discourses, is not totally inescapable: exercise of this type of contingent agency is difficult because particular ways of thinking have been naturalised and normalised and herein lies the power of public relations. Goffman suggested that 'we personally negotiate aspects of all the arrangements under which we live' and that we 'continue on mechanically as though the matter had always been settled' (1974, p. 2). In this way, Goffman (1974) acknowledged the agency we have in our lives, but the automatic acceptance of previous decisions means that once a public relations discourse is established, it may not have to do a lot to maintain the status quo. The deeply problematic issue here is that we are not always aware of the public relations machinations that are creating discursive frames and power relations for us to interpret and practice our lives, so resistance is unlikely. When it comes to consumption practices, we may automatically head to the mall and alternative discourses may struggle to undo the socialisation practices that have led us to think of shopping as a leisure activity rather than a chore. The power exercised in this instance is a form of contingent agency that relies on an anti-shopping or alternative discourse prevailing in order for us to have autonomy and the right to exercise alternative valuing systems.

Our online, social media interactions suggest that interpersonal power is an important dimension of our agential experiences with public relations. In the instance examined, civility was a significant form of power that enabled engagement and defused conflict and controversy. This is a neglected aspect of public relations studies that may yield important insights into both the exercise of and resistance to public relations, particularly in relation to our social media interactions. Choosing how we react in our online interactions safeguards the right to freedom of expression and conveys a form of identity and reputational power which we control.

Choices about how we spend our leisure time are subject to public relations efforts. Within our everyday working lives, it may not be possible to exercise significant agency but the spillover of work into our leisure time represents a type of enculturated, normalised dominance – driven by fear and/or positive motivation. Agency in this situation may simply be the refusal to work outside legislated hours or it be the choice to use leisure time to only work on those things that matter to individuals. Ethical institutions respect the need for work to be balanced by leisure and moderate expectations. Working in leisure time may be a response to institutional narratives, an attempt to create and manage our own reputational narratives or a form of pleasure. These types of public relations practices not only act as socialising influences – they also allow us to be our best, preferred selves and exercise choice.

Our leisure activities are inextricably bound up with multiple public relations discourses. For example, a seemingly simple day at the beach may evoke multiple traces of sociocultural, economic and political influences. In settler nations, beaches are colonised spaces and professional forms of public relations may be employed to maintain the status quo. Resistance to colonising impacts requires effort and information along with commitment and care. By identifying all of the communicative rights outlined above – information, identity, cultural sense making, and autonomy – the chapter established them as key considerations for all public relations work and demonstrated how they are brought into play when leisure is politicised, commodified or captured. The paradox of public relations as a socialising machine within popular culture is that choices are made from multiple yet limited sets of options. Thus, I argue, agency plays out as various modalities within the popular culture engagements examined in this chapter: an embodied force; contingent preferences; civility; and justice-oriented, rights-based systems of decision making. In Foucauldian terms, these modes of agency offer nuance to the technologies of the self framework and highlight the possibilities for promoting or resisting the power of public relations efforts – or popular culture itself – in our everyday lives.

References

Alvesson, M., & Willmott, H. (1992). On the idea of emancipation in management and organization studies. *Academy of Management Review, 17*(3), 432–464.

Bourdieu, P. (1984). *Distinction* (R. Nice, Trans.). Cambridge, MA: Harvard University Press.

Bridgen, E., & Verčič, D. (Eds.). (2018). *Experiencing public relations: International voices*. London, England: Routledge.

Clegg, S. R., Courpasson, D., & Phillips, N. (2006). *Power and organizations*. Newbury Park, CA: Pine Forge Press.

Clegg, S. R., & Haugaard, M. (Eds.). (2009). Discourse of power. In *The Sage handbook of power* (pp. 400–465). London, England: Sage.

Davenport, S., & Leitch, S. (2005). Circuits of power in practice: Strategic ambiguity as delegation of authority. *Organization Studies, 26*(11), 1603–1623.

De Certeau, M. (1984). *The practice of everyday life* (S. Rendall, Trans.). Berkeley, CA: University of California Press.

Denzin, N. K. (2009). The elephant in the living room: Or extending the conversation about the politics of evidence. *Qualitative Research, 9*(2), 139–160.

Doherty, B. (2017, October 19). 'Unacceptable': UN committee damns Australia's record on human rights. *The Guardian*. Retrieved from www.theguardian.com/australia-news/2017/oct/19/unacceptable-un-committee-damns-australias-record-on-human-rights

Edwards, L. (2016). The role of public relations in deliberative systems. *Journal of Communication, 66*(1), 60–81.

Ellis, C., & Bochner, A. (2000). Autoethnography, personal narrative, reflexivity: Researcher as subject. In N. K. Denzin & Y. S. Lincoln (Eds.), *Handbook of qualitative research* (2nd ed., pp. 733–768). Thousand Oaks, CA: Sage.

Fairclough, N. (1992). *Discourse and social change*. Cambridge, England: Polity Press.

Fairclough, N. (2005). Discourse analysis in organization studies: The case for critical realism. *Organization Studies, 26*(6), 915–939.

Finkelstein, J. (1991). *The fashioned self*. Cambridge, England: Polity Press.

Foucault, M. (1978). *The history of sexuality: An introduction* (R. Hurley, Trans.). London, England: Penguin.

Foucault, M. (1979). *Discipline and punish: The birth of the prison*. London, England: Penguin.

Foucault, M. (1980). *Power/knowledge: Selected interviews & other writings 1972–1977 by Michel Foucault*. New York, NY: Pantheon.

Foucault, M. (1984). *The use of pleasure: The history of sexuality* (R. Hurley, Trans.). London, England: Penguin.

Foucault, M. (1988). Technologies of the self. In L. Martin, H. Gutman, & P. Hutton (Eds.), *Technologies of the self: A seminar with Michel Foucault* (pp. 16–48). Amherst, MA: University of Massachusetts Press.

Foucault, M. (1996). *Foucault live (interviews, 1961–1984)*. New York, NY: Semiotext(e).

Foucault, M. (1997). The ethics of the concern for the self as a practice of freedom. In P. Rabinow (Ed.), *Michel Foucault: Ethics, subjectivity and truth* (pp. 281–301). New York, NY: New York University Press.

Goffman, E. (1959). *The presentation of self in everyday life*. New York, NY: Doubleday.

Goffman, E. (1974). *Frame analysis: An essay on the organization of experience*. Cambridge, MA: Harvard University Press.

Hardy, C., Palmer, I., & Phillips, N. (2000). Discourse as a strategic resource. *Human Relations, 53*(9), 1227–1248.

Heath, R. L. (1992). The wrangle in the marketplace: A rhetorical perspective of public relations. In E. L. Toth & R. L. Heath (Eds.), *Rhetorical and critical approaches to public relations* (pp. 17–36). Hillsdale, NJ: Lawrence Erlbaum Associates.

Hein, H. (1993). Refining feminist theory: Lessons from aesthetics. In H. Hein & C. C. Korsmeyer (Eds.), *Aesthetics in feminist perspective* (pp. 3–18). Bloomington, IN: Indiana Press.

Holt, N. L. (2003). Representation, legitimation, and autoethnography: An autoethnographic writing story. *International Journal of Qualitative Methods, 2*(1), 18–28.

Ihlen, Ø., & van Ruler, B. (2009). Introduction: Applying social theory to public relations. In Ø. Ihlen, B. van Ruler, & M. Fredriksson (Eds.), *Public relations and social theory: Key figures and concepts* (pp. 1–20). New York, NY: Routledge.

The Institute for Civility in Government. (n.d.). *What is civility in government?* Retrieved August 29, 2019, from www.instituteforcivility.org/who-we-are/what-is-civility/

Labi, S. (2016, June 17). Five powerhouse foods. *Body and Soul*. Retrieved from www.bodyandsoul.com.au/nutrition/nutrition-tips/five-powerhouse-foods/news-story/d5b8823ce689d31f65da61680ee243b9.

Moloney, K., & McKie, D. (2016). Changes to be encouraged: Radical turns in PR theorization and small step evolutions in PR practice. In J. L'Etang, D. McKie, N. Snow, & J. Xifra (Eds.), *The Routledge handbook of critical public relations* (pp. 151–161). London, England: Routledge.

Motion, J., Heath, R. L., & Leitch, S. (2016). *Social media and public relations: Fake friends and powerful publics*. London, England: Routledge.

Motion, J., & Leitch, S. (1996). A discursive perspective from New Zealand: Another world view. *Public Relations Review, 22*(3), 297–309.

Motion, J., & Leitch, S. (2018). On Foucault: Engaging with Foucault's critical theory and methods. In Ø. Ihlen & M. Fredriksson (Eds.), *Public relations and social theory: Key figures, concepts and developments* (pp. 334–353). New York, NY: Routledge.

Neff, C. (2012). Australian beach safety and the politics of shark attacks. *Coastal Management, 40*(1), 88–106.

O'Sullivan, T., Hartley, J., Saunders, D., Montgomery, M., & Fiske, J. (1994). *Key concepts in communication and cultural studies*. London, England: Routledge.

Plumwood, V. (2002). Decolonizing relationships with nature. *Pan, 2,* 7–30.

Rabinow, P. (Ed.). (1997). Introduction: The history of systems of thought. *Michel Foucault: Ethics, subjectivity and truth* (pp. XII–XLII). New York, NY: New York University Press.

Reed-Danahay, D. (1997). *Auto/ethnography.* New York, NY: Berg.

Richardson, L. (2000). New writing practices in qualitative research. *Sociology of Sport Journal, 17,* 5–20.

Sabatier, P. A., Hunter, S., & McLaughlin, S. (1987). The devil shift: Perceptions and misperceptions of opponents. *Western Political Quarterly, 40*(3), 449–476.

Sabatier, P. A., & Jenkins-Smith, H. C. (1999). The advocacy coalition framework: An assessment. *Theories of the Policy Process,* 117–166.

Sabatier, P. A., & Weible, C. M. (2007). The advocacy coalition framework. *Theories of the Policy Process, 2,* 189–220.

Vesper, S. (2008). Bronte. *The Dictionary of Sydney.* Retrieved from https://diction aryofsydney.org/entry/bronte

Weible, C. M., Sabatier, P. A., & McQueen, K. (2009). Themes and variations: Taking stock of the advocacy coalition framework. *Policy Studies Journal, 37*(1), 121–140.

Weinstein, E. (2013, September 30). Public relations and the democratization of popular culture. *The Holmes Report.* Retrieved from www.holmesreport.com/latest/article/public-relations-and-the-democratization-of-popular-culture

Yeomans, L. (2016). Imagining the lives of others: Empathy in public relations. *Public Relations Inquiry, 5*(1), 71–92.

3   Trending . . . fortune tellers, dream weavers and charlatans

Judy Motion

Introduction

How do we know what is hot, what is not and what is trending in popular culture? Through a series of vignettes and narratives, this chapter seeks to critique the role that public relations may play in the creation of popular culture and social change. Writing at this disheartening time, when shameless, blatant lies dominate political systems, social justice concerns are multiplying and environmental justice is critical, understanding the possibilities that popular culture may offer to effect social change is vital. This chapter was inspired by chance encounters. A number of years ago, very early one morning while I was staying in Singapore, a stopover on my way to public relations conferences in Europe, I was out running by the river and encountered an elaborately dressed South Asian man who looked like a seer or holy man. He greeted me. He was exceedingly charming, complimented me and asked if I would like my fortune told. I was curious, so I agreed. He wrote down some notes on a piece of paper then asked me a series of questions and, when I looked at the notes, he had written a series of abbreviations that seemed to identify my favourite flower, number and age. He then asked me for money. At the same time, a friend and former colleague, who was also heading to public relations conferences in Europe and also running to cope with jetlag, came around the corner. The fortune teller vanished. Later, on reflection, I couldn't figure out if he really was a fortune teller or a charlatan, or perhaps the two are indistinguishable. I knew there was a trick to what he did and later realised that he had not actually predicted my future. It was, however, certainly a compelling performance. From this experience, I became interested in making sense of fortune telling and investigating the discipline of future studies, an interest shared by public relations scholars, McKie and Munshi (2007), who have also written on this topic.

The connections and intersections between popular culture, social change and public relations foresight form the focus of this chapter. McKie and Munshi (2007) argue that a reconfigured public relations that contributes to environmental responsibility, social justice and global enterprise requires a 'forward-looking orientation' that considers connections between past and present trends in combination with 'predicted futures' (p. 132). Examining how public relations foresight plays out in online contexts may potentially open up possibilities for social and environmental change. The apparent randomness of social media trends needs to be considered in relation to broader sociocultural conditions that mediate popular culture. In particular, here I focus on the ways in which spreadability (Jenkins, Ford, & Green, 2013) and the sharing (John, 2012) affordabilities of social media are impacting popular culture trends. Alongside these considerations, the algorithms that form the basis of our social media experiences need to also be taken into account. The conditions that give rise to trends may be part of a broader social fault line that impact professional public relations or they may be deliberately manufactured and driven for public relations purposes. Within this chapter, I draw upon future studies to think through the ways that public relations seeks to influence popular culture and impact social change. Future studies, as an academic discipline, is concerned with 'both past change and possibilities for the future different from the present' (Bell, 2002, p. 239). Forecasting techniques draw upon information extrapolated from past events and data (Tsoukas & Shepherd, 2004). So, the past and future are entangled in webs of predictions. McKie and Munshi (2007) argue that uncertainty is a starting point for preparing for the future and that such processes move 'from the domain of exact science towards imagination-influenced territory' (p. 133). Uncertainty seems a more reliable and likely, but less appealing, predictor of the future than drawing upon the past. At the same time, hope and positivity may be maintained as part of the imagination process that uncertainty provokes. Shared objectives of various future studies approaches include making the world a better place, exploring potential futures, integrating knowledge and values into social design, increasing engagement in designing the future and communicating and advocating for a particular future (Bell, 2002). Webb (2017) explains that futurists look for and recognise early patterns, what she terms 'pre-trends', in the fringes where experimentation and innovation take place (p. 55). Although traditional futurist approaches emphasised prediction, forecasting and scenario building, in contrast, critical futures studies emphasise the social construction of meanings and the power relations inherent in futurists' service to particular interests, projects and institutions (Son, 2015). 'Critical futures studies', Son argues, 'focus on the critique of official futures, radical transformation of the existing order, and the emphasis on value and power relationships' along with 'community-oriented alternative futures' (2015, p. 133). Critical discursive and political perspectives of future studies are drawn upon here to critique two public relations approaches to the prediction of trends: forecasts and surveys.

Forecasting may be undertaken by organisations for various public relations purposes or by public relations firms as a form of promotion. Some firms may be dedicated to future trend forecasting, such as the website-based 'Trendhunter. com' (www.trendhunter.com/), which describes itself as an inspirational, sharing community that anticipates and shares trends. Trendhunter.com claims to deliberately drive media attention to education, eco-awareness and social business. Such trendsetting sites play an important role in identifying popular culture trends with the potential for social transformation. Understanding what is likely to be popular and why that is so may generate insights into how public sentiment and participatory moments occur. However, it is also critical to understand the multiple roles that organisations such as Trendhunter.com play in the production of popular culture and the maintenance of neoliberalism. Questions need to be asked about the funding models that underpin their efforts, who they represent, the valuing systems they advocate and the meanings of messages they promote. Such organisations act as cultural fortune tellers in this trend-setting space, along with charlatans who mislead us. Their discursive practices are analysed here in order to highlight some of the ways that popular culture is produced and promoted, the ways we engage with popular culture and the implications for public relations.

Trendhunter.com describes itself as 'the world's largest, most popular trend community, with 20,000,000 monthly views'. To identify trends, Trendhunter. com claims to draw upon research from 'big data, human researchers and AI'. The statistics about reach and impact are impressive: they claim to 'empower' more than 500 brands, billionaires and CEOs, including Coca-Cola, Adidas, Victoria's Secret, IBM, Cisco, Microsoft and NASA. The Trendhunter.com head office is based in Toronto, Canada, and they have a global network of 200,000 contributors and 3,000,000 fans. According to the website, at the time of writing, Trendhunter.com is currently studying more than 350,000 cutting edge ideas using over 3 billion choices from 150,000,000 people. The 'About us' web page that offers this information is part of the organisation's public relations efforts to promote the corporate identity and establish its corporate reputation as a legitimate business. In many ways, the 'About Us' page is standard fare, dedicated to promoting the company and the work it does. The narrative is factual rather than story-based. The 'About Us' web page advertises three promotional videos. In the first video still, a young woman appears on the page banner with the text 'Join the world's #1 trend firm or learn more about our culture' and a neon sign with the Trendhunter name and a bank of computer screens feature in the background. The second still is for a promotional video for Trendhunter magazine, 'a minute documentary', with an image of a youngish male. The third video advertisement is titled 'Trendhunter – The Series' with, I am guessing, a Victoria Secret model, who is clad in a skin-tight sports t-shirt with a cut-out revealing a bra and, in the background, what appears to be angel wings cut from ice. So, something to appeal to everyone? Not really, the faces are white and young which provides possible insight into preferred staff and audiences, and who the future is intended for. Scrolling further down the page reveals a staff photo. It would indeed seem that trendsetters are primarily white and young. Except that much of the work they do is not predicting trends; it is more likely to be writing content and rewriting press releases. Trendhunter is a promotional site rather than a trend prediction site.

In contrast to the 'About Us' page, the 'Home' page looks like a crowded online shopping site with a list of top 20 trends on the left, that are actually just products, and promotional text about Trendhunter.com on the right side of the page. Scrolling down, the next section is titled 'Data trends' by Trendhunter AI and comprises a series of lists labelled insights, topics, places, events, products, people, brands – each with ten click-throughs to various promotions for products – some at concept development stage. A series of photographic images for products then follow, including hand-sculpted marble skulls, textile-based exosuits [a robotic joint-support suit], speedy underwater diver scooters, wearable outdoor sleeping bags, architect-interpreted handbags, distraction-limiting smart watches, and so on. The next section is the TrendHunter megatrends framework – a table of six patterns of opportunity and top 18 megatrends – a section designed to inform organisations about trends that will influence consumers. A large banner advertising Trendhunter Future Festival follows the megatrends framework. Future Festival is an innovation conference that promises **'next year's trends** from the #1 trend firm, **while prototyping 5–10 disruptive ideas** using the same **award-winning innovation workshops** we've used to help **NASA prototype the journey to Mars'** [bold in original]. The banner is then followed by infinite scrolling: screeds of seemingly never-ending photographic images for innovative ideas, practices and products. A section titled 'hottest galleries' profiles branding trends, interactive trends, travel trends, health trends, food trends, youth trends, transportation trends and so on. The 'Home' page concludes with the usual footer details.

Although Trendhunter is promoted as a trend prediction site, it actually resembles an online shopping site and may be understood as a form of mimesis (Benjamin, 1970) in that it imitates and reproduces the format and content of online shopping sites. Much like unsolicited postal catalogues that market odd/strange gadgets, innovations and inventions, Trendhunter promotes many useless things that nobody needs alongside clever new gadgets. Clicking through the dashboard/sidebar at the top of the web page leads to a page titled 'culture' and a sub-category titled pop culture. The page is primarily dedicated to consumer goods, such as Vape-like inhalable nutrient pens, precision sunscreen applicators, a deep sleep enabling clock that uses AI to help you sleep, performance-tracking mouthguards, on-the-go coffee bars, and perhaps the most useless product of all, non-alcoholic gin spirits. However, it also claims to showcase how elements of mainstream media influences societal behaviour and consumer goods, featuring everything from viral videos to film merchandise and political satire. A problem is that in order to move beyond consumer goods to learn about popular culture trends, users need to subscribe.

A striking feature of the site is the language that is deployed to predict future trends. The language mimics that of the wellness industry. For example, it is claimed that as part of a 'Distraction Defense', consumers seek products and services in the tech space to help stay 'present'. In other words, we are told that consumers want products that contribute to a sense of wellness and an absence of the addictive properties of technology. Behind each popular culture aspect profiled there is an effort to promote or sell something. For Trendhunters, popular culture is synonymous with consumer culture and promotion. What that means from a public relations perspective is that Trendhunters is an ideal space to promote and commercialise client innovations and inventions, but it also means that it less likely to contribute significantly to social or environmental change.

An alternative approach is offered by Future Crunch (https://futurecrun.ch/), a website that presents a very positive model of future trends from 'a group of scientists, artists, technologists and entrepreneurs' who believe that science and technology will create 'a more peaceful, transparent and abundant world'. 'Intelligent optimism' is a slogan proclaimed on the page banner, which is suggestive of an alternative to the usual negativity encountered in trend sites and expanded upon in additional maxims: 'We give you rocket fuel for the brain. We show you how the world is getting better. We help organisations navigate the future. We're your field guides for the next economy'. The approach is highly positive and upbeat. Much of the language mimics that of academia. Here mimesis is also at play – imitating academia conveys a form of cultural value and legitimacy.

The aim of Future Crunch is to assist organisations to offer presentations and create stories that they claim will help people contribute to the future. The business model is a speaker bureau that promotes motivational speakers who present on topics such as adaptability, the next economy, technology trends, imagining futures and optimism. A free fortnightly email newsletter is provided that reports on good news, scientific breakthroughs and positive stories. Future Crunch philosophy is based upon positivity. They acknowledge that a key issue for those driving social change is 'how to avoid being overwhelmed by problems'. The site does deliver on positivity. Clicking on the tab titled 'Good news' leads through to the newsletter and a range of good news stories that include the doubling of the wild tiger population in Nepal, cessation of coal plant construction by a Japanese company, a decrease in the youth crime rate in California, the compulsory use of plastics in road construction in India and a 60% fall in deforestation in Indonesia. Although these stories are not about the future, they do create a sense of hope and optimism about the future and suggest possibilities for social change. Rather than the more typical negative messages of mainstream media, Future Crunch's examples of potential solutions establish a set of case studies and practices for alternative media futures. This approach fits with a broader mimesis of academic discourses that Future Crunch draws upon for credibility and legitimacy. Like academia, Future Crunch seeks to establish its position as a thought leader by generating knowledge and innovative solutions to societal problems. What we see here is that instead of the negative messaging deployed by media, Future Crunch uses positivity or constructive positioning as a primary public relations strategy that is often summed up as 'accentuate the positive, eliminate the negative'. This type of public relations aligns with the aim of popular culture to be relatable and tell positive stories. It is possible (or likely) that social change may more readily emerge from the progressive, constructive elements of popular culture rather than links to the consumer aspects of popular culture.

Shifting from the forecasting industry to examine how public relations organisations engage in trend forecasting draws attention to a range of promotional strategies. Edelman, a public relations organization founded in 1952, describes itself as 'an independent global communications firm that partners with businesses and organisations – long-established and just-emerging – to evolve, promote and protect their brands and reputations. Our global network comprises 6,000 practitioners in more than 60 offices whose work spans brand, reputation, digital, and advisory and is powered by analytics, planning, creative and media relations' (Edelman, 2019). As a global public relations organisation, Edelman offers its global clients access to a series of findings from research projects it undertakes to inform them of current trends and to establish its own areas of expertise. For example, the Edelman 'earned brand study' is a mechanism for Edelman to position itself as knowledgeable about trends and consumers. The term 'earned brand' suggests that customer loyalty must be earned. This sort of jargon implies that Edelman has something unique to offer. We learn from the website that

> Ideology dominates the cultural conversation. Around the globe, consumers are putting their personal convictions front and centre. From the grocery aisle to the car dealership, they're buying on belief. Willing or not, brands of all kinds and sizes are navigating this new reality. And in a lightning-quick digital world, the rewards and risks are equally high. The 2017 Edelman Earned Brand study reveals that

> - 57% of consumers boycott brands based on a social or political issue
> - 65% of belief driven buyers will not buy a brand if it stays silent on relevant issues.
>
> (Edelman, 2017)

The opening statement, that ideology dominates the cultural conversation, could be interpreted as Edelman co-opting or mimicking academic jargon and positioning itself as having expertise in ideology, culture and conversations. On a different tack, the Edelman 2019 Trust barometer study suggests that 'My employer' is the most trusted institution because of deep dissatisfaction with the system (Edelman, 2019). The working hypothesis or supposition is that trust has become more localised and moved to relationships within one's control, which means that there are expectations that the organisations we work for will be more responsible. The Trust Barometer research has also found that pessimism about the future is likely to mean that protests will become more mainstream and that CEOs are expected to lead the fight for change. These are provocative findings that shift the responsibility for social and environmental change from government to organisations. It is unclear how influential the Trust Barometer is in terms of impact and change but it certainly is an important discursive shift. This goes beyond some of the empty rhetoric of corporate social responsibility – employee expectations about the locus of control are now localised. Although Edelman posits that it marks a shift to relationships within our control, that is a stretch – many employees are unlikely to agree that such relationships are in any way controllable. But it is important to note that regardless of how valid or verifiable the study findings are, Edelman is highlighting the need for CEOs and organisations to meet social expectations. This is not a novel approach but the reference to protest brings a sense of urgency and suggests that it should be taken seriously.

Weber Shandwick, a multinational public relations company, was formed in 2001 through a series of mergers and acquisitions and is a member of the Interpublic Group of Companies. Weber Shandwick's trend forecasting primer, 'Media Genius' offers insights into 'the trends, tech and strategies that are actively changing our world' (Weber Shandwick, n.d.). Media Genius is positioned as a live study guide that explains how intelligent technology is transforming media and assists in understanding and adapting to the transformations. It is derived from, and updated regularly by, posts for the Weber Shandwick online newsletter titled 'Solving for X'. The Media Genius manual covers five key trends: Artificial Intelligence (AI) and machine learning; platform economy; synthetic content; media forensics; and content experience. It also suggests possible implications for each trend and provides a selection of independent online courses that develop understanding of each trend. The general content of the guide is a series of statements about each trend and a series of opportunities and risks afforded by each trend. For example, it is claimed that 'AI is helping brands deliver marketing efficiencies and customer value. . . . AI is exposing companies to new forms of risk' (Weber Shandwick, n.d.). The Media Genius guide provides insights into the business development strategies of Weber Shandwick and the type of expertise that Weber Shandwick pitches to clients. It offers a hook to start a conversation with clients and create business around those conversations. The guide also functions as a form of brand building. By prioritising AI as a key trend, Weber Shandwick is positioning itself as current and innovative. Prioritising media forensics works in much the same way. The term 'forensics' suggests the use of scientific techniques and connects to our familiarity with popular culture crime television genres. Media Genius functions as part of their own public relations strategy – it is a tool that signals what is hot and what Weber Shandwick can do. Weber Shandwick may be understood to be positioning itself as a type of investigator that deploys evidence-based data to develop communication strategies. These types of trend reports offer a general market analysis to suggest how clients may navigate contemporary challenges and open up business opportunities in ways that imply a scientific legitimacy. Here, again, a mimetic strategy is at play but, in this instance, it is more a form of imitation than reproduction or representation. Within cultural theory, distinctions between representation and imitation are significant. Public relations scholarship may draw upon these distinctions to examine how other disciplines are appropriated, co-opted, re-interpreted and transformed and determine the cultural value and contributions of such strategies. The relationship between public relations and popular culture may be critiqued according to intent and outcome – is popular culture deployed as a resource for social change or are worlds of illusion created for business development purposes? Thinking through what response is demanded is another mode of evaluating public relations strategies. Public relations firms also imitate one another.

Smaller public relations agencies that do not have the funds to develop trend forecasts for their clients may borrow from the forecasting that is conducted by multinational public relations companies. They may also rely on and adapt publicly available information. For instance, the well-known Megatrends forecasts that analyse and speculate on global, broad and transformative shifts or changes may be appropriated. Consultancy firm, PWC, identifies five megatrends or global shifts that they claim are reshaping the world, which may then be adapted and applied to client problems and responses developed. An alternative forecasting resource is public relations media, such as *Public Relations Today*, which offers a series of insights into various developments such as content marketing, email marketing, social media trends and diverse case studies throughout the year. A further alternative for small public relations agencies is, for example, consulting the work of firms such as LEAD Innovation, a spin-off from the Vienna University of Economics and Business, that specialises in international trend research. LEAD Innovation defines a trend as 'an assumed development in the future that will have a long-term and lasting effect on and change something' (LEAD, Innovation, n.d). The firm's website offers a series of insights into how to manage for trends, how to identify trends and how integrate those trends into strategy. The core strength is trend research methods. Public relations consultancies may 'borrow' content from firms such as LEAD Innovation. The word 'borrow' is used here as a tactful way of saying that many smaller agencies rely on secondary research – they assemble, summarise, and amalgamate existing research – and offer second-hand interpretations. So, when attempting to understand how particular trends become popular it would seem that, rather than the 'forward-looking orientation' that McKie and Munshi (2007) call for, what we see here is sideways borrowing, copying and appropriating – a type of pirating – of future trend predictions. This is not out of order for understanding how popular culture works – it too is often based on these types of practices. In terms of thinking about how the relationship between public relations and popular culture may drive social change, what we see at play is that sometimes an assemblage of miscellany has the potential to create new and innovative solutions. The challenge is to get the mix right and popularise those solutions.

A discussion of trending would be incomplete without consideration of the role that algorithms play in the relationship between popular culture, public relations and social change. Algorithms are the mathematical models that are built into computer programs and predetermine the media selections available. Donovan and boyd's (2019) work on algorithms and accountability in the amplification role of social media underscores the importance of taking into account how technology design impacts people, public relations and popular culture. Donovan and boyd (2019) argue that algorithms mask political decisions in social media and influence how people may connect, collaborate and organise. Algorithms have become proxy decision makers that advance the economic interests of those who have them designed and, as Donovan and boyd (2019) point out, there is no appeals process. Donovan and boyd (2019) argue that as we move more of our lives online, we are allowing algorithmic management to take more control of our lives. This cultural change means that community organising and socially driven change is put at risk. However, Donovan (2018) identifies a type of 'hypercommons' in which skills, knowledge and resources transfer within and across movements in time and space. Although intended as a community space, it is also a space that public relations may intervene in. It is critical that a deliberative or conversational space is maintained for community organising that is outside the confines of algorithms and commodified popular culture. Perceptions of popular culture trends may simply reflect a particular algorithm that prioritises certain trends and de-prioritises or ignores other trends. Such algorithms are connected to the interests of the organisations that design them and therefore what may seem to be a popular culture trend may actually just be a reflection of a corporate algorithm. We need to ask: How do we determine genuine popular culture trends – is there even such a thing? Or is it that all trends are genuine – just that some are corporatised and commodified and others are community derived? What are the popular cultures we want to create and engage in? These questions are central to thinking through the types of worlds we want to create and live in. A range of popular culture ephemera, from news, to social media conversations and images, are also important for us to understand because popular culture trends are not only about significant issues. We also need to understand the appeal and value of a quirky angle or humour. What may be seemingly mundane is, potentially, of vital importance for understanding how everyday values and concerns are reinserted into popular culture and how political and commercial public relations efforts are ignored or subverted.

Conclusion

I would like to conclude this chapter with a story about another chance encounter. At a party in Sydney, I met two filmmakers who had become intrigued by psychics and were producing a documentary on the topic. They told compelling tales of divination, telepathy and clairvoyance, noting how psychics were able to connect people with their deceased loved ones and tell fortunes. Psychics seem an old-fashioned phenomenon, rather than a contemporary popular culture trend, yet it was clear the filmmakers were spell-bound and the topic had captured their imagination. To me, this seemed a clear-cut case of charlatanism, trickery or self-delusion. I researched everything I could find on the phenomena of psychics because I wanted to know how it worked. There was no compelling scientific evidence to support psychic claims; instead a number of techniques were identified such as 'reading' a person and covert research. So, no special paranormal powers – just investigative preparation and smart reading of people and situations. This chapter about fortune telling points to how academic research and aspects of popular culture may be co-opted for various future-oriented, legitimate or dodgy/suspect/dubious purposes. Trend forecasting is a commercial undertaking designed to enhance business development opportunities and sell products. Future forecasting or foresight for public relations purposes in popular culture may involve research, grandiosity or deception. It is challenging to determine how public relations may advance positive change when there is minimal evidence of attention to social and environmental issues in the examples discussed.

A key strategy for creating trends that is identified in this chapter is mimesis – mimicking already recognisable and accepted phenomena and approaches to leverage popularity. The relationship between public relations and popular culture is mimetic and imitative. What that means in practice is that borrowing and copying are standard practice in both public relations and popular culture – innovation evolves from creative combinations that hold appeal. Motion, Weaver, and Leitch (2015) suggest that popularisation is more likely to occur when concerns are escalated, everyday practices are mobilised and meaningful mechanisms are developed for navigating social issues. Popular culture should offer meaningful ways of imagining, visualising and speaking about issues and innovations that connect with people's sense of self and their everyday experiences (Motion et al., 2015, p. 507). A vital aspect of future forecasting is the importance of creating deliberative spaces and allowing opportunities for spontaneous deliberative moments so that civil society may open up and articulate issues, set agendas and establish stakes in issues. The commercial aspects of future forecasting identified in this chapter need to be countered by re-establishing societal and environmental priorities and inserting them in governance policies and practices.

In writing this chapter I have come to wonder more generally about popular culture. Is it actually a form of culture or simply a series of promotional moves? Are we confusing consumption and entertainment with culture – and is public relations complicit in creating this confusion or does it merely exploit it? Perhaps the answers to these questions about the nature of popular culture may be found in our own everyday lives rather than mass experiences. Increasingly it is becoming apparent that even public forums such as Facebook, that we originally believed were interactive and that we were actively sharing and participating in, are being controlled by algorithms, advertising revenue, business imperatives and controlling interests. For culture to be meaningful and matter, we need to have some influence, control and active involvement in popular sense making. So, this chapter points to the vital role that public relations can play in popular culture and driving social change – the democratisation of mediatised spaces – rather than trying to drive popular opinion through faux trend research and forecasting.

References

Bell, W. (2002). A community of futurists and the state of the futures field. *Futures*, *34*, 235–247.

Benjamin, W. (1970). The work of art in the age of mechanical reproduction. In H. Arendt (Ed.), *Illuminations* (H. Zohn Trans., pp. 214–218). London, England: Fontana.

Donovan, J. (2018). After the #keyword: Eliciting, sustaining, and coordinating participation across the occupy movement. *Social Media + Society*, *4*(1), 1–12.

Donovan, J., & boyd, D. (2019). Stop the presses? Moving from strategic silence to strategic amplification in a networked media ecosystem. *American Behavioral Scientist*, https://doi.org/10.1177/0002764219878229

Edelman. (2017, October 2). *Earned brand*. Retrieved from www.edelman.com.au/research/earned-brand-2017

Edelman. (2019, January 20). Edelman trust barometer reveals my employer most trusted institution. News and Awards. Retrieved from www.edelman.com/news-awards/2019-edelman-trust-barometer-reveals-my-employer-most-trusted-institution

Jenkins, H., Ford, S., & Green, J. (2013). *Spreadable media: Creating value and meaning in a networked world*. New York, NY: New York University Press.

John, N. A. (2012). Sharing and Web 2.0: The emergence of a keyword. *New Media & Society, 15*(2), 167–182.

LEAD Innovation. (n.d.). Trend research: How to identify relevant trends. Retrieved from www.lead-innovation.com/english-blog/trend-research

McKie, D., & Munshi, D. (2007). *Reconfiguring public relations: Ecology, equity and enterprise*. London, England: Routledge.

Motion, J., Weaver, C. K., & Leitch, S. (2015). Popularizing dissent: A civil society perspective. *Public Understanding of Science, 24*(4), 496–510.

Son, H. (2015). The history of Western futures studies: An exploration of the intellectual traditions and three-phase periodization. *Futures, 66*, 120–137.

Tsoukas, H., & Shepherd, J. (2004). Organisations and the future: From forecasting to foresight. *Management Today, 20*(7), 18–23.

Webb, A. (2017). The flare and focus of successful futurists. *MIT Sloan Management Review, 58*(4), 55–58.

Weber Shandwick. (n.d.). *Media at the intersection of content and intelligence*. Retrieved from https://solveforx.webershandwick.com/genius

4 Undead PR

Theorising public relations and popular culture[1]

Kate Fitch

Introduction

This chapter investigates zombie public relations in order to understand the ways in which public relations activity is embedded in society and culture and yet is often conceptualised in line with an undead paradigm. It draws on scholarship on public relations and popular culture to argue the need to rethink and retheorise public relations in relation to contemporary culture. Recognising popular culture as a transformative and critical space, this chapter engages with the popular zombie trope, a key cultural motif in the twenty-first century, and its use in public relations as well as its potential as a metaphor for exploring public relations theory. My interest in zombies is not just because of the resurgence of their popularity but because of their global and cultural significance as a metaphor for neoliberalism. Precisely because the zombie is located at the threshold between life and death (Luckhurst, 2016), it is a useful device for crossing, and investigating the construction of, boundaries and public relations' double game and entanglement with neoliberalism.

Karen Miller, in documenting fictional representations of public relations on screen, identified an early depiction of a zombie public relations practitioner, and significantly one that denies any responsibility for organisational action: 'I don't know a damn thing. I play tour guide and I write press releases' says Randi James, 'in charge of PR', in the movie *Dead Heat* (1988) (cited in K. Miller, 1999, p. 8). Here, the public relations role is an (undead) mouthpiece without any reflexivity or ethical conscience around the work performed. I've previously written about undead public relations, focusing on vampire spokesperson Nan Flanagan in *True Blood* (Fitch, 2015). Flanagan, like Randi James, disintegrates on termination. In writing that paper, in which I offered a postfeminist Gothic reading, I became interested in the monstrous in terms of how the vampire genre offered multiple and contradictory discourses around public relations in popular culture, and, in particular, of how public relations was frequently represented as mind/mass media manipulation and persuasion techniques. In this chapter, I tease out my ideas around public relations' spectral haunting – or to draw on Fawkes (2020), its Shadow – to make visible its promotional impulses and privileging of hegemonic and commercial interests. Given the zombie's boundary-crossing and polysemic identity, and its capacity for massification, the zombie trope enables a (sometimes playful) rethinking of public relations and its 'invisible' work in promoting neoliberalism.

Public relations engages with popular culture and cultural texts, frequently referencing popular tropes in campaigns and even changing their meaning in new contexts. The resurgence of the zombie in the twenty-first century offers rich material for thinking through public relations, not only in terms of popular culture representations, but in the ways in which public relations engages with contemporary culture and is implicated in the processes of globalisation and neo-liberalism. For example, the historical development of public relations is closely linked with the dissemination of the neoliberal project and furthering the aims of capitalism (Cronin, 2018; Surma & Demetrious, 2018). I therefore build on ideas around 'undead PR' in this chapter by unpacking the zombie trope and teasing out what it might mean for not just understanding the links between popular culture and public relations but for how we perceive and theorise public relations and its work furthering the processes of capitalism and consumption. I also argue the zombie metaphor allows an examination of the construction of boundaries between public relations and propaganda and a stronger understanding of the links between public relations and neoliberalism.

The aim of this chapter is twofold: (1) to illustrate how public relations, as a promotional industry, engages with the popular and (2) to excavate the links between public relations work and neoliberalism. This chapter is structured in four sections. First, I identify public relations as a promotional industry and the zombie-like pervasiveness of functionalist approaches and their continuing influence on shaping the field. I identify how public relations is concerned with persuasion and practitioners regularly seek to manipulate public opinion to support government and business interests. I then discuss the zombie trope in the second section: its mutable identity, its cultural history and its resurgence in popular culture in the twenty-first century. I consider how the zombie is the 'other' human, as it symbolises the loss of what makes us human in response to market forces and is therefore useful for describing the experience of neoliberalism. In the third section, I analyse the use of the zombie trope in public relations campaigns in order to highlight the cultural work of public relations, its engagement with the everyday and its use of popular tropes to engage audiences. Finally, I draw on the zombie discussion in this chapter to discuss the often unacknowledged cultural work of public relations alongside the real, and often hidden, societal impact of public relations.

Public relations and promotional culture

Public relations is widely recognised as one of a number of promotional industries, alongside, for example, marketing, advertising, lobbying and the growing influencer industry. Lee Edwards argues that public relations practitioners are 'promotional intermediaries', that is 'cultural intermediaries working in the promotional industries' whose work is 'ideological in that it invokes or contests existing hierarchies of power' and draws on both 'popular and "high" culture for their creative inspiration' (2018, p. 51). Public relations is cultural work in that it engages with meaning making, produces symbolic texts and works with cultural norms and values (Edwards, 2015, 2018; Hesmondhalgh, 2013). However, public relations and promotional culture texts are rarely perceived as '*culture*' worthy of study: 'as reflective, artistic, worthy of engagement, and as perhaps contributing positively to the mediasphere' (Gray, 2010, p. 307). There has been limited scholarly investigation into public relations' cultural intermediary role or, subsequently, recognition of its quest for symbolic power (Edwards, 2012). Instead, public relations tends to be framed as propaganda, manipulative and superficial (Gray, 2010).

The widely touted – and accepted – historical development of the public relations industry towards a modern, ethical profession tends to dominate disciplinary understandings of public relations globally (Fitch, 2016). This progressive narrative that positions modern strategic public relations as somehow separate from propaganda and unethical practices continues to frame mainstream understandings of the discipline and is reproduced by industry representatives, professional associations and educators. In one of the foundation texts for public relations, *Managing Public Relations*, Grunig and Hunt acknowledge 'the profession has its roots in press agentry and propaganda . . . [but has] made great strides in its sophistication, ethics, responsibility, and contribution to society' (1984, p. 4). What is elided in such conceptualisations of public relations, and in more contemporary conceptualisations that promote the occupation as an ethical and socially responsible practice that contributes to a better society, is the social and cultural impact of public relations activity and its entanglement with power. Such accounts are by no means unique to public relations. Davis, for example, acknowledges how the standard historical narrative touted by promotional industries – that once 'dubious, ad hoc and questionable occupations have evolved to become "respectable" pillars of business and society' – is nothing short of 'deceptive' and distorts the impact of these industries on the modern media and markets (2013, pp. 19, 24). The emphasis on strategic public relations as a business, management function that supports organisational goals similarly fails to consider the broader ways public relations activity engages with contemporary culture, framing issues, connecting with the zeitgeist and fostering or enabling trends.

In fact, there is compelling evidence that persuasion and manipulation underpin public relations activity, are routine in the industry and are embedded in everyday tasks (Edwards, 2018). For example, despite the condemnation by professional public relations associations, the Cambridge Analytica-Facebook scandal that erupted amid concerns over the manipulation of the US 2016 election and the Brexit poll through disinformation, fake news and the widespread and unethical use of personal data in micro-targeting campaigns are both associated with public relations (Edwards, 2018). Similarly, the work of former UK-based public relations firm, Bell Pottinger, which declared bankruptcy following the scandal associated with their racist 'white monopoly' campaign in South Africa, may not be exceptional even though both UK professional associations, Public Relations and Communication Association and Chartered Institute of Public Relations issued strong statements distancing the industry from Bell Pottinger (Burne Jones, 2017; Edwards, 2018; Sweney, 2017). In another example, Mercer PR was linked with the communication activities of the Republic of Nauru in relation to the contentious Australian offshore detention centres (McKenzie-Murray, 2015).[2] According to news reports, the Public Relations Institute of Australia [PRIA] modified their statement condemning Mercer PR for identifying the victim of an alleged rape on Nauru to the media, following the threat of legal action (see Hasham, 2015; Mackenzie, 2015, 2016; Robin, 2019; Ward, 2015). In 2019, the Federal Treasury found that Mercer PR had breached the woman's human rights (Robin, 2019). Mercer describes his company's role as 'limited to assisting in the flow of information between the government of Nauru and the Australian media' (cited in McKenzie-Murray, 2015), a position which frames public relations as a neutral activity. These examples, however, highlight the inability of the industry to regulate ethical practice and suggest the impact of public relations is not benign.

In this book, we view practitioners as cultural intermediaries, whose promotional work depends on the culture in which it is situated and uses popular culture as a resource (Davis, 2013). We recognise that the interaction between consumers and audiences and promotional work produces meaning, but not necessarily in the prescribed ways. Meaning, in promotional texts, is co-created and reappropriated by consumers and audiences (Davis, 2013, pp. 40–41). It is therefore not just organisations and practitioners who draw on culture in their public relations work, but 'individuals *productively use culture and commodities*' (emphasis in original) (Davis, 2013, p. 40). Audiences resist, challenge and subvert meanings constantly (Barthes, 1977; Davis, 2013; Fiske, 2010). Consumption can be subversive, creative and productive (Davis, 2013). The zombie metaphor, with its dense, if slippery and mutating, network of meanings, as I discuss in the following section, therefore becomes less fanciful in its application to understanding the cultural work of public relations.

Zombie histories and cultures

Zombies are a global, twenty-first-century phenomenon even though historically they emerged out of colonisation and global capitalism and later twentieth-century Hollywood to become the modern Gothic monster (Luckhurst, 2016). The zombie represents the undead, an uncomfortable space that emerges between living and death and threatens the existence of both categories. In terms of the themes of this book, the zombie is a useful device for discussing boundaries and boundary riding as zombies are by definition: 'threshold people' (Victor Turner, cited in Luckhurst, 2016, p. 9). They have always been 'low-brow' popular culture and this marginality allows transgression and boundary crossing. Although the zombie trope is often employed to stand for mindless mass media audiences in response to technological change, there is no single definition of a zombie. The zombie signifies many things and a precise meaning remains ambiguous and elusive. Zombies therefore offer a metaphor that can mean almost anything, allowing them to operate as a metatrope, a kind of mass metaphor (Rutherford, 2013). In this section, I consider the infinite meanings of zombies, drawing on literature from various disciplines to illustrate the diverse ways in which this popular cultural trope is employed and its potential for illuminating understandings of public relations.

The zombie is a pervasive and popular trope that crosses boundaries and cannibalises other genres. In popular culture, the ubiquitous zombie trope demonstrates some common attributes. Webb and Byrnand (2008) theorise these characteristics as unrelenting hunger and therefore an easy metaphor to use in relation to capitalism: ceaseless consumption; lack of free agency (and therefore mindless and lacking in judgement); colonisation (like a virus, they infect, multiply and spread); and a close similarity to, but not the same as, humans. The zombie represents the loss of human soul or thought, as Sinead Murphy poetically describes in her book on the neoliberal university: 'When you enter the gates of the post-university, you enter the orifice of a zombie, in which all that brought it to be is emptied out' (2017, p. x). Zombies therefore represent a monstrous other to humanity in that they lack free agency and the capacity to think and to know.

Across disciplines, the term zombie is employed to signify some kind of loss, often of truth or authenticity, in relation to market-driven forces. John Quiggan (2012), for example, coined the term zombie economics to express how the dead ideas (of market liberalism such as deregulation and free enterprise) still walk among us. Similarly, ideas around excellence in public relations continue to have currency, but this updated Grunigian paradigm masks the ways in which public relations ultimately serves corporate and government interests rather than the publics it purports to represent (Bourne, 2019).

Teasing out the significance of these ideas for understandings, Katz identifies how the 'zombification of social institutions . . . occurs when the machinery that enables the neoliberal growth imperative is accepted uncritically' (2016, p. 3). Public relations is an intrinsic part of that machinery. In an example that serves to illustrate how public relations is oriented to serve business interests, Charlton (2008) developed the term 'zombie science' to describe using science as propaganda to further commercial aims, often through corporate funding of academic research. This is, in fact, a typical public relations activity, well documented by Marion Nestle (2015) who writes about science tainted by lobbyists and corporate funding of academic research in relation to the food industry. The public relations 'investment' in academic work taints by distorting truth and lacking in authenticity. Further, Katz coins the terms 'Zombilingo' and 'corpspeak' to describe the 'means of disseminating a worldview maintained by faith in market forces' (2016, p. 2). The question for both this chapter and this book is the extent to which public relations reproduces and disseminates – and whether there is a capacity for challenging and resisting – that world view.

Zombie campaigns

There are many examples of zombies used in promotional campaigns. Even public relations trade media and industry blogs draw on the popular zombie trope, for example promoting tongue-in-cheek articles with clickbait headlines include '4 things zombies can teach PR pros' (E. Miller, 2016) and 'Bad PR: 13 sure signs you're a PR zombie' with pithy advice such as 'Your news releases are vapid, coma-inducing, Dead Sea scrolls' (Domansky, n.d.). To offer another example, Weber Shandwick highlights learning outcomes from the zombie apocalypse for modern public relations practice in a blog (see Tsang, 2012). As Rutherford says so eloquently and succinctly, 'Zombie sells' (2013, p. 22).

In this section, I discuss the US Center for Disease Control (CDC)'s Zombie Apocalypse campaign, which began in 2011, as a way of thinking about public relations activity as promotional work that creates and circulates meaning. This example highlights the gaps in standard approaches to thinking about public relations as a 'strategic' practice that relies on research and evaluation to show its impact on business objectives. The campaign was designed to raise awareness of disaster preparation among young adults. CDC's initial plan was for a week-long social media campaign to engage new and younger audiences and to revitalise their annual campaign about disaster preparedness (Fraustino & Ma, 2015; Kruvand & Silver, 2013). They spent $87 on a stock photo and relied on their existing staff to run the campaign. The unexpectedly high levels of engagement led to the campaign running for 16 months and included the development of graphic novels, teaching resources for schools and universities and invitations for the campaign managers to attend fan conventions such as Comicon. CDC was even approached about the possibility of Hollywood films and novels although these offers were declined on the grounds they were too commercial. By most measures, the campaign was successful in terms of awareness raising and had a global impact. Like a zombie infection, the campaign went viral and attracted global attention.

However, some public relations scholars maintain that the campaign was unsuccessful in that it failed to bring about the desired behavioural change. Fraustino and Ma (2015) argue – based on an 'experiment' with university students and the apparent lack of audience research to underpin the campaign – that the use of zombies weakened rather than strengthened the likelihood of disaster kit preparation. I question the quantitative approach to this research (as they analysed their statistics drawn from their experiment with university students) and the somewhat linear thinking (borrowed from management and illustrated through the usual structures of public relations planning: goals, targets, objectives, strategy) that underpins their study. The 'scientific method' underpins much writing and theorising about public relations work, as part of claims gesturing towards the field's management status and a disciplinary alignment with business. Their conclusion draws heavily on a normative and functionalist paradigm of public relations, one that as I suggested earlier, is like the undead in that it continues to have currency in theorising public relations despite criticism from critical and interpretive scholars. My concern is how such approaches structure neoliberal logic into the very 'DNA' (Bourne, 2019, p. 110) of public relations work.

What interests me about such scholarly responses to the Zombie Apocalypse campaign is that despite its unexpected success, its virality, and I would argue its successful use of popular culture tropes, it is considered a failure. That leads me to question what is going on, given the campaign had an impact that exceeded any expectations its originators could have anticipated. The answer might lie in thinking differently about promotional texts, including those texts that are the outputs of public relations activity. For example, Gray points to the meaning making which occurs when audiences engage with promotional texts, in this case, with advertisements:

> Ads, though, do not just produce profits, dupes and the ills of capitalism; they also produce engagement, reflection, interest, meanings, and interpretative introductions to much of the culture that advertising's staunchest critics generally regard as more legitimate, artistic, uplifting and hence worthy of aesthetic analysis.
>
> (2010, pp. 307–308)

Promotional texts work precisely because they are enmeshed with cultural meaning-making processes (Edwards, 2018). In framing public relations as a promotional industry, Edwards argues that 'the business of public relations is therefore to ensure that meaning is created and campaigns devised in ways that maximise circulation' (2018, p. 53). The virality, then, of CDC's Zombie Apocalypse campaign does point to its success as does the playfulness and engagement that promoted a more serious message as part of a recurring annual campaign around disaster preparedness.

While the CDC campaign is just one example, there are many others. Zombies tend to be used playfully as a popular cultural icon that can engage a knowing audience familiar with the zombie genre. For example, Toyota developed a series of screen advertisements that offered mini-filmic narratives. At two minutes in length, they were longer than the standard television car advertisement and broke the generic boundaries of car advertising. Zombie texts only 'work' because the audience is familiar with the zombie genre and can playfully engage with the narrative knowing that it is a promotional text but one in which the audience can also engage with pleasure. So, the promotional text is not simply persuasive but also pleasurable. Edwards argues that public relations is 'a prolific source of meaning' (2018, p. 28) and it is this meaning making and sometimes pleasure making that is neglected in more linear and strategic framing of public relations that attempt to evaluate and measure campaign success through predetermined objectives and key performance indicators.

Considering the zombie as a cultural trope allows me to explore how public relations texts, as promotional texts, create and circulate meaning and as texts with which knowing audiences playfully engage. Public relations here is reframed as a cultural activity and it highlights the ways in which practitioners engage with social trends and cultural norms. The zombie offers another useful analogy for this chapter. In order to illustrate how public relations 'instrumentalises' culture, Edwards argues that:

> practitioners disembed socio-cultural norms and practices from their original context, relocate them into new environments, and repurpose them in communication that serves specific ends. In this way, public relations both intervenes in and instrumentalises different aspects of society and culture.
>
> (2018, p. 4)

Like the genre-crossing and mutating zombie, then, the very work of public relations rearticulates and repurposes cultural tropes and artefacts. This work creates new meanings and resonates with audiences who are familiar with these tropes. In fact, this is not new: professional communicators have always sought to harness trends and topical events in their promotional work in order to engage audiences.

Public relations and neoliberalism

Public relations as an occupational practice traditionally is concerned with persuasion on behalf of a client or employer and about researching publics in order to better target them. It has also been about lobbying behind the scenes and setting the news agenda, and such 'behind the scenes' work has thrived on a lack of public visibility and accountability (Bourne, 2016; Fitch, 2017). The point is 'promotional intermediaries . . . serve primarily those that employ them' (Davis, 2013, p. 22). From a cultural studies perspective, promotional industries are tainted by their association with the market. There is no doubt that promotional industries, such as public relations, are integral to markets, media and culture, but more research is needed to understand the ways in which public relations has shaped market-based democracies, human imaginations and public discourse in line with a neoliberal logic (Cronin, 2018; Davis, 2013). In this section, therefore, I consider the ways public relations is intertwined with neoliberalism.

The rise of consumer society, and correspondingly, media audiences, in the twentieth century, and probably from the late nineteenth century, contributed to the historical development of public relations (Davis, 2013). In turn, as critical scholars have established, public relations reinforces neoliberalism and protects hegemonic interests (Cronin, 2018; Miller & Dinan, 2008; L'Etang, 1996; Roper, 2005). But, the 'confluence' between public relations and neoliberalism is perhaps more insidious in that public relations has played a significant role in communicating and implementing the neoliberal project across the twentieth century (Demetrious & Surma, 2019, p. 106). As a result, public relations permeates the everyday with a market orientation:

> public relations, not only as an industry but also as a communicative process and mode, seeps into and affects all areas of our lives – professional, corporate, domestic, political, activist and technological. As an industry, public relations

is intimately interwoven with and, often, invisibly, amplifies the tenor and reach of neoliberal ideology. As a communicative process, and therefore as a mode and style of being and relating to others in the contemporary social world, public relations plays a significant social role in the 'harmonising' or dissolving of contradiction and difference, as well as marginalising or even muting those questions of power and control that organise and regulate our personal, social, professional and political relationships.

(Demetrious & Surma, 2019, p. 106)

Public relations is transformative in that it creates publics and opportunities for engagement but it does so in line with a neoliberal logic (Cronin, 2018). Despite adopting democratic values and rhetoric, the work of public relations is to enact what Cronin argues is a 'commercial democracy' that has significant social and political impact (2018, pp. 3, 54, 112). Cronin describes 'commercial democracy' in her book *Public Relations Capitalism*:

Commercial democracy is a new vernacular form of democracy that speaks the language of representation and agency but is disconnected from the practices and formal legitimacy of conventional representative democracy. It displaces the political and, in the public's eyes, it relocates politics, power, and agency to the popular, the everyday, and especially to consumption.

(2018, p. 4)

For Bourne (2019), one of the more disturbing aspects of public relations work is the way it appears to give publics a voice, even as that work privileges corporate and commercial interests. Ultimately, this means that public relations tends to work against democracy, in that it shuts down opportunities for dissenting voices and alternative perspectives (Bourne, 2019).

In trying to understand how public relations inflects neoliberalism into the everyday, Surma and Demetrious (2018) draw on Poerkson's concept of 'Plasticwörter' [plastic words] to describe words that lack precise meaning but have nevertheless become everyday commonsense words. These words are imbued with neoliberal language and market discourse and relate closely to the ideas around zombies I have presented in this chapter. Like zombies, these plastic words are 'hollowed out' and have lost the original meanings of their historical context (Surma & Demetrious, 2018, pp. 100–101). They are Katz's (2016) 'corpspeak' and 'Zombilingo'. The significance is these plastic words – such as management, freedom, progress – can reveal the subtle ways in which ideas based on the market and free enterprise are propagated so that they appear to be the commonsense norm (Surma & Demetrious, 2018). This observation points to the hidden work of public relations we identify in this book. Davis describes public relations as 'the Trojan horse of marketisation' in its promotion of neoliberalism and consumption (2013, p. 198). However, for Cronin, 'public relations practices parade in plain sight market rationalities such as brand distinctiveness and competition while simultaneously weaving them into the fabric of institutional thinking and practice' (2016, p. 11). The hidden work of public relations, then, despites its protestations of democratising impulses, is the stealthy promotion of neoliberalism and its insertion into the everyday.

Conclusion

In this chapter, I have presented different conceptualisations of the zombie and its relevance for theorising public relations. Slightly tongue in cheek, I have pointed to the zombie as an apt metaphor for functionalist and normative approaches to public relations, arguing that like the undead, they keep reanimating despite a growing and significant body of work that offers rich alternatives for theorising public relations. As a boundary-dweller between life and death, the zombie as monstrous other can also threaten the neat boundary constructions of public relations as a strategic business discipline that serves organisational interests and as 'not propaganda', manipulation or unethical persuasion.

The close links between zombies and capital also allow us to glimpse less tangible aspects of public relations work. That 'dark side' embraces public relations' shadowy work that is not always visible in its double game of relationship building and engagement and at the same time, promoting and framing consumption and instrumentalising publics. Zombies threaten the institutional boundaries we construct and zombie narratives 'interrogate the impact of neoliberal ideology' (Blake, 2015, p. 29). Like a zombie, the neoliberal project mutates and reanimates in new forms. Blake argues:

> The zombie apocalypse has provided audiences with a means of looking at and working through the contemporary deliquescence of a body politic infected by neoliberalism. The zombie is, in short, the monster of choice for a generation tired of a decade of governmental facilitation of the anti-democratic impulses of neoliberal corporatism allowing . . . an urgent reconsideration of who we have become under the auspices of a failed economic model that . . . refuses to lie down and die.
>
> (2015, p. 28)

In trying to understand how public relations engages with the popular, I have investigated the popularity of the zombie trope. Drawing on the CDC disaster preparedness campaign, I have also considered the zombie as a cultural trope that allows me to explore how public relations texts, as promotional texts, create and circulate meaning and as texts with which knowing audiences playfully engage. Public relations here is reframed as a cultural activity and it highlights both the ways in which practitioners engage with social trends and cultural norms that resonate with audiences and audiences engage and take pleasure in promotional texts. Rethinking public relations through the lenses of cultural production enables a new emphasis on the ways it engages audiences with meaning and pleasure making.

I conclude with reference to an independent Canadian zombie movie, *Fido*, where, post-apocalypse, the nation state has yielded to a corporation (Blake, 2015). Through public relations, the corporation controls every aspect of peoples' lives, including employment, housing, media and schools. Zombies are indentured labourers and in servitude to further capitalist production until ZomCom Corporation's propaganda lies are exposed. Most of the rather unpleasant husbands are killed in a factory accident, and the women and children live out a peaceful and pleasant existence served by their docile and kind zombie companions. The happy ending points to the failure of consumer capitalism in developing a fair and just society. The zombie is useful, then, in drawing attention to public relations' 'hidden' work in promoting the neoliberal project and potentially in pointing the way forward to new ways of imagining and promoting more socially oriented and community driven forms of public relations. It may be pushing the zombie trope too far, but deconstructing the organisation-public boundary and exposing public relations' entanglement with neoliberalism enables different understandings of public relations and its role in society to emerge.

Notes

1 I thank Philip Young (2013) for coining 'Undead PR' in his blog, which included a review of my conference paper on *True Blood*.
2 Australia's actions exiling asylum seekers in Nauru have been condemned by organisations such as the United Nations (Davidson & Vasefi, 2018), Amnesty International and Human Rights Watch (2016).

References

Barthes, R. (1977). *Image-music-text* (S. Hath, Trans.). New York, NY: Hill and Wang.

Blake, L. (2015). 'Are we worth saving? You tell me': Neoliberalism, zombies and the failure of free trade. *Gothic Studies, 17*(2), 26–41.

Bourne, C. (2016). *Trust, power and public relations in financial markets.* Abingdon, England: Routledge.

Bourne, C. (2019). AI cheerleaders: Public relations, neoliberalism and artificial intelligence. *Public Relations Inquiry, 8*(2), 109–125.

Burne Jones, S. (2017, September 20). CIPR 'condemns without reservation' Bell Pottinger's South Africa work as it confirms withdrawal of DA complaint. *PR Week.* Retrieved from www.prweek.com/article/1445211/cipr-condemns-without-reservation-bell-pottingers-south-africa-work-confirms-withdrawal-da-complaint

Charlton, B. G. (2008). Zombie science: A sinister consequence of evaluating scientific theories purely on the basis of enlightened self-interest [Editorial]. *Medical Hypotheses, 71*(3), 327–329.

Cronin, A. M. (2016). Reputational capital in 'the PR university': Public relations and market rationalities. *Journal of Cultural Economy, 9*(4), 396–409.

Cronin, A. M. (2018). *Public relations capitalism: Promotional culture, publics and commercial democracy.* Cham, Switzerland: Palgrave Macmillan.

Davidson, H., & Vasefi, S. (2018, October 16). UN body says Australia breached human rights laws and needs to review migration act. *The Guardian.* Retrieved from www.theguardian.com/australia-news/2018/oct/16/un-body-says-australia-breached-human-rights-laws-and-needs-to-review-migration-act

Davis, A. (2013). *Promotional cultures.* Cambridge, England: Polity Press.

Demetrious, K., & Surma, A. (2019). In ordinary places: The intersections between public relations and neoliberalism [Editorial]. *Public Relations Inquiry*, *8*(2), 105–108.

Domansky, J. (n.d.). Bad PR: 13 sure signs you're a PR zombie. *The PR Coach*. Retrieved from www.theprcoach.com/bad-pr-13-signs-youre-a-pr-zombie/

Edwards, L. (2012). Exploring the role of public relations as a cultural intermediary occupation. *Cultural Sociology*, *6*(4), 438–454.

Edwards, L. (2015). Understanding public relations as a cultural industry. In K. Oakley & J. O'Connor (Eds.), *The Routledge companion to the cultural industries* (pp. 371–381). Abingdon, England: Routledge.

Edwards, L. (2018). *Understanding public relations: Theory, culture and society*. London, England: Sage.

Fawkes, J. (2020). The contribution of public relations to promotional culture: Taking the long view. In I. Somerville, L. Edwards, & Ø. Ihlen (Eds.), *Public relations, society and the generative power of history* (pp. 15–29). Abingdon, England and New York, NY: Routledge.

Fiske, J. (2010). *Understanding popular culture* (2nd ed.). London, England: Routledge.

Fitch, K. (2015). Promoting the vampire rights amendment: Public relations, postfeminism and *True Blood*. *Public Relations Review*, *41*(5), 607–614.

Fitch, K. (2016). *Professionalizing public relations: History, gender and education*. Basingstoke, England: Palgrave.

Fitch, K. (2017). Seeing 'the unseen hand': Celebrity, promotion and public relations. *Public Relations Inquiry*, *6*(2), 157–169.

Fraustino, J. D., & Ma, L. (2015). CDC's use of social media and humor in a risk campaign – 'preparedness 101: Zombie apocalypse'. *Journal of Applied Communication Research*, *43*(2), 222–241.

Gray, J. (2010). Texts that sell: The culture in promotional culture. In M. Aronczyk & D. Powers (Eds.), *Blowing up the brand: Critical perspectives on promotional culture* (pp. 307–326). New York, NY: Peter Lang.

Grunig, J., & Hunt, T. (1984). *Managing public relations*. New York, NY: Holt, Rinehart and Winston.

Hasham, J. (2015, October 14). Mercer PR condemned by peak body for releasing rape victim's name. *Sydney Morning Herald* [online]. Retrieved from www.smh.com.au/politics/federal/mercer-pr-condemned-by-peak-body-for-releasing-rape-victims-name-20151014-gk95m5.html

Hesmondhalgh, D. (2013). *The cultural industries* (3rd ed.). London, England: Sage.

Human Rights Watch. (2016, August 2). Australia: Appalling abuse, neglect of refugees on Nauru. Retrieved from www.hrw.org/news/2016/08/02/australia-appalling-abuse-neglect-refugees-nauru

Katz, L. (2016). Feeding greedy corpses: The rhetorical power of Corpspeak and Zombilingo in higher education, and suggested countermagics to foil the intentions of the living dead. *Borderlands*, *15*(1), 1–25.

Kruvand, M., & Silver, M. (2013). Zombies gone viral: How a fictional zombie invasion helped CDC promote emergency preparedness. *Case Studies in Strategic Communication*, *2*, 34–60.

L'Etang, J. (1996). Corporate responsibility and public relations ethics. In J. L'Etang & M. Pieczka (Eds.), *Critical perspectives in public relations* (pp. 405–421). London, England: International Thomson Business Press.

Luckhurst, R. (2016). *Zombies: A cultural history*. London, England: Reaktion Books.

Mackenzie, E. (2015, October 16). Mercer PR considers legal position in response to PRIA statement. *Bandt*. Retrieved from www.bandt.com.au/mercer-pr-considers-legal-position-in-response-to-pria-statement/

Mackenzie, E. (2016, March 23). Journos should consider their own conduct says Mercer PR after PRIA statement clarification. *Bandt*. Retrieved from www.bandt.com.au/mercer-pr-considers-legal-position-in-response-to-pria-statement/

McKenzie-Murray, M. (2015, October 17). The man paid to protect Nauru's image. *The Saturday Paper*. Retrieved November 7, 2019, from www.thesaturdaypaper.com.au

Miller, D., & Dinan, W. (2008). *A century of spin: How public relations became the cutting edge of corporate power*. London, England: Pluto Press.

Miller, E. (2016, August 2). 4 things zombies can teach PR pros. *Ragan's PR Daily*. Retrieved from www.prdaily.com/Main/Articles/4_things_zombies_can_teach_PR_pros__19098.aspx

Miller, K. (1999). Public relations in film and fiction: 1930 to 1995. *Journal of Public Relations Research, 11*(1), 3–28.

Murphy, S. (2017). *Zombie university*. London, England: Repeater Books.

Nestle, M. (2015). *Soda politics: Taking on big soda (and winning)*. New York, NY: Oxford University Press.

Quiggin, J. (2012). *Zombie economics: How dead ideas still walk among us*. Princeton, NJ: Princeton University Press.

Robin, M. (2019, July 11). Federal treasury slams PR firm for human rights breach. *Financial Review* [online]. Retrieved from www.afr.com/rear-window/federal-treasury-slams-pr-firm-for-human-rights-breach-20190710-p525vl

Roper, J. (2005). Symmetrical communication: Excellent public relations or a strategy for hegemony? *Journal of Public Relations Research, 17*(1), 69–86.

Rutherford, J. (2013). *Zombies*. Abingdon, England: Routledge.

Surma, A., & Demetrious, K. (2018). Plastic words, public relations and the neoliberal transformation of twentieth century discourse. *Ethical Space: The International Journal of Communication Ethics, 15*(1–2), 92–107.

Sweney, M. (2017, September 5). Bell Pottinger expelled from PR trade body after South Africa racism row. *The Guardian*. Retrieved from www.theguardian.com/business/2017/sep/04/bell-pottinger-expelled-from-pr-trade-body-after-south-africa-racism-row

Tsang, J. (2012, July 12). What the zombie apocalypse and modern PR have in common [Blog]. Weber Shandwick Seattle. Retrieved from http://webershandwickseattle.com/2012/07/zombie-apocalypse-modern-pr/

Ward, M. (2015, October 15). PRIA condemns Mercer PR's actions in releasing identity of Nauru sexual assault victim. *Mumbrella*. Retrieved from https://mumbrella.com.au/pria-condemns-mercer-prs-actions-in-releasing-identity-of-nauru-sexual-assault-victim-324724

Webb, J., & Byrnand, S. (2008). Some kind of virus: The zombie as body and as trope. *Body and Society, 14*(2), 83–98.

Young, P. (2013, July 5). Conferences: Image and reputation, or the undead and the unsaid. *Mediations*. Retrieved from https://publicsphere.typepad.com/mediations/2013/07/conferences-image-and-reputation.html

5 'The PR girl'

Gender and embodiment in public relations

Kate Fitch

Introduction

This chapter offers a feminist perspective on the construction of meanings in relation to the public relations occupation, focusing on the role of embodied cultural capital in constructing a professional identity. The majority of studies within public relations acknowledge the body only peripherally, if at all, but feminist scholars outside public relations have been interested in the body for decades. Feminist scholars have identified a strong relationship between consumption and the body, an intersection in which promotional work plays a key role in shaping notions of femininity and promoting both neoliberalism and consumerism (Elias, Gill, & Scharff, 2017; Gill & Elias, 2014; McRobbie, 2004). Social media scholars have also investigated socially mediated representations of the body (see for example, Abidin, 2014, 2016; Warfield, 2016). In this chapter, I consider how such ideas play out in relation to diverse representations of public relations' bodies and in the management and gendering of an occupational identity.

The genesis for this chapter emerges out of my interest in visual images of public relations, and how female practitioners – in popular culture, in trade media, in historical archives, and, more recently, on social media platforms – are portrayed. Most popular culture representations of female practitioners are white women who are coded as middle class through dress and education and as sexually available (Miller, 1999; Johnston, 2010; Saltzman, 2012). Some representations are humorous in their depiction of absurd caricatures, for example, Edina Monsoon in *Absolutely Fabulous*. However, scholars are beginning to problematise the ways an occupational identity is constructed for public relations and represented visually through the body via popular culture (Fitch, 2015, 2018; Lambert, 2017). It is not my intention in this chapter to focus on the representation of the practitioner body in fiction, but rather, to use such examples as a starting point for acknowledging the virtual body in the digital images of practitioners and to consider how the body intersects with discourses concerned with gender and professionalism.

The aim of this chapter is therefore to investigate socially mediated representations of the female practitioner through a corporeal lens. Investigating diverse representations of the public relations body allows an understanding of its construction, and the tensions that underpin and delineate public relations' occupational identity. This chapter is structured in four sections. First, in 'Absent Bodies', I review the marginalisation of the body from much public relations theorising, and identify recent scholarship that suggests a new focus on the body and the links between aesthetic labour and professionalism. In the second section, 'Sex(ual)ised Bodies', I discuss the persistent association between public relations and women, focusing on their appearance, an association that is perceived to threaten professional legitimacy. I also introduce Kristin Demetrious's work on the clothes-body complex, which navigates the links between professionalisation and sexualisation through an analysis of public relations' dress codes. In the following section, 'Professional Bodies', I discuss representations of the public relations body in order to understand the representation of the female body and its significance for understandings of public relations in:

- the celebrity-style, self-presentation practices on Instagram of an Australian public relations practitioner, Roxy Jacenko; and
- the online images shared by practitioners via the website of a professional public relations association.

In the final section, 'PR Bodies and Occupational Identity', I consider the significance of a somatic turn for public relations and the ways in which focusing on the body potentially disrupts carefully constructed boundaries around a gendered professional occupational identity and allows a stronger understanding of the links between neoliberalism, consumption and promotional work.

Absent bodies

Many studies within public relations acknowledge the body only peripherally, if at all. However, a small handful of recent studies, particularly those that adopt an intersectional or critical feminist perspective, suggest the beginning of a somatic turn (see, for example, Vardeman-Winter, 2012; Place & Vardeman-Winter, 2016, for a discussion of the body in public health campaigns and Weaver, 2013 on the use of women's bodies in activism). Theorising about public relations is often underpinned by what Acker, writing on organisations, identifies as an abstract, bodiless practitioner 'who occupies the abstract, gender-neutral job, has no sexuality, no emotions, and does not procreate' (1990, p. 151; see also, Acker, 2006). Similarly, Elias, Gill and Scharff note how 'the body corporeal – fleshy, feeling, embodied – is not prominent but 'disappears' in these accounts' of work and labour (2017, p. 8). Good examples of how this understanding of professional practice is internalised can be found in studies of practitioner perspectives; indeed, one interview participant in L'Etang's historical study stated that public relations has 'always been a sexless trade' (2015, p. 363) and male and female interview participants perceived public relations work as ungendered (2015, p. 362). In addition, L'Etang identified the invisibility of certain public relations activities, particularly the work performed by 'Girl Fridays' (2015, p. 360).

Similarly, Pieczka found in public relations case studies that 'gender is noticeable in the case narratives by its absence' and concluded that 'the emphasis on rationality, control, and objectivity' ensures that professional conceptualisations of public relations are framed as masculine (2007, pp. 347–348). But the body is neither absent from public relations work nor gender neutral and as these examples reveal, professional norms are highly gendered (Fitch, 2016a, 2016b; Fitch & Third, 2014).

Investigating the body is therefore useful in considering how gender is encoded into the occupational identity of public relations. Similar research in other service professions, accounting and law, confirms that the physical body embodies particular aspects of professional identity along gendered lines (Haynes, 2012). Recent public relations scholarship has begun to disrupt abstract assumptions about a professional – but bodiless – identity. These studies restore aspects of lived, bodily experiences, including the sexuality, emotions, and even procreation identified by Acker (1990). For example, Yeomans (2014, 2019) explored gendered identity work in public relations practice, focusing on emotional labour, and Surma and Daymon (2014) investigated the significance of care, particularly in terms of nurturing, across personal and professional domains. While these studies do not focus specifically on the body, they do attempt to restore, or engage with, an emotional dimension – which Acker (1990) identified as lacking – within understandings of public relations and gender. Research into power and diversity has also revealed the significance of race and class to occupational fit (L. Edwards, 2014, 2019). Munshi and Edwards (2011) argued that public relations suffers from institutional whiteness and Vardeman-Winter and Place (2017) called the field 'lily-white'. Other researchers have challenged the heteronormative dimensions of professional conceptualisations of public relations (Ciszek, 2018; Tindall & Waters, 2013).

Building on this work, an investigation of the body in public relations can reveal new insights into the construction of a professional identity. Power is inscribed on the body through social practices, organisational practices and institutional norms (Acker, 1990, 2006; Butler, 2008). Not only does the physical appearance embody and project a professional identity, in that '*looking* professional becomes inseparable from *being* professional' (Muzio & Tomlinson, 2012, p. 461), but for Butler (2008), that professional identity is an ongoing performative process. Fitch and Third (2014) reported interview participants – female public relations practitioners – discussing the ways they negotiated gendered professional norms through dress in the 1970s and 1980s, and, drawing on Butler (2008), provided examples of the performative dimensions of feminised gender constructions. Aesthetic labour is concerned with how 'worker corporeality is appropriate and transmuted for commercial benefit', which translates into 'stylistic choices' to ensure 'the right look' (Mears, 2014, pp. 1330, 1333–1334). It foregrounds embodiment, in terms of lived bodily experience and the ways in which power is inscribed on the body (Acker, 1990; Butler, 2008; Bryant & Jaworski, 2011). The embodied professional identity articulates what is 'valuable, marketable or desirable' (Haynes, 2008, p. 330) within public relations and determines occupational fit (L. Edwards, 2014). Golombisky (2015) argues that a notion of gendered embodiment can open up feminist public relations scholarship to better account for both intersectionality and material bodies.

Sex(ualis)ed bodies

This chapter investigates contemporary coding of the feminine body in order to understand the ways in which power is incorporated into particular constructions of the occupational identity of public relations. In understanding then, what an archetypal image of a female practitioner might be, it is revealing to look at what is not considered representative. Searching digitised Australian library collections led me, using the search terms, 'public relations' and 'women', to a 1983 image by acclaimed photographer Rennie Ellie. It is labelled:

> P.R [i.e., Public relations] lady and beach girl, Qld. [i.e., Queensland] [picture]/ Rennie Ellis.
> Summary: Unidentified woman, almost three-quarter-length, full face, standing behind a table in a marquee, wearing white singlet top over swimsuit

Such images, that is, scantily clad women, are typically rejected by the industry, as not representative of professional practice. For example, Johnston and Zawawi (2000), in an early Australian textbook, refer to a similar image about bikini-wearing women who put money in parking meters in Queensland ('meter maids'), arguing that this activity is not public relations. Yet the sexualisation of practitioners continues to inform aspects of the industry's occupational identity.

The persistent association with young, attractive women – 'the PR girl' or even 'the PR chick' – is one an industry seeking to establish itself as a strategic, management profession finds troubling. It is also longstanding. Various national histories acknowledge its association with attractive women but fail to consider the implications (Fitch & L'Etang, 2017). For example, in the 1950s in Jamaica, public relations was primarily practised by 'fair-skinned, attractive young women' (C. Edwards, 2014, p. 35) and in Zimbabwe, public relations was 'largely a female position and appointments were mainly based on organizing ability and appearance' (Mawerera, 2014, p. 28). L'Etang (2015) documented various references to the Jennifer Syndrome, Eve in PR, and even dolly-birds in her interviews with practitioners about the UK industry in the 1950s and 1960s. A study in Germany identified the prevalence of the 'PR bunny' stereotype (and even 'PR sluts' according to one interview participant) (Fröhlich & Peters, 2007, p. 242).

In a contemporary study of gendered codes and meanings in public relations work, Demetrious identified three themes around dress:

- classic, where the code was conservative, professional and corporate, yet 'nudged boundaries with notions of sexy communications';
- sexualised, where 'the "PR girl" trope was highly represented and connoted a young, nubile female, unmarried, with a degree of sexual power'; and finally,
- lifestyle public relations, which embraced a more casual and even fun dress code in that it 'relaxed the boundaries that encode status' (2014, p. 32).

Two important points for this chapter emerge from this study. First, despite the emphasis on individual agency, particularly with regard to promoting the self and developing a career, the practitioner conforms to public relations occupational codes around fashion; and second, the contradictory and ambiguous links between professionalisation and sexualisation in public relations, evident in the clothes-body complex, should not be ignored (Demetrious, 2014).

The stock photograph of a blonde woman chosen for the cover image of a recently published book is worth noting in terms of the apparent resistance to gendered norms. *Experiencing Public Relations: International Voices* (Bridgen & Verčič, 2018), according to the promotional copy, aims to explore everyday, lived experiences of public relations. The blonde, heavily tattooed woman is clearly in an office, at work and gazing at a mobile phone screen in a thoughtful pose. Far from being the object of the camera gaze (although she is), her attention is elsewhere – presumably her work. And although increasingly mainstream, the tattooed body is far from a corporate look, and certainly not representative of the corporatised, sanitised public relations – the management discipline and strategic business practice – that is often theorised within the dominant paradigm. The provocative image therefore raises questions about both the archetypal image and contemporary identity of the female practitioner.

Professional bodies

Celebrity bodies

In this section, I want to consider specifically one celebrity-practitioner body: that of high-profile Australian public relations practitioner Roxy Jacenko, through an analysis of her Instagram account. I have previously written about Jacenko, who in addition to establishing her own public relations consultancy and writing several novels on public relations, has worked studiously to develop and indeed monetise her online profile and that of her children (Fitch, 2017). Jacenko's public relations work thrives on visibility; it crosses boundaries between more traditional public relations practice and digital influence. In addition to a lifestyle public relations consultancy, Sweaty Betty PR, Jacenko established an agency, Ministry of Talent, to manage digital influencers. Influencers are important stakeholders in public relations activity, yet the extent to which this digital labour overlaps with public relations activity is understudied. But in the monetisation of her online profile, Jacencko deliberately blurs the boundaries between professional and private. Nor are there clear boundaries around what constitutes public relations work and what does not, given Jacenko's clients and brand partners feature on her social media accounts and those of her children. I therefore draw on scholarship on aesthetic, glamour and visibility labour in cultural industries to consider the ways in which the body is used here and the implications for understandings of public relations.

In analysing Jacenko's Instagram, which had attracted 250,000 followers in late 2019, there is a curious mix of professional and personal. Rettberg identifies the need to study 'cumulative self-presentations' of social media feeds rather than isolated images, in order to understand both the technological filters of production and the processes of consumption around reading and sharing (2014, p. 35). The account name anchors Jacenko to her work: Roxy Jacenko/Sweaty Betty PR, and the brief bio acknowledges that Jacenko is a director of Sweaty Betty PR and the Ministry of Talent as well as various and changing roles as an Australian brand ambassador, ranging from Enjo (environmentally friendly cleaning products) to Toni & Guy hair salons. Instagram posts in the week ending 5 October 2017 include children playing on beds; Jacenko having her hair coloured in a Toni & Guy salon; Jacenko at work in the office, with clients or client products, or eating in restaurants; Jacenko modelling clothes, often in mirror or elevator selfies; and, frequently, Jacenko working out in the gym. Jacenko's body features prominently in many posts, showcasing clothes and fashion accessories but also Jacenko's body. Often the product is acknowledged, for example a headless gym selfie is captioned 'new running gear thanks @runningbare83' and an elevator selfie tags Louis Vuitton and other luxury brands. In a recent pilot for a reality television show, *I am Roxy* (2019), Jacenko's voiceover states: 'You're the face of the business so I need to look good' as we see her get a facial, before undertaking light therapy and being made up by a professional makeup artist at her desk. Jacenko's worked on, working out body is also a product: its commodification is integral to the Jacenko brand. Jacenko's body is a clotheshorse for high fashion and on trend items, and for gym and running gear, and for hair and beauty products. Far from being absent from her professional work, the body is an intrinsic part of that work.

Jacenko's feed illustrates much of the work that comprises fashion and lifestyle public relations that aims to promote consumerism. Marwick argues that Instagram fosters a particular kind of self-presentation strategy closely aligned with celebrity culture and notes that 'the Instafamous tend to be conventionally good-looking' and 'work in cool industries' (2015, p. 139). The body is central to such work. Scholars have recognised the cultural work necessary to manage both physical and online identity, noting the blending of life, work and the body by models through terms such as 'glamour labour' (Wissinger, 2015) and by influencers through 'visibility labour' (Abidin, 2016). The work required to stay on-trend, define cool and maintain visibility is little acknowledged within scholarship on public relations, yet is recognised in other cultural industries, including fashion blogging (Duffy & Hund, 2015), new media and dot.com workers (Gill, 2002; Neff, Wissinger, & Zukin, 2005) and in advertising and magazine publishing (Nixon & Crewe, 2004). Although Jacenko is often criticised for her extensive self-promotion, that work is pivotal to her brand. While this work might not conform to normative, professional conceptualisations of public relations, it highlights the links between presentation, glamour and consumption that are seldom acknowledged within public relations scholarship. Jacenko's broader narrative around her self-made success conforms precisely to the neoliberal project (Fitch, 2017), and the visibility and self-branding that are required to be successful in 'cool jobs' (Neff et al., 2005). Further, that visibility and branding hinges on a commodified body that is disciplined within postfeminist discourses of individual agency, aspiration, choice and consumption.

Industry bodies

In this section, I want to consider the ways in which female public relations practitioners are – and historically, were – represented visually in professional contexts. In a study of public relations' trade media, Edwards and Pieczka (2013) argued that such media construct occupational archetypes that have a disciplinary effect on practitioners in the communication of professional norms and values. The focus of that study was a critical discourse analysis of a weekly trade publication, rather than specifically its visual texts. However, the authors identified that practitioner profiles were highly gendered in that physical appearance and self-presentation were regularly included in female, but not in male, practitioner profiles, and closely linked with understandings of professional competence (Edwards & Pieczka, 2013, p. 19). An analysis of Australian trade media in the 1960s and early 1970s found there were more depictions of women's bodies and body parts than of senior female practitioners (Fitch, 2020). This 'body' theme was primarily the result of collaborations with photographers, illustrators and designers whose work featured in the journal pages. Its significance is the linking of feminised labour with the body (Mayer, 2013), precisely in the years more women began working in public relations.

In order to understand the contemporary construction of institutional norms, I analysed the images contained in the Public Relations Institute of Australia's newsroom (see PRIA.newsroom.com.au) on 10 October 2017; the newsroom is described as 'an online resource for PRIA members, to help share your media stories'. Mostly consultants, rather than in-house practitioners, post to the PRIA newsroom. There were 424 photos in the multimedia section and I analysed the most recent 100 images, which ranged in date of posting from 26 May 2016 to 14 September 2017. Nearly a quarter (23) were images of products, graphics or brand logos but the remaining images were of practitioners, mostly posted to announce new appointments, new agencies or clients, or at awards ceremonies. The majority of these self-selected images related to practitioners working for consultancies and my analysis focuses on the ways in which industry professionals choose to represent themselves visually to a practitioner audience.

One-third (32) of these images were of solo practitioners, with a 12/20 male/female split. The male portraits are more likely to be formal head shots, often a studio portrait, wearing a suit (although not necessarily a tie). In contrast, female solo portraits include casual, smiling headshots that appear to have been snapped on an iPhone while a few are more formally styled. For example, two black and white portraits show the full body of the 'smart but casually' attired female practitioner in a stylish office or art gallery. The more formal portraits, male and female, were generally linked to status in that they were provided with announcements of high-level appointments such as CEO or Director. The less formal ones were linked with lower status roles. Even when the submitted photograph of a single female practitioner is to announce a new position or the establishment of their own agency, the portrait is styled, often as doing work rather than a standard head and shoulders portrait, that is, there is a studious avoidance of a corporate head shot.

Almost half the images featured two or more practitioners. Only a few featured two or more men. One example announcing 'Cruise Line Industry Association Sets Sail with Primary Communication' shows two men casually posed in jackets in Sydney Harbour, with a cruise ship and the iconic Harbour Bridge in the background. Teams of female and male/female practitioners are often styled but in ways that demonstrate the consultancy is 'cool' and 'on trend'. Tailor Maid Communications, a fashion and lifestyle consultancy, announce the launch of their 'social, content & digital arm' with a photo of both directors dressed in white with black accessories posing in a grey streetscape. Their stance claims power, as does the high fashion look. In contrast, Straight Up PR, a self-described 'health, wellbeing & lifestyle PR' agency, features four young women in active wear looking at each other rather than the camera. This photograph, tagged with a media release headline 'healthy growth with client wins' illustrates the agency brand; the release refers to 'its real and authentic approach to PR and communications' and that Straight Up PR 'spread[s] trusted health and wellbeing messages to all Australians'. Other teams, and although rarer, mixed gender teams, are styled in arguably funky, often black and white clothes, sometimes in a white studio.

Three themes emerged from the analysis of self-selected practitioner images. First, the corporate look, including formal headshots and suits, although few in number, was more likely to represent older, male practitioners. Some portraits of female practitioners do fall into this category, but they are often creatively styled in terms of dress or setting. Second, the visual iconography could be mostly characterised as fashionable but edgy. That the majority of practitioners featured in the newsroom worked for consultancies, often in fashion, lifestyle and consumer public relations, is significant in that it points to the significant cultural work that underpins public relations in these sectors. The self-branding can be characterised as 'cool'. The third category is related to the second in that it demonstrates a studied casualness, either styled or, more rarely, an informal and poor-quality headshot snapped on an iPhone. Young, female practitioners are more likely to be casually attired, especially outside of award ceremonies and other more formal activities. This category mirrors Mears' observation of the alignment of workers' looks and identity with ideas that contemporary work should be 'fun' and 'flexible' (2014, p. 1332). These themes broadly align with Demetrious's categories, which identified corporate/professional; young/sexy/female; and the relaxed lifestyle public relations' dress codes. I suggest that the relative rarity of branding one's self as corporate points to a strong alignment, at least in the consultancy sector, with creative and cultural industries. The self-selected visual representation of practitioners suggests a shift away from corporate public relations. Nevertheless, these bodily representations reproduce gendered hierarchies that reveal tensions around status and work.

PR bodies and occupational identity

In documenting diverse, mediated representations of the practitioner body, I have attempted to draw attention to a somatic turn in thinking about public relations. This turn can be found in the work of feminist public relations scholars, particularly in investigations of lived experiences, and by scholars thinking more broadly about the raced, heteronormative and intersectional identities of public relations (see, for example, Ciszek, 2018; Munshi & Edwards, 2011; Place, 2015; Tindall & Waters, 2013). I need to acknowledge the difficulty in discussing gender in isolation from other social forces. Nevertheless, studying visual representations of public relations practitioners in Australia confirms the institutional whiteness of public relations (Munshi & Edwards, 2011; Vardeman-Winter & Place, 2017). In addition, some attention must be paid to the public sharing of these images online and the significance of the socially mediated body (Highfield & Leaver, 2016; Warfield, 2016) in order to understand the construction of contemporary occupational identities for public relations. Given our interest in navigating boundaries in this book, I am interested in how the body offers 'a variable boundary', subject to political and cultural signification (Butler, 2008, p. 189). Further, the socially mediated body must be understood in relation to constructed and dynamic boundaries between the practitioner and the image, and in terms of its 'networked, material-discursive entanglements' (Warfield, 2016, pp. 1, 7). In this chapter, I have therefore attempted to move beyond a discussion of popular culture representations of female practitioners to consider the self-presentation of the socially mediated practitioner body.

For Jacenko, the body constitutes work, in that she works out to maintain a body that can then be used to showcase clients' products, a glamorous lifestyle and indeed the Jacenko brand. Drawing on celebrity studies reveals the significance of the wealth and status symbols in Jacenko's Instagram feed (see Abidin, 2014; Marwick, 2013, 2015), which cannot be read in isolation from the other media texts, including reality television, news and entertainment stories, her novels and the monetised social media feeds of her children, surrounding Jacenko. Given the prominent reference to her public relations work, it is difficult to ignore an association with meaning making around public relations, even acknowledging the visual and self-presentation practices are not exclusive to Jacenko or to public relations practitioners. Nevertheless, displaying the body confirms feminist scholarship on the links between femininity, consumption and the celebratory body (Gill & Elias, 2014). The worked-on and commodified body becomes one of the status symbols promoting luxury, wealth and, in turn, consumption (Abidin, 2016; Wissinger, 2015).

Industry self-presentation practices on a professional association website are designed to engage other practitioners and are carefully framed, edited and selected to showcase images that point to the unwritten rules concerning dress and other occupational codes of the industry – rules that do not conform to the more traditional, corporate, management and business image of public relations.

Aesthetic labour is concerned specifically with the stylistic choices and the display of the body, where the worker's appearance, in the reproduction of certain cultural norms, plays a central role in their capacity to ensure occupational fit and belonging (Abidin, 2016; Mears, 2014; Wissinger, 2015). As Demetrious argued in response to fashion advice offered to aspiring practitioners, such choices are 'not an insignificant frivolous activity but anticipate a complex presentational performance linked to sexual hierarchy, authoritarianism and capitalism' (2014, p. 33). The casual, fun and relaxed style that Demetrious (2014) and Mears (2014) identified is particularly associated with lifestyle, fashion and entertainment public relations, but other sectors demand conformity with implicit occupational codes underpinned by significant aesthetic labour. These findings confirm studies of related occupations associated with new media and cultural industries, which identified common themes around informal, fun, stylish and cool dress and appearance (Duffy & Hund, 2015; Gill, 2002; Neff et al., 2005; Nixon & Crewe, 2004). It is not difficult to draw parallels with the self-presentation of public relations practitioners. The examples in this chapter highlight the kinds of aesthetic choices needed to successfully do public relations work. This success, at least in the consultancy sector closely associated with entrepreneurial work, depends on self-promotion and visibility.

A postfeminist and a neoliberal sensibility emerges in the self-presentation practices of female practitioners working in the Australian consultancy sector. There is rejection of a 'fluffy bunny' image, in part to claim public relations work as a serious business (see Yeomans, 2014), yet many of the practitioner bodies conform to normative societal expectations of attractiveness and physical fitness. The growing rejection of corporate suits and conservative dress evident in my analysis of the self-promoted images of practitioners working primarily in fashion, lifestyle and consultancy sectors reveals other aspects of sectoral cultural norms. The selection of clothing and styling suggests practitioners are creative, and have the agency to make informed choices (Demetrious, 2014). Further, the performative elements of their identity point strongly to autonomy, individualism and defying convention; these practitioners work hard to show they are on-trend and cool. This is typical of cultural work and labour that demands aesthetic, visibility and glamour labour on the part of the practitioner (Abidin, 2016; Mears, 2014; Wissinger, 2015). Given the ubiquitousness of visual imagery, the (fashionable) body is central to this performative identity as a cultural and/or promotional worker.

The analysis of bodily representations enables the construction of gendered occupational identities and the negotiation of gendered occupational norms to be observed. Through their self-presentation practices, practitioners produce a new understanding of 'professionalism' of public relations. These images reject an alignment with corporate business and management, a position that I have previously criticised in terms of professional associations and industry perspectives in relation to public relations education (Fitch, 2016a). However, even within cultural industries, there is a gendered segregation of labour with women more likely to perform public relations, marketing and even production roles than more prestigious creative positions, which tend to be coded masculine (Hesmondhalgh & Baker, 2015). Hesmondhalgh and Baker (2015) attribute this in part to strong historical associations between creativity and masculinity. Women claiming creativity through stylistic choices could therefore be read as resistance to gendered hierarchies within public relations work.

However, the postfeminist sensibility that practitioners are empowered to make certain fashion choices is fraught. Workplaces remain hierarchical and sexualised and fashion choices can significantly impact careers in public relations (Demetrious, 2014). Even as female and younger practitioners seek to express their individuality, autonomy and rejection of a corporate hierarchy through both fashion choices and the visual iconography of their self-selected images, such empowerment is far from autonomous or without influence of existing gendered power structures. On the one hand, practitioners can seek to express their knowledge of cultural work through choices around clothing and styling. An edgy, fashionable look can be interpreted as practitioners claiming power within cultural sectors by asserting a creative identity. But this self-branding also occurs within a consumer marketplace and public relations activity helps define what is cool and on-trend. The relatively stylish yet informal dress codes and occupational norms do not reject sexualised discourses of public relations and could be conceived as a neoliberal illusion, in that they reinforce gendered hierarchies.

Conclusion

This chapter has attempted to illuminate a little discussed aspect of the professional identity of public relations: that of the body and the challenges for practitioners in negotiating gendered professional norms in terms of having 'the right look' to ensure occupational fit. The discrimination along gender lines in the industry – evident in the gender pay gap and the relative lack of representation of women at senior levels – is well documented (Fitch, 2016b; Fitch & Third, 2010). Aesthetic labour also drives inequality along gender, race and class lines (Mears, 2014), and is reflected in the socially mediated images of the practitioner body, which are entangled with networked dimensions of power (Warfield, 2016). The images I have discussed encapsulate very real tensions around professionalism (and therefore gender) in public relations discourses. These tensions play out on the gendered representation of the body and the disciplining of the female body in line with institutional norms in public relations. In response, this chapter identifies the significance of the virtual, mediated body in promotional work and explores how the gendered embodiment of public relations replicates sexual hierarchies and norms. The findings in this chapter confirm a repositioning of the public relations industry within a new set of cultural norms, where women's bodies and the commodification of the mediated self are closely linked to employability and entrepreneurship (Adkins & Dever, 2016; Hearn, 2008), and the performance of aesthetic labour and the corresponding commodification of the body is necessary to confirm an occupational fit and, in turn, economic success.

References

Abidin, C. (2014). #In$tagLam: Instagram as a repository of taste, a burgeoning marketplace, a war of eyeballs. In M. Berry & M. Schleser (Eds.), *Mobile media making in an age of smartphones* (pp. 119–128). New York, NY: Palgrave Macmillan.

Abidin, C. (2016). Visibility labour: Engaging with influencers' fashion brands and #OOTD advertorial campaigns on Instagram. *Media International Australia*, *161*(1), 86–100.

Acker, J. (1990). Hierarchies, jobs, bodies: A theory of gendered organizations. *Gender and Society*, *4*(2), 139–158.

Acker, J. (2006). Inequality regimes: Gender, class and race in organizations. *Gender & Society*, *40*(4), 441–464.

Adkins, L., & Dever, M. (Eds.). (2016). *The post-Fordist sexual contract: Living and working in contingency*. Basingstoke, England: Palgrave Macmillan.

Bridgen, E., & Verčič, D. (Eds.). (2018). *Experiencing public relations: International voices*. London, England: Routledge.

Bryant, L., & Jaworski, K. (2011). Gender, embodiment and place: The gendering of skills shortages in the Australian mining and food and beverage processing industries. *Human Relations*, 1345–1367.

Butler, J. (2008). *Gender trouble: Feminism and the subversion of identity*. Abingdon, England: Routledge.

Ciszek, E. (2018). Queering PR: Directions in theory and research for public relations scholarship. *Journal of Public Relations Research*, *30*(4), 134–145.

Demetrious, K. (2014). Surface effects: Public relations and the politics of gender. In C. Daymon & K. Demetrious (Eds.), *Gender and public relations: Critical perspectives on voice, image and identity* (pp. 20–45). Abingdon, England: Routledge.

Duffy, B., & Hund, E. (2015). 'Having it all' on social media: Entrepreneurial femininity and self-branding among fashion bloggers. *Social Media + Society*, 1–11.

Edwards, C. (2014). The Caribbean. In T. Watson (Ed.), *Latin American and Caribbean perspectives on the development of public relations: Other voices* (pp. 30–44). London, England: Palgrave Macmillan.

Edwards, L. (2014). *Power, diversity and public relations*. Abingdon, England: Routledge.

Edwards, L. (2019). *Understanding public relations theory, culture and society*. London, England: Sage.

Edwards, L., & Pieczka, M. (2013). Public relations and 'its' media: Exploring the role of trade media in the enactment of public relations' professional project. *Public Relations Inquiry*, *2*(1), 5–25.

Elias, A., Gill, R., & Scharff, C. (Eds.). (2017). *Aesthetic labour: Beauty politics in neoliberalism*. London, England: Palgrave Macmillan.

Fitch, K. (2015). Promoting the vampire rights amendment: Public relations, postfeminism and *True Blood: Public Relations Review*, *41*(5), 607–614.

Fitch, K. (2016a). *Professionalizing public relations: History, gender and education*. London, England: Palgrave Macmillan.

Fitch, K. (2016b). Feminism and public relations. In J. L'Etang, D. McKie, N. Snow, & J. Xifra (Eds.), *Routledge handbook of critical public relations* (pp. 54–64). London, England: Routledge.

Fitch, K. (2017). Seeing 'the unseen hand': Celebrity, promotion and public relations. *Public Relations Inquiry*, *6*(2), 157–169.

Fitch, K. (2018). 'Can you see me?' Images of public relations in *Babylon*. In E. Bridgen & D. Verčič (Eds.), *Experiencing public relations: International voices*. London, England: Routledge.

Fitch, K. (2020). Wives, secretaries and bodies: Representations of women in an Australian public relations journal, 1965–1972. In I. Somerville, L. Edwards, & Ø. Ihlen (Eds.), *Public relations, society and the generative power of history* (pp. 61–80). London, England: Routledge.

Fitch, K., & L'Etang, J. (2017). Other voices? The state of public relations history and historiography: Questions, challenges and limitations of 'national' histories and historiographies. *Public Relations Inquiry*, 6(1), 115–136.

Fitch, K., & Third, A. (2010). Working girls: Revisiting the gendering of public relations. *Prism*, 7(4). Retrieved from www.prismjournal.org/uploads/1/2/5/6/125661607/v7-no4-a1.pdf

Fitch, K., & Third, A. (2014). Ex-journos and promo girls: Feminization and professionalization in the Australian public relations industry. In C. Daymon & K. Demetrious (Eds.), *Gender and public relations: Critical perspectives on voice, image and identity* (pp. 247–267). Abingdon, England: Routledge.

Fröhlich, R., & Peters, S. (2007). PR bunnies caught in the agency ghetto? Gender stereotypes, organizational factors, and women's careers in PR agencies. *Journal of Public Relations Research*, 19(3), 229–254.

Gill, R. (2002). Cool, creative and egalitarian? Exploring gender in project-based new media work in Europe. *Information, Communication & Society*, 5(1), 70–89.

Gill, R., & Elias, A. (2014). 'Awaken your incredible': Love your body discourses and postfeminist contradictions. *International Journal of Media & Cultural Politics*, 10(2), 179–188.

Golombisky, K. (2015). Renewing the commitments of feminist public relations theory from velvet ghetto to social justice. *Journal of Public Relations Research*, 27(5), 389–415.

Haynes, K. (2008). (Re)figuring accounting and maternal bodies: The gendered embodiment of accounting professionals. *Accounting, Organizations and Society*, 33, 328–348.

Haynes, K. (2012). Body beautiful? Gender, identity and the body in professional services firms. *Gender, Work & Organization*, 19, 489–507.

Hearn, A. (2008). 'Meat, mask, burden': Probing the contours of the branded 'self'. *Journal of Consumer Culture*, 8(2), 197–217.

Hesmondhalgh, D., & Baker, S. (2015). Sex, gender and work segregation in the cultural industries. *The Sociological Review*, 63(1), 23–36.

Highfield, T., & Leaver, T. (2016). Instagrammatics and digital methods: Studying visual social media, from selfies and GIFs to memes and emoji. *Communication Research and Practice*, 2(1), 47–62.

I am Roxy [television]. (2019). Channel 10, Australia.

Johnston, J. (2010). Girls on screen: How film and television depict women in public relations. *Prism*, 7(4). Retrieved from www.prismjournal.org

Johnston, J., & Zawawi, C. (Eds.). (2000). *Public relations: Theory and practice*. Crows Nest, Australia: Allen & Unwin.

Lambert, C. A. (2017). Post-racial public relations on primetime television: How *Scandal* represents Olivia Pope. *Public Relations Review*, 43(4), 750–754.

L'Etang, J. (2015). 'It's always been a sexless trade'; 'It's clean work'; 'There's very little velvet curtain': Gender and public relations in post-second world war Britain. *Journal of Communication Management*, 19(4), 354–370.

Marwick, A. (2013). *Status update: Celebrity, publicity, and branding in the social media age.* New Haven, CT: Yale University Press.

Marwick, A. (2015). Instafame: Luxury selfies in the attention economy. *Public Culture, 21*(10), 137–160.

Mawerera, R. (2014). Botswana, Zambia and Zimbabwe. In T. Watson (Ed.), *Middle Eastern and African perspectives on the development of public relations: Other voices* (pp. 22–33). Houndmills: Palgrave Macmillan.

Mayer, V. (2013). To communicate is human; To chat is female: The feminization of US media work. In C. Carter, L. Steiner, & L. McLaughlin (Eds.), *The Routledge companion to media and gender* (pp. 51–60). Abingdon, England: Routledge.

McRobbie, A. (2004). Post-feminism and popular culture. *Feminist Media Studies, 4*(3), 255–264.

Mears, A. (2014). Aesthetic labor for the sociologies of work, gender and beauty. *Sociology Compass, 8*(12), 1330–1343.

Miller, K. (1999). Public relations in film and fiction: 1930 to 1995. *Journal of Public Relations Research, 11*(1), 3–28.

Munshi, D., & Edwards, L. (2011). Understanding 'race' in/and public relations: Where do we start and where should we go? *Journal of Public Relations Research, 23*(4), 349–367.

Muzio, D., & Tomlinson, J. (2012). Researching gender, inclusion and diversity in contemporary professions and professional organizations. *Gender, Work and Organization, 19*(5), 455–466.

Neff, G., Wissinger, E., & Zukin, S. (2005). Entrepreneurial labor among cultural producers: 'Cool' jobs in 'hot' industries. *Social Semiotics, 15*(3), 307–334.

Nixon, S., & Crewe, B. (2004). Pleasure at work? Gender, consumption and work-based identities in the creative industries. *Consumption, Markets & Culture, 7*(2), 129–147.

Pieczka, M. (2007). Case studies as narrative accounts of public relations practice. *Journal of Public Relations Research, 19*(4), 333–356.

Place, K. R. (2015). Binaries, continuums, and intersections: Women public relations professionals' understandings of gender. *Public Relations Inquiry, 4*(1), 61–78.

Place, K. R., & Vardeman-Winter, J. (2016). Science, medicine, and the body: How public relations blurs lines across individual and public health. In J. L'Etang, D. McKie, N. Snow, & J. Xifra (Eds.), *The Routledge handbook of critical public relations* (pp. 259–271). Abingdon, England: Routledge.

Rettberg, J. W. (2014). *Seeing ourselves through technology: How we use selfies, blogs and wearable devices to see and shape ourselves.* London, England: Palgrave Macmillan.

Saltzman, J. (2012). The image of the public relations practitioner in movies and television, 1901–2011. *The IJPC Journal, 3*, 1–50. Retrieved from http://ijpc.org/page/journal.html

Surma, A., & Daymon, C. (2014). Caring about public relations and the gendered cultural intermediary role. In C. Daymon & K. Demetrious (Eds.), *Gender and public relations: Critical perspectives on voice, image and identity* (pp. 46–66). Abingdon, England: Routledge.

Tindall, N., & Waters, R. (Eds.). (2013). *Coming out of the closet: Exploring LGBT issues in strategic communication with theory and research.* New York, NY: Peter Lang.

Vardeman-Winter, J. (2012). Medicalization and teen girls' bodies in the Gardasil cervical cancer vaccine campaign. *Feminist Media Studies, 12*(2), 281–304.

Vardeman-Winter, J., & Place, K. (2017). Still a lily-white field of women: The state of workforce diversity in public relations practice and research. *Public Relations Review, 43*(2), 326–336.

Warfield, K. (2016). Making the cut: An agential realist examination of selfies and touch. *Social Media + Society*, April–June, 1–10.

Wissinger, E. (2015). #NoFilter: Models, glamour labor, and the age of the blink. In J. Davis & N. Jurgenson (Eds.), Theorizing the Web 2014. *Interface, 1*(1), 1–20.

Yeomans, L. (2014). Gendered performance and identity work in PR consulting relationships: A UK perspective. In C. Daymon & K. Demetrious (Eds.), *Gender and public relations: Critical perspectives on voice, image and identity* (pp. 87–107). Abingdon, England: Routledge.

Yeomans, L. (2019). *Public relations as emotional labour.* Abingdon, England: Routledge.

6 Fashionable ephemera, political dressing and things that matter

Judy Motion

Introduction: on mattering

Considerations of 'fashion' have tended to be neglected by public relations scholarship, yet it is a significant popular culture enterprise that uses public relations extensively to build brands and sell commodities. Fashion is entangled in mutually beneficial and expedient relationships with other promotional culture endeavours, such as art, film and music. Together, bound by creativity, they signal contemporaneity and provide cultural capital. What is not always clear is the political role that fashion plays and how fashion and popular culture act as arbiter or indicator of social change. Fashion, here, is theorised as a form of politics that acts as a weather vane for social transformation – pointing to emergent directions. Borrowing from Hatmaker's (2014) work on mattering, this discussion of fashion, public relations and popular culture concentrates on thinking through what matters – what is significant, important and worthwhile – what we value, and how and why we value it. Mattering may also refer to thinking about matter – materiality – the physical substance of objects. Examination of fashion requires a focus on temporality, significance and impact – our infatuations with various popular culture trends may be fleeting or long-term, deep or shallow and have the potential to contribute to or undermine positive social change. This chapter deals with the seemingly ephemeral nature of fashion to ask: what conditions, movements and connections form these modes of meaning production and sense making? How do particular instances of fashion signal what matters? What affective work are we called upon to enact and what are the possibilities for social change? Drawing on archival research, this chapter stitches together juxtaposed fashion stories and offers a reconsideration of the promotional efforts of public relations that influence the significance of fashion.

The philosopher's clothes

My first encounter with the French philosopher and sociologist, Bruno Latour, was in Paris. Latour was a conference keynote speaker and, because I could only get a seat at the back of the hall, I struggled to see and hear his presentation. It was a disappointing experience. However, my second, more memorable encounter took place in Gothenburg where Latour was, again, a keynote speaker. As Latour entered the stage a male colleague leaned over and remarked, *di sotto*, 'It's hard to take seriously an academic wearing a black velour track suit'. On the contrary, I thought, he now has me really interested; he breaks conventional rules. Rather than the standard, deadly dull keynote, both the outfit and the talk were highly memorable and I became a fan of Latour and his work. I recall that he talked about the importance of intersectionality – working across multiple boundaries – rather than siloed thinking. For public relations, this concept of intersectionality is both affirming and challenging – earlier discussions of the mimetic practices of public relations suggest a profession that is adaptable and flexible, but it also raises questions about genuine innovation.

I was recently reminded of this conference experience when reading an article about Latour's work in the magazine section of the *New York Times* (Kofman, 2018). Although the article primarily concentrated on explaining Latour's scholarship, it also inserted commentary on what Latour was wearing alongside the line of argument. What was the intention of this commentary on his sense of style? From the article, we learned that Latour

> was wearing a purple turtleneck sweater, his favourite burgundy slacks and sensible black walking shoes. He has a full head of dark, dishevelled hair, and his vigorously overgrown eyebrows sweep several unsettling centimetres up beyond the rim of his round spectacles, like a nun's cornette.
>
> (Kofman, 2018)

This description is equally disconcerting and distracting because it transposes the gendered media focus on appearance that women have long complained about onto a male academic. In the article, discussion of a talk Latour presented included a description of his appearance – 'dressed in a striking suit (straw-colored tie, blue waistcoat)' (Kofman, 2018). Again, his clothing seems irrelevant. In the same article, when Latour met with collaborators, we learned that he 'had paired his usual aqua Lacoste messenger bag and burgundy slacks with a brown suede jacket, pumpkin scarf and flat tweed cap, which gave him the appearance of a Wes Anderson character'. Perhaps this description of Latour's appearance is meant to render him more accessible, more popular? On a visit to a mountain-top laboratory, Latour's appearance is also remarked upon: 'In addition to several sweaters and a coat, Latour was wearing a brightly patterned red ascot, which seemed to be his way of subtly acknowledging the significance of the business at hand' (Kofman, 2018). It is difficult to know how to interpret these commentaries on Latour's appearance – are they intended to convey his French sense of style, popularise an academic aesthetic sensibility or to humanise him? Regardless of intention, the overall effect is to downplay his contributions to knowledge. Although some journalists offer impressions of their interviewees in personality profiles, in this instance the article is accompanied by photos so readers are actually able to make their own independent assessments and interpretations of his appearance. Questions of relevance and appropriateness arise that are linked to feminist criticisms of emphases on appearance. Adjusting the gendered approach of focusing on women's appearance so that men are also included is not a mechanism for overcoming sexism. Writing a profile on a contemporary French philosopher is not an easy task, so this style of reporting is most likely an effort to popularise the article, to give it a certain cachet and render the discussion of his work less daunting and complicated. Ironically, it also resonates with Latour's work on critique that examines the relationship between matters of fact and matters of concern. For Latour (2004), critique is not just a matter of presenting facts – communication efforts should be framed in line with public concerns. The challenge then, is not to move away from facts by incorporating concerns – it is actually to get 'closer to facts' (Latour, 2004, p. 231) Latour explained that 'Matters of fact are only very partial and . . . very polemical, very political renderings of matters of concern' (2004, p. 232). Critique, Latour suggested, needs to offer something. Application of these theoretical insights to media reporting reveals the problem with journalism that focuses on appearance – it fails the 'matters of concern' test if we ask what is being offered and how does it connect us closer to facts? In an article primarily reporting on philosophical arguments about climate change, a focus on Latour's appearance and clothes undermines the facts and concerns. Yet, at the same time, it positions Latour within popular culture and makes him and his messages seem more accessible. How we tell these stories about climate change matters. The assumption that our concerns lie with appearance and clothing is largely erroneous – our concern lies with what they mean and how they matter. The conundrum is that individuals cannot simply be transposed into popular culture; instead, it is vital to be actively engaged in order to gain 'popular' capital. Opening the chapter with this example is designed to establish an argument that although popular culture is a highly commodified space, it is not some sort of currency for public relations. Increasingly, popular concerns about contemporary issues circulate and punctuate commercial practices in popular culture. Authenticity is a critical norm. This chapter explores how our expectations of fashion have coalesced with concerns about what matters and social and environmental justice initiatives. Each of the examples that follows examines particular public relations modes of meaning production and sense making, how instances of fashion signal what matters, the affective work we are called upon to undertake and the possibilities for social change.

Opening up and redirecting the gaze to things that matter

Michel Foucault (1984, 1988, 1989) asserted the need to create the self as a work of art – for women the art lies in meeting unspoken/unspecified rules for appearance. A delicate balancing act is often required that acknowledges the need to pay attention to aesthetics but not to appear as though it is the dominant priority. Women subjected to an intense, continuous media and public gaze may choose diverse public relations approaches – such as to either embrace fashion as a feature of their mediatised identity or manage it in ways that advance their priorities. Michelle Obama, in reflecting upon her time as the First Lady of the United States, was well aware of the public relations balancing act required and the need to manage perceptions. She demonstrated her understanding that matters of fact and matters of concern coalesce – in order to concentrate on her messages and what matters she must get appearance right. She noted that 'it seemed that my clothes mattered more to people than anything I had to say . . . optics governed more or less everything in the political world and I factored this into every outfit. It required time, thought, and money – more money than I'd spent on clothing ever before' (Obama, 2018, pp. 332–333). As part of her expenditure, Michelle Obama employed a personal stylist, a hairdresser and a makeup artist to assist her. Although at first she found that 'discomforting', she realised that women in public life have such support and referred to it as 'a built-in fee for our societal double standard' (Obama, 2018, p. 334). Part of that built-in fee was paying for her clothes and accessories – except for formal events where designers lent her gowns. Michelle Obama was cognisant of the role that race would play in assessments of clothing choices:

> As a black woman, too, I knew I'd be criticised if I was perceived as being showy and high-end, and I'd be criticised also if I was too casual. So I mixed it up. . . . For me, my choices were simply a way to use my curious relationship with the public gaze to boost a diverse set of up and comers.
>
> (2018, p. 333)

She tried to use the power of such situations and reframe them as public relations opportunities by promoting causes she supported, particularly advancing diversity through her choice of designers such as Jason Wu and Narciso Rodriguez. Such choices open up possibilities for diversity to be normalised and introduce cultural changes within the fashion industry. She explained that, 'People seemed to want to dial into my clothes, my shoes, and my hairstyles, but they also had to see me in the context of where I was and why. I was learning how to connect my message to my image, and in this way I could direct the American gaze' (Obama, 2018, p. 372). The importance of connecting message and image meant that she welcomed the public relations opportunities afforded by social media and popular culture to promote her social justice agendas.

As her connections to popular culture increased they were seen as a campaign asset – her husband, President Barack Obama, referred to her as 'Joe Public' and asked her to comment on campaign slogans and strategies (Obama, 2018). As she actively identified ways to connect with Americans through social media, she ensured that the media attention and gaze moved beyond herself to include those who undertook social justice work that she supported, such as working with veterans, commenting that 'the gaze belonged here' (Obama, 2018, p. 373).

In her role as First Lady of the United States, she was expected to conform to expectations that she would play a supporting role. She explained, 'I tried to be somewhat unpredictable, to prevent anyone from ascribing any sort of message to what I wore. It was a thin line. I was supposed to stand out without overshadowing others, to blend in, but not fade away' (Obama, 2018, p. 333). This balancing act meant that she played a double game – but foremost was her desire to advance issues of race and encourage young people of colour: 'I offered testament to the idea that it was possible, at least in some ways, to overcome invisibility' (Obama, 2018, p. 405). In these instances, fashion was a vehicle to create visibility for social issues and associated public relations efforts were strategically managed to advance her social justice agenda.

By using fashion as a political, public relations vehicle to render herself visible and to make her messages matter, rather than to blend in, Michelle Obama developed popular culture as a communicative milieu for advancing issues of social justice, particularly race, equity and diversity. Playing the fashion game and demonstrating a substantive commitment to and active engagement in popular culture accorded Michelle Obama a form of socially situated agency. Her embrace of contemporary culture – art, music, dance, fashion – meant that since leaving the White House, Michelle Obama has been able to achieve iconic status in popular culture. She has published a best-selling book, titled *Becoming*, undertaken a book tour, appeared on numerous chat shows and continued to speak on social justice issues. She has adopted a new look, wearing fewer dresses and more trousers and jumpsuits – her more recent look inspired the following comment: 'There's an appetite for the nuanced way Mrs. Obama used fashion both as a tool and a celebration (as opposed to, say, a defensive measure)' (Friedman, 2018). Her stylist, Meredith Koop, acknowledged the challenges in dressing Michelle Obama:

> You have to anticipate every avenue of attack and every possible outcome. Everyone has an opinion: This dress is too informal; that is too frilly; this is expensive; that is too conceptual. You have to celebrate fashion but also be aware of the message people are going to take away. Fashion can bolster communications in the best-case scenario, or be a silent partner, or actually distract.
>
> (Friedman, 2018)

These challenges have necessitated thinking through every possible scenario and response. The work that goes into appearance is part of the built-in fee for women who wish to succeed. It is an added task, a burden, a tax, that women must meet and master. Koop observed that 'It's so complicated now to be a woman. You want to be yourself, and you want to look good, but you don't want to be objectified, and you don't want to wear a bag' (Friedman, 2018). That is not to say that fashion is entirely pleasure-free – for many women it is a delight that is willingly engaged with. Fashion is not only a form of domination but also conveys a sense of power. Somehow, a double game must be played in which pleasure is derived from conforming to, but also bending, the rules. Koop commented that Michelle Obama now needs to look 'powerful and chic' in ways that reflect her values (Friedman, 2018). The challenge for others is to apply the approach adopted by Michelle Obama to clothing choices that represent values in their everyday lives, to decide what matters and how to advance those concerns. Popular culture capital is accrued through active engagement rather than purchased.

Controversial fashion

As the next First Lady of the United States, Melania Trump has made a number of controversial fashion choices. Her first appearance went well from a public relations perspective; she wore a light blue suit that kept her warm, looked good and seemed uncontroversial. We learned that the suit was created by an American designer, so that chimed with President Trump's brand (Rao, 2018) and motto of 'making America great again'. Some journalists/commentators noted that it echoed an outfit worn by Jacqueline Kennedy; the implication was that the First Lady's choice lacked originality – or that she was a copy-cat. This was also possibly an indirect reference to her borrowing from a speech given by Michelle Obama. Although most women who are judged on their appearance have no training or preparation, Melania Trump is a former model which indicates some expertise in this fashion sphere. Judgements about women's appearance have long been criticised (Motion, 1997). From a feminist perspective, questions we should ask include 'Does it really matter what she wears, do we over-analyse her choices?' An understanding of semiotics would suggest that it does matter, that we continually read visual images as symbolic texts and therefore we will be making judgements about the connotative as well as denotative meanings (Williams, 1976). Thus, a coat is not only an item of clothing (denotative meaning), it is an artefact with multiple cultural meanings that conjure various associations such as status, expense, aesthetic sensibilities and, of course, fashionability (connotative meanings). According to Finkelstein (1991, p. 148), 'the fashionability of an object prescribes its social meaning, thereby relieving us of the discursive problem of analysing and evaluating it. This is a crucial point – fashion is about social meaning – it has inscribed discursive significance and interpretation. Fashion also communicates what is acceptable and desirable. It imposes a social hierarchy, enforces standards and designates what is of value (Finkelstein, 1991, p. 115). Finkelstein (1991, p. 24) pointed out 'appearances become a matter of conscious effort, a kind of technical achievement, and a measure of individual competence with the tools and resources available to transform the human body. No matter how we may wish it were different, from a public relations perspective, we know that it does matter what Melania Trump wears. In her high-profile role as First Lady, her fashion choices will be scrutinised and analysed by the media, the public and even academics. Perhaps, instead, we should ask, for someone in such a high-profile role, can her choices ever be neutral or not matter? Fashion choices fit within a broader cultural context – and some of Melania Trump's choices have created controversy. The decision to wear a Zara jacket with the text 'I really don't care, do u?' printed on the back of the jacket while visiting a shelter for migrant children has been criticised as inappropriate and insensitive. Wearing this jacket may indicate a lack of understanding about the connotative meanings of fashion. In this instance, the expectation is that Melania Trump does care about children living in a shelter. The politics of care, Puig de la Bellacasa suggests, 'have been at the heart of concerns with exclusions and critiques of power dynamics in stratified worlds' (2011, p. 86). To imply lack of care is to adopt an elite, marginalising and callous position. Yet, in order to contribute to 'liveable worlds', we need to ask 'how to care' in each situation (Puig de la Bellacasa, 2011, p. 100). Questions about whether the First Lady cares are answered by the text on her jacket. Wearing the jacket seems like a type of popular culture gesture: Melania Trump is trying to accrue cultural capital or cachet by wearing a jacket with a contemporary, cool message. However, because the text contradicts expectations that she cares about the visit to the shelter, it is actually popular culture appropriation – fake care and fake popular culture. The response from the White House was that there was no underlying message: 'It's a jacket. There was no hidden message' (Herschfeld, Rogers, & Haberman, 2018). So, the message was visible and explicit – Melania Trump does not care. Although less contentious and more risible, her decision to wear pink Louboutin high heels and a Valentino skirt that cost $4,000 while planting a tree at the White House (Cocozza, 2018) was possibly a reaction to media coverage that had mocked her earlier attempt at casual clothing for gardening when she wore an expensive, checked Balmain shirt and immaculately clean sneakers. The First Lady is not interested in pretending she gardens: 'of course, Trump looks glamorous, but she isn't really gardening and neither is she pretending to' (Cocozza, 2018). This is a Marie Antoinette moment, a simple message that she is rich and wears expensive clothes. Ostentatious displays of wealth may be considered bad taste or vulgar. Wilson's (2019) discussion of vulgarity suggests that fashion choices may be a type of showing off 'to demonstrate social power and wealth' that is the 'opposite of kindness and sensitivity' (p. 8). Vulgarity, then, moves beyond bad taste – it establishes a contestation between democratic and elitist ideals (Wilson, 2019). For public relations, this contestation creates possibilities for rethinking how identities are represented, power relations play out and the values that are epitomised. When social and environmental justice principles and practices are over-ridden by vulgarity, fashion becomes complicit in disempowering practices that normalise elitism.

During a visit to Kenya, Melania Trump's decision to wear a safari-type outfit and pith helmet, usually associated with colonial rule of Africa, was also deemed insensitive and inappropriate (Burke, 2018). Scott (2018) argued that her choice to wear the pith helmet was about 'race, power and privilege on display' rather than just a hat to keep off the sun. Scott (2018) considered it 'a symbol of how race and colonialism ghosts shape the African landscape when it comes to safari, poaching and trophy hunting'. The contradiction between wearing a pith helmet/safari outfit that validates imperialism, racism and big game hunting and visiting an elephant sanctuary is too significant to assume it is anything but deliberate. Another complicating issue is that President Trump's family have been criticised for big game hunting. In response to media criticism, Melania Trump suggested that the media should '[f]ocus on what I do, not what I wear' (Herschfeld et al., 2018). This is a seemingly reasonable suggestion, yet to do so would require a range of cultural compromises in regards to knowledge production and media responsibilities. It is disingenuous for a former model to suggest we ignore what she wears. The fashion choices Melania Trump makes are positioned within a broader agenda to advance right wing Republican agendas, promote President Trump and enhance the Trump fortune. Melania Trump's fashion choices are a form of 'political dressing' (Delgado, 2018) that amplify cultural divisions and discord. She is playing a double game. Although her actions may imply a concern for social issues, the visual images she presents resonate with populist right-wing sentiments and acquire a social power to amplify Trump's messages. The first lady is unable to gain popular traction for her fashion choices or causes because connotative meanings over-ride the denotative meanings – matters of fact are subsumed by matters of concern and care. It is important to recognise that the First Lady's fashion choices are part of a political network of conditions and communicative efforts that make certain knowledges legitimate and signal complicity in President Trump's contentious, contemptuous regime. Melania Trump's fashion choices have not been widely adopted – instead, her primary influence on popular culture has been that she has sparked a range of memes that mock and reject her double game. She is perceived as an outsider, an elite who does not belong in popular culture. In contrast to Melania Trump's elitist practices, the following sections examine how fashion may be shaped to advance democratic ideals and practices.

It is in the resistance to President Trump that we see clothing becoming a feature of popular culture and being adopted as a democratising political statement. In contrast to Melania Trump's role in normalising a divisive and deeply troubling form of power, resistance to the Trump regime pays attention to issues of social justice – poverty, class, gender, sexuality and race. The Women's March that took place in Washington in 2017 was an initial response to President Trump's election and his misogynist treatment of women. As a symbol of resistance, women knitted and wore pink pussy hats to oppose and confront Trump's vulgar comment 'Grab them by the pussy'. The hats were, more broadly, a symbol of support for women's rights and political resistance. In another instance, celebrities chose to wear black clothing to award ceremonies to signal support for the #MeToo movement. Although these fashion trends that have emerged from resistance movements may be fleeting, the movements that they symbolise are expanding and strengthening. Influential connections between fashion and mattering are authentic and emerge from engagement in popular culture rather than elitist imitations or appropriations.

A right royal transformation

Actress meets prince, they fall in love, get married and live happily ever after. A perfect fairy tale for popular culture. In 2018 the marriage of Meghan Markle, an American actress in the popular television show, *Suits*, to Prince Harry, the Queen of England's grandson, was an important moment for popular culture and fashion. Markle, currently the Duchess of Sussex, is a black American, and her acceptance into British royalty marked a significant cultural transformation. The Duchess of Sussex makes very deliberate political fashion choices. Like Michelle Obama she mixes high and fast fashion and supports local and indigenous fashion.

She also supports environmentally sustainable brands. She has become a fashion leader and the outfits she wears sell out immediately. The ability to set trends means that she is an important commercial asset, or brand addition, for the royal family. Although she has been subjected to significant media coverage it had been primarily positive, apart from some commentary from her own family. However, more recently Meghan Markle has been subjected to insidious media rumours and criticism that she is a tyrant, her staff are leaving and the queen is taking charge and controlling her (Elser, 2019). This type of media coverage is not new; both Princess Diana and Sarah Ferguson, Duchess of York, were subjected to similar coverage. By stepping outside the rigid expectations of royalty, women marrying into the royal family who are non-royalty or commoners are viewed as subverting the rules and subjected to harsh media criticism. Most recently, Markle has been blamed for the decision the Sussexes have made to establish their independence from the Royal family institution.

It takes courage to continue to open up possibilities for change. Meghan Markle, at a panel convened for International Women's Day, talked about problems created for young women's education in developing nations by the shame connected with menstruation. She explained,

> At the end of the day, we're doing our part just to normalise the conversation. . . . This is 50 percent of the population that's affected by something, that can also end up creating the most beautiful thing in the world. So it's a strange one that it's ended up becoming so stigmatized.
>
> (Barry, 2019)

This discussion marks a strong feminist commitment to improving the educational opportunities for women and normalising women's bodily functions. It is part of a broader popular culture discourse that attempts to remove the shame, stigma and costs associated with menstruation. It may be argued that royal support for causes has been radicalised – a taboo subject is being opened up and normalised through the endorsement of a royal member who has a significant celebrity status in popular culture. In this instance, fashion acts as a type of enabler for change. By successfully managing the media gaze on her outfits, Meghan Markle has been able to garner the coverage she needs to advance more serious issues. And herein lies the difference between Latour and Markle's media coverage. Latour has well-established legitimacy to comment on serious issues through his status as one of the world's leading philosophers; he is not a fashion leader, so the focus on his style of clothing does not add popular culture status. But, for Markle, the focus on her sense of fashion amplifies her popular culture status and lends her a legitimacy and credibility to comment on contemporary issues. So, it is important to understand the relative relationship between expertise and credibility and how to leverage expertise or how to develop credibility and it is here that notions of mattering come into play. Menstruation is not a conventional topic of discussion for members of royalty but Markle is able to use her popular culture capital to introduce the topic. She also has outsider status, or the common touch, which may lend her credibility in creating public relations for this issue.

Ministerial leadership and kindness

In 2017 Jacinda Ardern was elected Prime Minister of New Zealand. At 37 years of age, she was the world's youngest female head of government and is the second to give birth during office. Prime Minister Ardern's politics and policies are regarded as socially progressive. She has successfully navigated the politics of aesthetic expectations by choosing and supporting New Zealand designers. Overall, the media gaze has been more political in nature rather than gendered.

In 2018 she undertook her first international engagements. During a toast to the Commonwealth, Prime Minister Ardern spoke of the need to address climate change, oceans and democracy. She asked what is the most important thing in the world – and responded in *Te Reo Māori* and English language: '*he tangata, he tangata, he hangata*, it is the people, the people, the people'. Her use of *Te Reo Māori*, the language of the Indigenous people of New Zealand, along with wearing a traditional Māori cloak, affirmed her respect and support for Indigenous people. The *kahu huruhuru*, a Māori cloak adorned with feathers, is bestowed on chiefs and dignitaries to convey prestige, respect and power (Roy, 2018). The image of a pregnant female world leader wearing an Indigenous garment was an important moment. It conveyed that she was an inclusive female leader and was a subtle reminder to the Crown and Commonwealth leaders to prioritise Indigenous peoples and culture.

In her 2018 debut speech to the United Nations, Prime Minister Ardern opened with a *Te Reo Māori* greeting, then talked about New Zealand values, the impact of climate change on South Pacific nations, the need for opportunities and the most basic dignities for women. She reaffirmed New Zealand's commitment to defending an open and inclusive world order based on universal values, to being pragmatic, empathetic and kind. Although she was wearing a designer white dress, that was not a focus of media reporting. Instead, her speech was interpreted as a counter to President Trump's nationalistic, America First, speech. Her call for kindness resonated and was internationally reported. This act was not only about controlling the gaze and getting the aesthetics right. It was an instance of advancing social transformation and the values that underpin cultural change.

Today as I continue to write about Jacinda Ardern, the Prime Minister of Aotearoa/New Zealand, and how she has used fashion choices to support her messages, we have woken up to a new reality – yesterday 50 people were killed here in Aotearoa/New Zealand by a terrorist white supremacist attack. What to say? Jacinda Ardern embodies all that makes me so proud to be a New Zealander – she is kind, caring and seeks to bring about positive social change. During this extraordinary tragedy, she is an exemplary leader. Three particular acts stand out. First, her messages convey inclusivity and empathy: 'They are us'; 'this is your home, you should have been safe here'; and 'Many of those who will have been directly affected by this shooting may be migrants to New Zealand, they may even be refugees here. They have chosen to make New Zealand their home, and it is their home' (Christchurch Mosque Shootings, 2019). These are messages of inclusion and belonging. When asked by President Donald Trump how to help, she replied, 'provide sympathy and love for Muslim communities' (Moore, 2019). That is a pointed response to a leader who seeks to capitalise on divisions. At one of the most troubling times in the history of Aotearoa/New Zealand, Prime Minister Ardern has excelled in prioritising both matters of fact and matters of concern in her communication and actions. Second, by wearing a hijab (head scarf) when meeting members of the Muslim community, Prime Minister Ardern demonstrates an appreciation of, and respect for, faith and culture. A sombre photo of the Prime Minister wearing the head scarf has reverberated around the world. Third, the offer to provide funding for the funerals of those massacred and to provide funding for their families demonstrates compassion and an understanding of the broader loss and impacts. New Zealand does not always get it right – it is a tough place for many Indigenous people who experience poverty, educational and health disadvantages and feature too highly in incarceration statistics. But it is a country that aspires to be inclusive and fair. And Jacinda Ardern promotes social justice for all. Fashion is being managed to substantiate and reinforce messages and actions that matter.

Conclusion

By opening the chapter with an example of how fashion is co-opted to serve mediatised aims through a reversal of the gendered gaze, my aim was to think through how public relations works in popular culture to elevate or undermine contemporary cultural transformation agendas and open up possibilities for change. The chapter has explored how and when a focus on fashion is useful and when it is inappropriate for public relations aims. As this discussion has highlighted, popular culture status may act as a type of capital that is exchanged for coverage of important issues. Thinking through what makes Michelle Obama's choices so right and Melania Trump's choices so wrong highlights the ways that popular culture works as a regulated, mediatised social space. While some of the evaluation of their fashion choices may be linked to their husband's politics and popularity [or lack of it], I would argue that it is more directly linked to popular culture status, savvy and sensitivity. Those whose fashion choices fit the expectations, norms and values and engage in mediatised popular culture spaces are more likely to be accorded cultural capital and gain public relations advantages. Getting it right or getting it wrong is strongly associated with the accrual of cultural capital through genuine engagement in popular culture rather than an instrumental public relations exploitation of popular culture as a type of currency or commodity. Popular culture operates more as a social milieu or space in these instances, rather than a currency or commodity, which means that entrée cannot simply be purchased. Fashion may open up entrée into popular culture if the choices support or amplify particular messages but when fashion and message clash, the judgements may be harsh.

The relationship between fashion, public relations, popular culture and social change is gendered and political. Women are required to play a double game. Sometimes they are expected to blend in and other times they need to stand out. They need to comply with unspoken/unspecified expectations and norms, but in order to be fashionable they need to break the rules – the key to negotiating and traversing this double game seems to increasingly be linked to mattering – those who connect with and engage in popular culture in ways that resonate with justice concerns are more likely to succeed. Melania Trump's double game backfired. Bourdieu's (1977) concept of habitus is helpful here for explaining the problem – Melania Trump does not have the cultural capital to leverage popular culture because her appearance is higher end or elite rather than fashionable and she is not engaged in popular culture. Attempting to use fashion as a currency to popularise her messages and activities, she transgressed the boundaries of popular culture and attempted to move beyond her regular habitus. Public relations often works best when it is unobtrusive. Blatant manoeuvres are less likely to succeed. Gaining influence through popular culture is tricky – navigating boundaries between vulgarity and popularity requires a deft understanding of the rules of popular culture. Crane suggests that 'fashion is one of the most visible markers of social status and gender and therefore useful in maintaining or subverting symbolic boundaries' (2000, p. 1). She suggests that '[v]ariations in clothing choices are subtle indicators of how different positions in society are experienced' (Crane, 2000, p. 1) and that changes in clothing indicate changes in social relationships and discourses. Although clothing can be used to negotiate status, fashion is more ambiguous and multi-faceted and therefore more challenging to negotiate (Crane, 2000). Popular culture is not the right milieu for Trump; fashion is a cultural product that resonates with some groups and not others. Stepping outside the elite fashion she has engaged with and trying to navigate the boundaries of popular culture was not possible because Trump does not belong to popular groups or speak to them. She also misinterpreted how to navigate politics of care. The lesson for public relations is that traversing popular culture boundaries in order to accrue capital is complicated – questions of authenticity along with relations of power are critical to success. This chapter demonstrates that although fashion and popular culture status may open up possibilities for interventions and social transformations, an amalgam of hybrid cultures needs to be navigated and relations of power de-emphasised. The political importance of popular culture in influencing social change is that it is a vehicle for affecting hearts and minds – simply wearing the right clothes is not enough. A key contribution of the chapter is the identification and discussion of mattering, the way that particular values and messages are advanced – in this instance through aesthetic choices – as the compelling dimension that convinces publics of the significance of issues that are being advanced by leading women.

References

Barry, E. (2019, March 11). Meghan Markle 'moved the dial' for British royalty in her first Q&A *Sydney Morning Herald*. Retrieved from www.smh.com.au/lifestyle/health-and-wellness/meghan-markle-moved-the-dial-for-british-royalty-in-her-first-q-and-a-20190310-p51338.html

Bourdieu, P. (1977). *Outline of a theory of practice.* Cambridge, England: Cambridge University Press.

Burke, J. (2018, October 6). Melania Trump criticized for wearing colonial style helmet during Kenyan safari. *The Guardian*. Retrieved from www.theguardian.com/world/2018/oct/05/melania-trump-in-pith-helmet-on-kenya-safari-likened-to-colonialist

Christchurch mosque shootings: New Zealand Prime Minister Jacinda Ardern describes one of 'darkest days'. (2019, March 15). *New Zealand Herald*. Retrieved from www.nzherald.co.nz/nz/news/article.cfm?c_id=1&objectid=12213100

Cocozza, P. (2018, August 29). Stilettos and a $4,000 skirt: Melania Trump's tree-planting outfit. *The Guardian*. Retrieved from www.theguardian.com/us-news/shortcuts/2018/aug/28/stilettos-and-a-4000-skirt-melania-trumps-tree-planting-outfit

Crane, D. (2000). *Fashion and its social agendas: Class, gender and identity in clothing.* Chicago, IL: University of Chicago Press.

Delgado, H. N. (2018, January 23). Fashion's potential to influence politics and culture. *The Conversation*. Retrieved from https://theconversation.com/fashions-potential-to-influence-politics-and-culture-90077

Elser, D. (2019, March 19). Hidden sign the Queen is moving to take control of Meghan and Harry. *New Zealand Herald*. Retrieved from www.nzherald.co.nz/lifestyle/news/article.cfm?c_id=6&objectid=12214412

Finkelstein, J. (1991). *The fashioned self.* Cambridge, England: Polity Press.

Foucault, M. (1984). *The use of pleasure: The history of sexuality* (R. Hurley, Trans.). London, England: Penguin.

Foucault, M. (1988). Technologies of the self. In L. Martin, H. Gutman, & P. Hutton (Eds.), *Technologies of the self: A seminar with Michel Foucault* (pp. 16–48). Amherst, MA: University of Massachusetts Press.

Foucault, M. (1989). The concern for truth. In S. Lotringer (Ed.), *Foucault live: Interviews, 1961–1984* (L. Hochroth & J. Johnston, Trans., pp. 455–464). New York, NY: Semiotext(e).

Friedman, V. (2018, November 15). Dressing Michelle Obama, then and now. *New York Times*. Retrieved from www.nytimes.com/2018/11/15/fashion/michelle-obama-stylist-meredith-koop.html?fbclid=IwAR2KqaH-9kGkizSh-Ae5_Im7O BAPLNVRGF54zpcWp8UDVHAVjlEtYibCAeE

Hatmaker, S. (2014). On mattering: A coal ash flood and the limits of environmental knowledge. *Environmental Humanities, 4*(1), 19–39.

Herschfeld, K., Rogers, J., & Haberman, M. (2018, August 17). Melania Trump, a mysterious first lady, weathers a chaotic White House. *New York Times*. Retrieved from www.nytimes.com/2018/08/17/us/politics/melania-trump-first-lady.html

Kofman, A. (2018, October 25). Bruno Latour, the post-truth philosopher, mounts a defence of science. *New York Times Magazine*. Retrieved from www.nytimes.com/2018/10/25/magazine/bruno-latour-post-truth-philosopher-science.html?

fbclid=IwAR2b8ECoyUNIfCCQdMwt9vj76IDBmZC6LuPuSr_nolvz2enrOD
lcsy_JXGk

Latour, B. (2004). Why has critique run out of steam? From matters of fact to matters of concern. *Critical Inquiry, 30*(2), 225–248.

Moore, S. (2019, March 18). Jacinda Ardern is showing the world what real leadership is: Sympathy, love and integrity. *The Guardian.* Retrieved from www.theguardian.com/commentisfree/2019/mar/18/jacinda-ardern-is-showing-the-world-what-real-leadership-is-sympathy-love-and-integrity.

Motion, J. (1997). Technologising the self: An art of public relations. *Australian Journal of Communication, 24*(2), 1–16.

Obama, M. (2018). *Becoming.* New York, NY: Crown Publishing Group.

Puig de la Bellacasa, M. (2011). Matters of care in technoscience: Assembling neglected things. *Social Studies of Science, 41*(1), 85–106.

Rao, P. (2018, January 19). What Melania Trump's clothes are actually saying. *In Style.* Retrieved from www.instyle.com/fashion/melania-trump-first-lady-fashion

Roy, E. (2018, April 19). Jacinda Ardern wears Māori cloak to Buckingham Palace. *The Guardian.* Retrieved from www.theguardian.com/world/2018/apr/20/jacinda-ardern-maori-cloak-buckingham-palace-new-zealand

Scott, J. L. (2018, October 14). Melania Trump's pith helmet is not just a hat. *The Conversation.* Retrieved from https://theconversation.com/melania-trumps-pith-helmet-is-not-just-a-hat-104824

Williams, R. (1976). *Keywords: A vocabulary of culture and society.* New York, NY: Fontana Press.

Wilson, E. (2019). The vulgar: Fashion redefined. *Fashion Theory, 23*(1), 109–119.

7 Public relations, race and reconciliation

Kate Fitch

Introduction

In 2015, leading Australian Rules footballer and Adnyamathanha man Adam Goodes – who had twice won the Brownlow Medal, the Australian Football League's (AFL) highest honour – retired from professional football following three years of sustained racial abuse from opposition fans. Ironically, in 2014, Goodes was awarded Australian of the Year for his anti-racism advocacy. In 2019, two documentaries *The Final Quarter* (Shark Island Production, 2019), based on archival news footage, and *The Australian Dream* (Madman Films, 2019), drawing on interviews with media commentators and other key players in the controversy around Goodes, were released. It was only in 2019, in anticipation of the release of these documentaries, that the AFL apologised for not better protecting and supporting Goodes and failing to address racism (ABC News, 2019; Black, 2019). I start this chapter with the Goodes anecdote to introduce contemporary race politics in Australia.

Australia is the only first world nation with a colonial history not to have constitutional recognition for First Nations people (RMIT ABC Factcheck, 2019), yet the Uluru Statement from the Heart (2017), which called for a First Nations voice to be represented in the constitution,[1] was rejected by the federal government. The ongoing trauma of colonisation points to the urgent need for better historical and cultural understanding of Indigenous disadvantage to address racial inequality. There is increasing recognition of the need for ongoing consultation and engagement of Indigenous people in the development of services and programs (Government of Western Australia, 2005; Zuckermann, 2015). Often such work falls broadly within public relations, be it through corporate or public affairs, community or stakeholder engagement functions or in event management and promotional activities. Beyond that, many organisations are publically committing to reconciliation and the Uluru Statement, as I discuss in this chapter.

This chapter investigates public relations and race in Australia, focusing on Indigenous Australians. It considers the role public relations might play in reconciliation and social justice, and highlights the need to locate public relations within social and cultural contexts and for an historical understanding of Indigenous people and public relations practices. Given the themes of this book, this chapter also explores how public relations, by organisations and in more community-driven conceptualisations of public relations activity, can challenge established power imbalances to promote greater social justice and allow a stronger understanding of public relations' role in social change. It therefore contributes an Australian perspective to the small body of critical scholarship focusing on public relations and race. Increasingly, organisations in Australia are committing to better practices in working with Indigenous people; this is evident in the inclusion of welcome or acknowledgement of country at the start of events[2] and in the development of formal Reconciliation Action Plans (RAP) at diverse organisations ranging from public relations consultancies, supermarket chains, and resource companies to universities. However, beyond the implications for practice, investigating the ways race is entangled with public relations offers an opportunity to deconstruct public relations and its discursive boundaries and to conceptualise how public relations might be harnessed for social justice and social change.

The chapter is structured in four sections. The first section, 'Race and Public Relations', reviews scholarship on critical race within the discipline to establish the ways in which public relations is underpinned by systemic discrimination and must be understood within its historical and social contexts. The second section, 'Reconciliation and Social Justice', outlines a brief history of Indigenous activism and government policy and the steps towards formal reconciliation. It offers a public relations case study, 'Deadly Questions', a groundbreaking and provocative Victorian state government campaign aimed at educating the wider community about Indigenous culture and heritage as the preparation for a state-based treaty. The following section introduces Indigenous Australia and the impact of colonisation to demonstrate contemporary racial inequality, evident in the stark and compelling disparities in health, life expectancy, income, incarceration rates and education between Indigenous and non-Indigenous Australians. It draws on activist use of public relations to bring attention to racial inequality and social justice issues, using an example of the campaigning around a tragic Death in Custody case in Western Australia. The final section draws on my experiences as an educator to advocate a critical pedagogy for public relations in Australia that specifically pays attention to the raced and violent history of Australia as a settler colony and the ongoing social disadvantage that results from this history (Wolfe, 2006). This chapter concludes by considering the role public relations can play in reconciliation and social justice.

Race and public relations

There is a long history of the use of public relations to protect existing power structures and hegemonic interests (Roper, 2005). To offer one example, Short (2008) identifies the vigorous public relations activities of mining and farming interest groups in Australia in response to the *Mabo* and *Wik* decisions in 1992 and 1996 respectively.[3] The mining industry promoted the idea that the Mabo decision threatened national interests and the farming lobby followed suit in order to protect pastoral leases (Short, 2008). Indeed, the National Council of Churches (1997, cited in Short, 2008, p. 75) identified one television advertisement produced by the National Farmers Federation as 'racist propaganda'. However, it is difficult to understand these campaigns without an appreciation of their social context and indeed the specific ways in which history has enabled the production of this public relations activity (Munshi & Edwards, 2011).

Public relations scholars need to understand how race is a systemic process that underpins structures of discrimination in public relations and contributes to inequity (Edwards, 2014, 2018, 2020). According to Edwards (2013, 2020), public relations is institutionally racist in that it is founded on concepts of whiteness and deeply embedded in capitalist systems. In discussing the history of public relations and race in the USA, Logan argues:

> Not only did mainstream public relations emerge as an economic discourse but it also emerged as a racialized discourse. This racialization was literally embodied in the forefathers of the field and in the racialized bodies of those denied access.
>
> (2016, p. 96)

For Logan (2016), the historic association of public relations with a neoliberal economic discourse and big business is closely linked with the history of a USA founded on slavery. Similarly, Edwards (2020), writing about the history of public relations in the UK, identifies close links with notions of white superiority and the British Empire. In Australia, the historical development of public relations in the twentieth century is closely linked with the Commonwealth (Fitch, 2016). However, it should also be understood in the context of Australia's status as a settler colony and the resultant ongoing disadvantage of Indigenous Australians.

Race and social justice were not a priority for most public relations scholars and it is only in recent years that a small number of critical scholars have begun to engage with issues of race (Logan, 2011, 2016; Waymer & Heath, 2016). Pompper first drew on critical race theory to argue how foregrounding race could address power and race within the discipline and enable public relations to 'be a change agent' (2005, p. 154). Scholars have noted the 'virtual invisibility' of race in public relations scholarship (Munshi & Edwards, 2011, p. 349), the limited research on race from a public relations perspective (Edwards, 2018), and even the ways race has been 'dysfunctionally studied', in that race is often instrumentalised to benefit organisations (Waymer & Heath, 2016, p. 299).

In the last decade, a small number of critical scholars have begun to engage with race, considering how normative understandings of whiteness inform campaigns (see, for example, Vardeman-Winter, 2011) and applied critical race theory to public relations campaigns. For example, Logan (2016) analysed Starbucks' #RaceTogether campaign and argued it was a proactive, if imperfect, attempt to address racial inequality in the USA. In New Zealand, there has been some scholarship on working with Indigenous stakeholders, arguing for the need to incorporate Indigenous knowledges and practices into public engagement as a way of confronting power imbalances between organisations and publics (Love & Tilley, 2014; Motion, Haar, & Leitch, 2012). However, in Australian public relations scholarship, there has been very little published research focusing on race, social justice and Indigenous Australians. A journal article investigates the perspectives of female Indigenous public relations practitioners and advocates incorporating Aboriginal and Torres Strait Islander cultural protocols as well as the potential for communicating for social change and self-determination for Aboriginal and Torres Strait Islander peoples (Clark, Guivarra, Dodson, & Hunt, 2019). Other research has addressed the experiences of minority practitioners, diversity and inclusion in the Australian industry and/or the need for cultural competence but without a specific focus on race (Fitch & Desai, 2012; Sison, 2016; Wolf, 2016). However, focusing on culture and cultural diversity instead of race is problematic, as I discuss below in relation to pedagogy.

One aspect around contemporary discussion of race that needs to be addressed is the idea that we live in a 'post-race' world, given the existence of legalisation, such as the *Racial Discrimination Act (1975)* in Australia. Post-racism assumes that racism no longer exists and racist ideologies and discrimination due to race are effectively rendered invisible (Edwards, 2020). As Lentin argues: ' "not racism" can be witnessed in definitions of racism that either sideline or deny race both as an historical phenomenon and as experienced by racialized people' (2018, p. 402). For example, Lambert identifies the fictional representation of a black public relations practitioner in *Scandal* as post-racist, given the 'racially charged stories that U.S. viewers encounter in mainstream news and social media channels exist only on the margins of the fictional world of Olivia Pope' or are safely confined in the past (2017, p. 572). Examples of post-racism can be seen in research based on interviews with practitioners of culturally diverse backgrounds, which leads to conclusions that whiteness and race are 'meaningless' and 'increasingly irrelevant' for public relations in Australia (Wolf, 2016, p. 71).

In the case of Goodes, many media commentators and football fans denied the booing of Goodes was racism (Coram & Hallinan, 2017; D'Cruz, 2018; de Souza, 2018). For example, conservative broadcaster Andrew Bolt argued the booing directed at Goodes was not because of his race but stemmed from an 'overreaction' by Goodes, and what Bolt called the 'racism industry', to a teenager for calling the dual Brownlow medallist an 'ape' (cited in Booker, 2015). Former state premiers, prominent media commentators and other footballers also argued the booing of Goodes was not racist (de Souza, 2018). In 2019, a national newspaper conducted an online poll regarding Goodes; out of approximately 60,000 participants, 19% said they had booed Goodes; 65% denied that such booing was racist; and 47% selected no to the question: 'Does Australia have a problem with racism?' (Johnson, 2019).

Reconciliation and social justice

Reconciliation in Australia constitutes complex processes around truth telling, remembering, apologising, educating, and reparating and contributes to an 'utopian social imaginary' that offers a 'narrative of nationhood' (Hattam & Matthews, 2008, p. 13). It involves identifying and redressing 'wrongs' and sources of conflict such as 'the forcible dispossession of Aboriginal peoples by the British, which began in 1788' (Short, 2008, p. 4). In 1991, the *National Report: Royal Commission into Aboriginal Deaths in Custody* (Johnston, 1991) was released; it made 339 recommendations aimed at reducing Indigenous incarceration rates, most of which have not been implemented (Klippmark & Crawley, 2018). The report concluded there was a need for reconciliation, which it defined as community relations to address 'a large reservoir of distrust, enmity and anger among Aboriginal people, and a lack of understanding amongst non-Aboriginal people' (Johnston, 1991, p. 14). Reconciliation Australia (n.d.), an independent, not-for-profit body established in 2001, views its role as 'building relationships, respect and trust between the wider Australian community and Aboriginal and Torres Strait Islander peoples'.[4] Acknowledging that reconciliation falls short of a full treaty, Hattam, Atkinson and Bishop nevertheless view reconciliation as positive:

> [R]econciliation can be seen as the optimistic, 'bright' side of our unsettling times; an engaged ethical turn that renews interest in our responsibility for one another; an attempt to map out an alternative world view to that proposed by social depredations of individualistic neo-liberalism and as a resistance against what Bauman has referred to as the 'social production of moral indifference' (1991, p. 18) and 'the dead silence of unconcern' (p. 74).
>
> (2008, p. 4)

Public relations work can play a pivotal role in building relations not just between organisations and Indigenous stakeholders, but in terms of locating organisations in society and considering their moral and social obligations and commitments to social justice. In Australia, diverse organisations – corporations, universities, schools, government, community organisations, and even some public relations consultancies – have committed to reconciliation, and formalised Reconciliation Action Plans (RAP). RAP specify how an organisation will build relationships between Indigenous peoples and the Australian community; develop respect for Indigenous cultures and create opportunities to improve socioeconomic outcomes for Indigenous Australians (Reconciliation Australia, n.d.). For example, major supermarket chain, Woolworths Group, launched its second RAP in 2019, which according to the CEO aims to bring prosperity to Aboriginal and Torres Strait Island peoples through: 'employment and supplier relationships and by nurturing lasting and impactful ties to communities through our national footprint of stores' (cited in Dickie, 2019). Adam Goodes is a member of their RAP's Indigenous Advisory Panel. In fact, Goodes has had a longstanding relationship with Woolworths (2016) through his role as a S.T.A.N.D. (Support Through Australian Natural Disasters) ambassador and advisor; in 2019, he continues to feature in advertising campaigns promoting Woolworths' fundraising to support disaster preparedness and recovery.

Leading companies, including airlines (Qantas), resource companies (BHP, Rio Tinto, Woodside), accounting firms (KPMG, PWC Accounting), universities, sports clubs, and law firms along with unions and industry bodies publically acknowledged support for the Uluru statement, even as the Australian government rejected it (AICD, 2019; Power, 2019). BHP's Manager for Indigenous Affairs, Libby Ferrari, acknowledged 'we've not always got this right in our history' (cited in Power, 2019). Goodes stated Woolworths and other organisations' commitment to the Uluru Statement represented 'a real opportunity for businesses to use their collective voices to continue to drive conversation about the importance of the Uluru statement and the potential for positive change it can bring' (cited in Dickie, 2019). In the Australian federal government's rejection of the Uluru statement and any immediate prospect of a treaty, a number of state governments have begun to work towards state-based treaties. The Victorian state government has the most developed plans, having committed to advancing self-determination for First Nations people in 2016. In 2019, 32 representatives were elected to negotiate a treaty framework (Dunstan & Willingham, 2019). A communication campaign aimed at educating Victorians about Indigenous culture and heritage in advance of the treaty is discussed below.

Deadly questions: a community campaign

Deadly Questions (see https://deadlyquestions.vic.gov.au/), a Victorian state government campaign launched in June 2018, is a risky, challenging communication campaign that offers Indigenous perspectives on a range of issues. Deadly in Aboriginal English means good or great. The website has the tag 'You ask. Aboriginal Victorians answer.' Anyone can submit questions and there are spoken, written and video responses by Indigenous Australians to questions that range from racist stereotyping, the significance of a treaty and even what deadly means. It was released in response to research that revealed Victorians knew little about Indigenous culture, heritage or politics, as part of the preparation required for community and political support for legislation around a state-based treaty (McDonnell, 2018). According to Simon Lamplough, Managing Director of Clemenger BDDO, their 'brief was to change perceptions and create work with cultural impact' (cited in Tutty, 2018), and that:

> Every element of the campaign was designed to provoke a response, so we knew that earned media was key to engaging the Victorian community and ensuring the campaign drove the discussion it needed to be successful
>
> . . .
>
> We wanted to use some of the division and misinformation that's out there to get people talking and get them to take notice of an issue that's been ignored for too long. (cited in McDonnell, 2018)

The campaign provoked additional controversy when two outdoor media companies refused to run campaign billboards, arguing that the content was discriminatory and potentially in breach of the advertising industry's own code of ethics (McDonnell, 2018). A spokesperson for Aboriginal Victoria acknowledged the controversy:

> We understand that some of the questions asked by the public – and that we are repeating in the campaign – are provocative, but that's the point. To have an open discussion we need to acknowledge that some ugly viewpoints exist.
> (cited in Tutty, 2018)

The campaign offers a good example of the use of public relations in educating and changing attitudes. The climate in Australia for talking about race under a conservative federal government is challenging. The campaign therefore represents something of a radical act by the Labor-held Victorian state government. Its focus shifted to the proposed treaty in the second phase of the campaign in September 2018 (Hutchins, 2018). The campaign contributed to the treaty legislation being passed in both the upper and lower houses of the Victorian state government and the subsequent creation of the First Peoples' Assembly to advise on the treaty (Allam, 2019; McDonnell, 2018).

Indigenous Australia and racial inequality

There is a long of history of activism around race and racial equality in Australia. In part, this activism was informed by international phenomena such as civil rights activism in the US in the 1960s and the anti-apartheid movement in South Africa (Clark, 2008), but it existed long before the 1960s. The loss of land, and therefore of cultural and spiritual connection to the land, as a result of colonisation is deeply significant and underpins Indigenous claims for political autonomy (Short, 2008). For example, McGlade (2017) offers a personal and detailed historical account of the impact of colonisation for Noongar people and the resultant activism and legal challenges. In late 2019, what might be the biggest land claim in the world – AUD$290 billion – was lodged in Australia's federal court on behalf of the Noongar nation in southwest Australia to compensate for the loss of native title (Higgins & Collard, 2019). It was another land claim, known as the *Mabo* decision, in 1992 that led to the recognition of *terra nullius* as a legal fiction that supported the British colonisers' claims over Australia.

In addition, the systematic removal of Indigenous children, in what is widely known as the 'Stolen Generations',[5] persisted throughout most of the twentieth century; it is documented in the landmark Human Rights and Equal Opportunity Commission's (HREOC, 1997) report, *Bringing Them Home: National Inquiry into the Separation of Aboriginal and Torres Strait Islander Children From Their Families*. The report documents the forced removal of children between 1910 and 1970 and calls it genocide. In addition to personal narratives, *Bringing Them Home* recommended an apology and compensation, among other measures. Prime Minister John Howard refused to apologise and the Senate response to *Bringing Them Home* was a 'corrective' report that sought to establish removing children was lawful and done with 'benign intent' (Surma, 2005). It was not until 2008 that Prime Minister Kevin Rudd made an historic apology to Indigenous peoples of Australia. The anniversary of the report, 26 May, is now National Sorry Day.

By most measures of wellbeing, Indigenous Australians, who make up 3.3% of the population in Australia, fare poorly in comparison to non-Indigenous Australians: in terms of a shorter average life expectancy; poorer health outcomes; lower levels of education, home ownership and employment; and higher rates of infant mortality and incarceration (ABS, 2017; Australians Together, n.d.). There is a 10-year gap in life expectancy between Indigenous and non-Indigenous Australians (ABS, 2017). In 2016, 47% of Indigenous Australians aged 15–64 were employed compared with 72% of non-Indigenous Australians (AIHW, 2019). Members of the Stolen Generations are particularly disadvantaged; compared with other Indigenous Australians born before 1972: they are 3.3 times more likely to have been incarcerated in the last five years; more likely to have experienced violence in the last 12 months; and are nearly twice as likely to receive government payments as their main source of income (AIHW, 2019). The annual *Closing the Gap* report records some progress in addressing inequality, but acknowledges that key targets such as halving the gaps between Indigenous and non-Indigenous Australians in employment and in reading and numeracy rates were not on track, nor is the target to close the gap in life expectancy (Department of Prime Minister, 2018).[6]

Drawing on scholarship on activism and public relations, I am interested in how public relations activity, as strategic communication, can be harnessed by activist groups and social justice movements to address power in society by resisting certain structures and bring about social change (see, for example, Ciszek, 2017; Demetrious, 2013). I therefore include in this section, a brief case study of a campaign, which involved a number of stakeholders – Deaths in Custody Watch Committee (WA),[7] Amnesty International, Maurice Blackburn Lawyers, journalists, academics, supporters, and family members of Ms Dhu – to draw attention to the circumstances of Ms Dhu's death in custody and ongoing social justice issues related to institutional racism.

Justice for Ms Dhu

Yamatji woman Ms Dhu was 22 years old when she died in police custody – she was in custody for outstanding civil fines – in Port Hedland in Western Australia.[8] Indigenous women are overly represented in the prison system, making up 34% of female prisoners nationally and double that figure in Western Australia (Deathscapes, 2017; Klippmark & Crawley, 2018; Walters & Longhurst, 2017). No charges have ever been laid in response to Ms Dhu's death from septicaemia, stemming from the broken ribs she had incurred as a victim of domestic violence, and pneumonia (Wahlquist, 2015a, 2015b). Ms Dhu's complaints were dismissed by police and by medical staff at the local hospital. A coronial inquest was held in Perth in two parts in November 2015 and in March 2016; historian and activist Ethan Blue (2017) describes the coronial inquest in detail. In addition to news reporting, partly in response to the protests held outside the coroner's court prior to the start of daily proceedings, activists maintained a strong social media presence that included tweeting, along with the journalists, from the inquest. In February 2016, prior to the second part of the inquest, a small group of activists began projecting images of Ms Dhu with hashtags such as #JusticeforMsDhu as well as the Aboriginal flag and hashtags such as #StopBlackDeathsInCustody and #BlackLivesMatter on state and other significant buildings in the city of Perth. One of them describes the action:

> Each evening, a small group of people loaded into a car with a projector and laptop, and travelled Perth's streets. We found prominent or symbolically resonant buildings – the East Perth lockup, the Western Power building, the Telstra Building, the Royal Perth Hospital, the Police Forensic Investigation Unit (an entirely unmarked building housing the investigators responsible for deaths in custody inquiries), Parliament House itself. We chose sites of death and of state power, institutions of infrastructure, communication, and capital formation. We stopped in alleyways and empty parking lots to set up the projector. Soon, giant, haunting images of Ms. Dhu lit the walls and overlooked the city. We stayed for as long as we could, until batteries ran out of power, or until local security ran us off.
> (Sherene Razack, cited in Blue, 2017, p. 308)

These deeply symbolic images drew attention to racial inequality and the use of hashtags such as #BlackLivesMatter connect Ms Dhu to global movements campaigning against state violence and racial inequality (Blue, 2017). They also offered a powerful counter-narrative to the historical erasure of Indigenous voices, calling attention to state violence and institutional racism (Klippmark & Crawley, 2018). According to Blue:

> By shining a light on places where human rights violations have taken place and on the city's centres of business, finance, state power, and communication, the projections reclaim the surfaces of a city that has grown rich from mining and real estate. Aboriginal people have been locked out of much of this growth, despite that the mineral resources come from Aboriginal lands.
> (2017, p. 309)

The point is that such acts of protest are communicative acts aimed to bring about social change and justice. They are not 'organisational communication' in the traditional, normative understanding of public relations, but they are – in the ways we seek a more transformative public relations concerned with social justice in this book – a highly visual and effective protest to draw attention to Ms Dhu and to ensure her visible presence in the city prior to the second part of the coronial inquest. These visual protests are 'talking back' (hooks, 1989) to the state and to institutions of power. Similarly, 'Ms Dhu', a protest song featuring Felix Riebl and the Marliya choir (Spinifex Gum, 2017) offers haunting lyrics with young Indigenous women's voices interspersed with actual CCTV footage of Ms Dhu from police cells in Port Hedland, news reports, protests in support of Ms Dhu, civil rights protests and even images of large-scale mine operations and corporate boardrooms confirming links with social justice, Indigenous disadvantage, the loss of land, white wealth and the corporate sector.

Critical pedagogy for public relations

One longstanding issue for the public relations curriculum is its historic reliance on industry expectations of practice and of the vocational training perceived as necessary for new graduates to 'hit the ground running' (Fitch, 2016). International and national professional bodies have developed guidelines for public relations curricula; these guidelines – and in the case of the Public Relations Institute of Australia [PRIA], a formal course accreditation process – attempt to define the curriculum and therefore the requisite body of knowledge (Fitch, 2016). Although these various frameworks acknowledge the need for both sensitive communication 'with stakeholders and communities across a range of cultural and other values and beliefs' and 'contextual intelligence (in terms of understanding local and global diversity in culture, values and beliefs)' (Fawkes et al., 2018, p. 7), they do not specifically address issues of race. The Australian recommendations point to the need for 'awareness of the country's multicultural and diverse society' and 'sensitivity to cultural values in communication messages' (Fawkes et al., 2018, p. 7). The PRIA course accreditation guidelines briefly mention the need to demonstrate how 'students learn about . . . the key characteristics of Australian indigenous and multicultural society' in relation to 'Australian and international politics, culture and society' (2017, p. 6). Yet, research with Australian employers of public relations graduates identified a significant gap across the industry in terms of cultural competency required to communicate and engage with Indigenous people, particularly in resource and government sectors (Fitch & Desai, 2012). The emphasis on cultural competence and cultural diversity in these various guidelines and frameworks fails to consider the histories and experiences of Indigenous Australians and the specific contexts and historical factors that led to systematic and widespread disadvantage along race lines. As Ahmed, drawing on research with Australian educators found, the problem with diversity is it 'become[s] detached from histories of struggle for equality' (2007, p. 235).

In response, I draw on the work of Professor Chelsea Bond (2017), who calls for greater racial literacy in the Australian health curriculum, to reflect on the need for greater racial literacy in the public relations curriculum. Curricula must do more than promote anti-racism and explicitly acknowledge the racialised structures in which they work. From Bond's perspective, addressing culture rather than race represents a problematic discursive shift that elides the impact of race and racism:

> While Indigenous people are not a 'race', 'Indigenous status' is a racial category and Indigenous bodies are inscribed with racialised logics, which are not absolved by using the term 'culture'.
>
> (Bond, p. 7)

For Bond, it is problematic to assume that culture is interchangeable with race, and to operationalise issues of race as 'cultural difference'. Instead, all students need to develop a critical racial literacy in relation to their studies to be able to understand and address racial inequality.

The failure to address race in curricula is not unique to the public relations discipline and Universities Australia, the peak body for 39 universities, has an *Indigenous Strategy 2017–2020* that states:

> By 2020, universities commit to have plans for, or have already in place, processes that ensure all students will encounter and engage with Aboriginal and Torres Strait Islander cultural content as integral parts of their course of study.
>
> This will give all Australian university graduates in the future the chance to develop their capabilities to work with and for Aboriginal and Torres Strait Islander people and communities.
>
> (2017, p. 30)

Universities Australia recommends all Australian curricula include and adapt for each discipline and service profession: concepts of culture, race, ethnicity and worldview; Indigenous culture and history; impact of government policies; current statistics regarding the disparities between Indigenous and non-Indigenous peoples; notions of whiteness, white privilege and power; and racism and anti-racist practices (2011, pp. 71–72). This framework reflects one of the recommendations of the *Bringing Them Home* (HREOC, 1997) report that all students receive 'education about the history and effects of forcible removal' (*Bringing Them Home*: Appendix 9 Recommendations, 1997).

My attempts to incorporate Indigenous perspectives into my teaching raised awareness of social inequality and disadvantage and of the complexity of contested knowledge spaces (Nakata, Nakata, Keech, & Bolt, 2012) and informed students' understanding of what socially responsible public relations might entail in relation to Indigenous stakeholders. Educating students about the need to understand the particular forms of disadvantage that persist for Indigenous Australia means a history lesson along with sound evidence of ongoing disadvantage and why that matters for professional communicators. I found it necessary to offer students an Indigenous history of Australia; this included key landmarks and showing Prime Ministers' speeches such as Paul Keating's Redfern Address and Rudd's historic apology to Stolen Generations. My teaching included iconic images such as Nicky Winmar, another Australian footballer whose response to racial vilification in 1993 is now commemorated in a statue (Wahlquist, 2019), to show that the booing of Adam Goodes is neither an isolated incident nor the result of Goodes' provocations. I provided compelling and at times depressing statistics to highlight the extent of Indigenous social disadvantage in Australia, despite Australia's self-identity as an egalitarian society (Universities Australia, 2011). I include these statistics so students can begin to understand why, as future professional communicators, they need to develop levels of cultural competency alongside literacy about race and race relations in Australia. Finally, I foregrounded that I could only offer a *wadjela* [white person in Noongar] perspective and therefore attempted to introduce Indigenous voices into the classroom, by setting readings by Indigenous scholars and in some years, Kylie Farmer's (2014) TedX talk on learning Noongar that concludes with her Noongar translation of a Shakespearian sonnet.[9] The introduction of language was important as no student could offer a single word of Noongar and the talk introduced them to some words and, significantly, the recognition that Noongar language was still spoken. A language map introduced students to more than 250 Indigenous languages across Australia. Feedback from students was enthusiastic in that they perceived new dimensions to public relations work, but they considered a single topic on Indigenous perspectives inadequate.

In reflecting on my attempts to introduce Indigenous perspectives into the public relations curriculum over several years, one challenge in a crowded curriculum focused on employability is an interrogation of the public relations discipline and the ways in which public relations is entangled with power and race. But, as Somerville, Purcell and Morrison found in their inclusion of terrorism in the public relations curriculum in Northern Ireland: 'focusing too narrowly on a managerialist orientation can lead to the exclusion, in any coherent sense, of consideration of the wider moral, political and social contexts of practice' (2011, p. 549), and they called for greater attention to challenging social issues and conflict without discounting the need for vocational aspects. Drawing on interviews with US educators, Waymer and Dyson argued:

> The question then is not 'Should we teach race in PR,' but, rather, 'How can scholars challenge and influence the curriculum in ways that lead to the inclusion and teaching of multiple standpoints, including race?'
>
> (2011, p. 464)

Scholars, not industry bodies, should consider how best to develop activities that are able to develop opportunities for reflection and self-awareness around race and white privilege. As I found in feedback from my students, Somerville, Purcell, and Morrison (2011) observed the majority of students welcomed the opportunity to discuss challenging and controversial topics as part of their public relations curriculum although a minority did not. Bond (2017) argues that concerns about student comfort and the need for positive statistics and stories are founded on notions of white privilege and fail to confront the very real health inequalities that Indigenous people experience. This leads me to consider the need for a critical pedagogy that not only incorporates Indigenous voices, case studies and expertise into public relations curricula, but which specifically considers race, power and knowledge production:

> 'Critical pedagogy' provides an 'emancipatory' social vision for pedagogical work that rejects views of pedagogy that are ahistorical, depoliticized and positivist. The critical pedagogue focuses on the way that power relations

exert an effect on how knowledge is (re)produced, and exchanged in any pedagogical act.

(Hattam, Atkinson, & Bishop, 2008, p. 6)

We need to educate students about race and social justice, and about specific cultural protocols (i.e., not simply in terms of cultural diversity or the multicultural other), but actually thinking specifically about Indigenous disadvantage and how public relations can intervene in that space. If the purpose of a university – still – is to challenge thinking and enable transformative learning around social justice outcomes, then public relations educators must consider a critical pedagogy that engages with the industry's role in reconciliation as well as its history in protecting hegemonic interests and in active resistance. In light of my reflections around teaching public relations in the Australian context, decolonising public relations and addressing Indigenous disadvantage should be fundamental concerns within the discipline.

Conclusion

In this chapter, I have examined race and public relations in Indigenous Australia in order to understand the historical and contemporary social contexts for public relations activity. I have not limited the discussion to public relations work done by well-resourced corporations in the mining sector and government departments seeking to engage Indigenous citizens. Instead, I have considered other kinds of public relations work, including activism that draws attention to high incarceration rates for Indigenous Australians, deaths in custody, and the unjust jailing of people for unpaid fines, a system which continues in Western Australia in 2020 and affects Indigenous women more than any other demographic. For me, this persuasive communication activity highlights racial inequality through media relations and events, using spokespeople and sophisticated messaging and visual imagery amplified through the strategic use of social media, acknowledging some scholars are wary of a simplistic conflation of activism and public relations (see, for example, Demetrious, 2013; Weaver, 2019; Wolf, 2018).

If we can understand public relations not as an organisational function but rather as communicative activity designed to persuade and transform, then campaigns such as #Justice4MsDhu and Deadly Questions can inform different understandings of public relations work and its impact. Both campaigns make visible the people and voices who might otherwise be marginalised or voiceless in mainstream Australia. They draw attention to social injustice: systemic and institutional racism in the case of Ms Dhu and to Indigenous knowledge and history in Deadly Questions in order to help Victorians understand the need for a treaty. In both cases, public relations is a resource for resisting and changing existing power relations and constitutes communication and advocacy for and by Indigenous Australians. These examples highlight the need not just for cultural competence but for racial literacy among professional communicators. Celebrations of multiculturalism or diversity and inclusion policies fail to acknowledge the significance of colonisation for Indigenous Australians. However, as I have discussed in this chapter, more and more organisations are committing to reconciliation.

Teaching students – future communicators – about Indigenous Australia and race offers an important opportunity to deconstruct public relations and its discursive boundaries. Public relations is a racialised practice (Edwards, 2018) and to date Australian professional bodies and public relations textbooks and curricula have not adequately addressed issues of race or social injustice. Although employers, particularly in government and resource sectors, identify a knowledge gap in their workforce around communicating with Indigenous people (Fitch & Desai, 2012), there is a larger issue around the need to develop an understanding of social justice as a graduate attribute. The introduction of Indigenous perspectives into the public relations curriculum enables students to consider the role public relations might play in reconciliation and social justice, and highlights the need to locate public relations within social and cultural contexts and for an historical understanding of Indigenous people and public relations practices. A critical pedagogy enables students and educators to reflect on what working with Indigenous people means in terms of professional public relations practice, in public relations education, and for me as an educator interested in a social justice framework for curriculum development. Such an approach requires opportunities for future practitioners to reflect on race and whiteness and to consider the ways public relations might challenge existing knowledge and power structures in order to bring about positive social change and social justice.

This chapter, then, highlights the need for racial literacy in public relations. It echoes calls by critical scholars in the USA and UK for greater attention to race, and argues that public relations cannot be understood as a universal practice but rather in relation to the unique historical and social contexts in which it is practised. Public relations is embedded in those contexts. In exploring the role public relations might play in reconciliation and social justice, this chapter drew attention to historical and contemporary race politics in Australia and the ways public relations, practised by organisations and by diverse activists, might contribute to social change. To conclude then, I return to the booing of Adam Goodes. In anticipation of the release of the two documentaries in 2019, the AFL apologised 'unreservedly' for their failure to call out racism and to support not only Goodes, but also 'all Aboriginal and Torres Strait Islander players, past and present' (Black, 2019). The AFL's Manager of Diversity and Social Policy, Torres Strait Islander Ms Tanya Hosch, stressed the AFL's apology was sincere 'rather than reputation management' (cited in ABC News, 2019). Although this comment serves to highlight that public relations activity may represent a superficial and self-serving act, the AFL's 'sincere' apology also suggests it is interested in real change and in addressing the ways in which racism is so embedded in public discourse that the booing of Goodes cannot be recognised as racist (Coram & Hallinan, 2017). Public relations may therefore play an important role in intervening in and challenging public discourse on race and power, and therefore contributing to processes of reconciliation.

Notes

1 The Uluru Statement From the Heart followed extensive consultation with Indigenous leaders across Australia and was the outcome of the First Nations National
 Constitutional Convention with 250 Aboriginal and Torres Strait Islander leaders
 held at Uluru in May 2017 (Chrysanthos, 2019).
2 A Welcome to Country draws on traditional cultural protocols; it can only be performed by Traditional Owners or Aboriginal and Torres Strait Islander people who
 have been given permission from Traditional Owners, to welcome visitors to country (Reconciliation Australia, 2017). In contrast, anyone can offer an Acknowledgement of Country, which respects Traditional Owners and recognises continuing
 connection with country (Reconciliation Australia, 2017).
3 In 1992, the High Court of Australia decided that *terra nullius* was wrongly applied
 in Australia and therefore recognised the land rights of Aboriginal and Torres Strait
 Islander peoples in what is widely known as the *Mabo* decision. In 1996, the High
 Court confirmed in the *Wik* decision the right to native title and that these rights
 were not extinguished by pastoral leases.
4 Reconciliation is not without its critics. According to Lloyd (2019), reconciliation both celebrates Indigenous history and culture and encourages private, voluntary action to address social inequality, even as it obscures the role of political and
 economic structures in supporting racialised hierarchies. For Russell-Mundine and
 Mundine, 'the language and intent of reconciliation has much in common with the
 language and intent of assimilation and protectionism' (2016, p. 85).
5 The *Bringing Them Home* report estimates between 10% and 33% of Indigenous
 children were removed from their families between 1910 and 1970 due to government assimilation policies, and recognises this systematic removal has resulted in
 ongoing trauma (HREOC, 1997).
6 This annual report to Parliament by the Prime Minister is the result of the Closing
 the Gap campaign and a promise made by Prime Minister Rudd during his apology
 to Indigenous Australians in 2008; it outlines the federal government's progress in
 addressing Indigenous disadvantage in health, education and employment.
7 The Deaths In Custody Watch Committee (WA) is the longest running of a number of state-based groups established in 1996 following a recommendation of the
 Royal Commission into Aboriginal Deaths in Custody in 1991; in 2017 it became
 the First Nations Deaths In Custody Watch Committee.
8 Removing jail terms for fines was a recommendation of the Royal Commission in
 1991; it remains a common practice in Western Australia and adversely affects Aboriginal women. A campaign, Free Her by Deb Kilroy, CEO of Sisters Inside, raised
 half a million dollars in 2019 to pay fines and encourages citizens to lobby the
 Western Australian government to change the law (Truu, 2019; Wahlquist, 2019).
 The Western Australian parliament passed a bill designed to end the imprisonment
 of people for unpaid fines only on June 16, 2020 (Shine, 2020).
9 I was then working in a university in Whadjuk Boodjar (the Noongar country that
 comprises the Perth coastal plains) in Australia, home of the Noongar people.

References

ABC News. (2019, June 9). AFL apologises unreservedly for failures over racism
 faced by Adam Goodes. *ABC News*. Retrieved November 28, 2019, from www.
 abc.net.au/news/2019-06-07/afl-apologises-unreservedly-for-failures-over-
 adam-goodes-racism/11191880
Ahmed, S. (2007). The language of diversity. *Ethnic and Racial Studies*, 30(2),
 235–256.

Allam, L. (2019, April 11). Victoria a step closer to Indigenous treaty with creation of first peoples' assembly. *The Guardian*. Retrieved November 28, 2019, from www.theguardian.com/australia-news/2019/apr/11/victoria-a-step-closer-to-indigenous-treaty-with-creation-of-first-peoples-assembly

Australian Bureau of Statistics [ABS]. (2017, October 31). *Aboriginal and Torres Strait Islander population, 2016*. Retrieved November 27, 2019, from www.abs.gov.au/ausstats/abs@.nsf/Lookup/by%20Subject/2071.0~2016~Main%20Features~Aboriginal%20and%20Torres%20Strait%20islander%20Population%20Article~12

Australian Institute of Company Directors [AICD]. (2019, July 1). This is Australia's opportunity to reset its relationship with the indigenous community. *Company Director Magazine*. Retrieved November 28, 2019, from https://aicd.companydirectors.com.au/membership/company-director-magazine/2019-back-editions/july/first-nations-voice

Australian Institute of Health and Welfare [AIHW]. (2019). *Australia's welfare 2019 in brief. Cat. no. AUS 227*. Canberra: AIHW. Retrieved December 3, 2019, from www.aihw.gov.au/reports/australias-welfare/australias-welfare-2019-in-brief/contents/table-of-contents

Australians Together. (n.d.). Retrieved from https://australianstogether.org.au/

Black, S. (2019, June 9). AFL, clubs unreservedly apologise to Goodes for not 'standing with him' [Media Release]. Retrieved November 28, 2019, from www.afl.com.au/news/2019-06-07/afl-clubs-unreservedly-apologise-to-goodes-for-not-standing-with-him

Blue, E. (2017). Seeing Ms. Dhu: Inquest, conquest, and (in)visibility in Black women's deaths in custody. *Settler Colonial Studies, 7*(3), 299–320.

Bond, C. (2017). Keynote presentation: Race is real and so is racism – making the case for teaching race in Indigenous health curriculum. *Lime Good Practice Case Studies*, vol. 4. Faculty of Medicine, Dentistry and Health Sciences, The University of Melbourne. Retrieved from www.limenetwork.net.au/wp-content/uploads/2017/10/Bond.C-GPCS-V4.pdf

Booker, C. (2015, July 30) Adam Goodes should admit he was wrong, says Andrew Bolt. *Sydney Morning Herald* [online]. Retrieved November 27, 2019, from www.smh.com.au/entertainment/tv-and-radio/adam-goodes-should-admit-he-was-wrong-says-andrew-bolt-20150730-gioa1o.html

Chrysanthos, N. (2019, May 27). What is the Uluru statement from the heart? *Sydney Morning Herald*. Retrieved January 12, 2020, from www.smh.com.au/national/what-is-the-uluru-statement-from-the-heart-20190523-p51qlj.html

Ciszek, E. (2017). Activist strategic communication for social change: A transnational case study of lesbian, gay, bisexual, and transgender activism. *Journal of Communication, 67*(5), 702–718.

Clark, J. (2008). *Aborigines & activism: Race, aborigines & the coming of the sixties to Australia*. Perth, Australia: University of Western Australia Press.

Clark, T., Guivarra, N., Dodson, S., & Hunt, Y. W. (2019). Asserting an Indigenous theoretical framework in Australian public relations. *Prism, 15*(1). Retrieved from www.prismjournal.org/v15-no1.html

Coram, S., & Hallinan, C. (2017). Critical race theory and the orthodoxy of race neutrality: Examining the denigration of Adam Goodes. *Australian Aboriginal Studies, 1*, 99–111.

D'Cruz, G. (2018). Breaking bad: The booing of Adam Goodes and the politics of the Black sports celebrity in Australia. *Celebrity Studies, 9*(1), 131–138.

Deathscapes: Mapping race and violence in settler states. (2017). Retrieved November 27, 2019, from www.deathscapes.org/

Demetrious, K. (2013). *Public relations, activism, and social change: Speaking up.* New York, NY: Routledge.

Department of the Prime Minister and Cabinet. (2018). *Closing the gap prime minister's report 2018.* Canberra, Australia: Department of the Prime Minister and Cabinet. Retrieved December 3, 2019, from www.pmc.gov.au/sites/default/files/reports/closing-the-gap-2018/sites/default/files/ctg-report-20183872.pdf?a=1

de Souza, P. (2018). What does racial (in)justice sound like? On listening, acoustic violence and the booing of Adam Goodes. *Continuum, 32*(4), 459–473.

Dickie, M. (2019, July 8). Woolworths reaffirms commitment to reconciliation. *National Indigenous Times.* Retrieved December 3, 2019, from https://nit.com.au/woolworths-reaffirms-commitment-to-reconciliation/

Dunstan, J., & Willingham, R. (2019, October 6). Victorian treaty vote for first peoples' assembly delivers a different kind of state election. *ABC News.* Retrieved December 10, 2019, from www.abc.net.au/news/2019-10-06/historic-aboriginal-victorian-treaty-assembly-voting-underway/11574078

Edwards, L. (2013). Institutional racism in cultural production: The case of public relations. *Popular Communication, 11*(3), 242–256.

Edwards, L. (2014). Discourse, credentialism and occupational closure in the communications industries: The case of public relations in the UK. *European Journal of Communication, 29*(3), 319–334.

Edwards, L. (2018). *Understanding public relations: Theory, culture, society.* London, England: Sage.

Edwards, L. (2020). History, racialisation and resistance in 'post-race' public relations. In I. Somerville, L. Edwards, & Ø. Ihlen (Eds.), *Public relations, society and the generative power of history* (pp. 81–95). Abingdon, England: Routledge.

Farmer, K. (2014, March 10). Keep our languages alive: Kylie Farmer at TEDx-Manly. *TedX.* Retrieved December 1, 2019, from www.youtube.com/watch?v=SAxhh6DguUo

Fawkes, J., Gregory, A., Falkheimer, J., Gutiérrez-García, E., Halff, G., Rensburg, R., & Sadi, G. et al. (2018). *A global capability framework for the public relations and communication management profession.* Retrieved December 1, 2019, from www.hud.ac.uk/media/assets/document/research/globalcapabilitiesinpublicrelationsandcommunicationmanagementgcpr/global-capability-framework-brochure.pdf

Fitch, K. (2016). *Professionalizing public relations: History, gender and education.* London, England: Palgrave Macmillan.

Fitch, K., & Desai, R. (2012). Developing global practitioners: Addressing industry expectations of intercultural competence in public relations graduates in Singapore and Perth. *Journal of International Communication, 18*(1), 63–78.

Government of Western Australia. (2005). *Consulting citizens: Engaging with Aboriginal Western Australians.* Department of Indigenous Affairs. Retrieved from www.dia.wa.gov.au/Documents/ReportsPublications/ConsultingCitizensSept2005.pdf

Hattam, R., Atkinson, S., & Bishop, P. (2008). Rethinking reconciliation and pedagogy in unsettling times. In P. Ahluwalia, S. Atkinson, P. Bishop, R. Hattam, & P. Christie (Eds.), *Reconciliation and pedagogy* (pp. 1–9). Abingdon, England: Routledge.

Hattam, R., & Matthews, J. (2008). Reconciliation as a resource for critical pedagogy. In P. Ahluwalia, S. Atkinson, P. Bishop, R. Hattam, & P. Christie (Eds.), *Reconciliation and pedagogy* (pp. 10–28). Abingdon, England: Routledge.

Higgins, I., & Collard, S. (2019, November 29). WA indigenous group's $290 billion compensation claim could become one of world's biggest payouts. *ABC News*. Retrieved November 29, 2019, from www.abc.net.au/news/2019-11-29/ $290-billion-wa-native-title-claim-launched/11749206

hooks, b. (1989). *Talking back: Thinking feminist, thinking black*. London, England: Sheba.

Human Rights and Equal Opportunity Commission [HREOC]. (1997). *Bringing them home: National inquiry into the separation of Aboriginal and Torres Strait Islander children from their families*. Retrieved November 30, 2019, from www. humanrights.gov.au/our-work/bringing-them-home-report-1997

Hutchins, N. (2018, September 20). Deadly questions shifts focus to treaty [Media Release]. Retrieved November 27, 2019, from www.premier.vic.gov.au/wp-con tent/uploads/2018/09/180921-Deadly-Questions-Shifts-Focus-To-Treaty.pdf

Johnson, P. (2019, July 19). Adam Goodes documentary: Sam Newman hits back, take our poll. *News.com.au*. Retrieved November 27, 2019, from www.news.com. au/sport/afl/poll-was-the-adam-goodes-booing-racist/news-story/810dc88378 d12361e751dd12dbb41985

Johnston, E. (1991). *Royal commission into Aboriginal deaths in custody: National report*. Canberra: Australian Government Publishing Service.

Klippmark, P., & Crawley, K. (2018). Justice for Ms Dhu: Accounting for Indigenous deaths in custody in Australia. *Social & Legal Studies, 27*(6), 695–715.

Lambert, C. A. (2017). Post-racial public relations on primetime television: How *Scandal* represents Olivia Pope. *Public Relations Review, 43*, 750–754.

Lentin, A. (2018). Beyond denial: 'Not racism' as racist violence. *Continuum, 32*(4), 400–414.

Lloyd, C. (2019). *Managing indigeneity, cultivating citizens: Reconciliation action plans in Australian organizations*. PhD thesis, Harvard University. Retrieved from https://dash.harvard.edu/handle/1/42013077

Logan, N. (2011). The white leader prototype: A critical analysis of race in public relations. *Journal of Public Relations Research, 23*(4), 442–457.

Logan, N. (2016). The Starbucks race together initiative: Analyzing a public relations campaign with critical race theory. *Public Relations Inquiry, 5*(1), 93–113.

Love, T., & Tilley, E. (2014). Acknowledging power: The application of Kaupapa Māori principles and processes to developing a new approach to organisation-public engagement. *Public Relations Inquiry, 3*(1), 31–49.

McDonnell, J. (2018, October 3). Behind Aboriginal Victoria's deadly questions campaign controversy. *AdNews*. Retrieved November 21, 2019, from www.adnews. com.au/news/behind-aboriginal-victoria-s-deadly-questions-campaign-contro versy#s37xyy3mlDPfMewz.99

McGlade, H. (2017). The McGlade case: A Noongar history of land, social justice and activism. *Australian Feminist Law Journal, 43*(2), 185–210.

Motion, J., Haar, J., & Leitch, S. (2012). A public relations framework for Indigenous engagement. In K. Sriramesh & D. Verčič (Eds.), *Culture and public relations* (pp. 54–66), New York, NY: Routledge.

Munshi, D., & Edwards, L. (2011). Understanding 'race' in/and public relations: Where do we start and where should we go? *Journal of Public Relations Research, 23*(4), 349–367.

Nakata, N. M., Nakata, V., Keech, S., & Bolt, R. (2012). Decolonial goals and pedagogies for Indigenous studies. *Decolonization: Indigeneity, Education & Society, 1*(1), 120–140.

Pompper, D. (2005). 'Difference' in public relations research: A case for introducing critical race theory. *Journal of Public Relations Research, 17*(2), 139–169.

Power, J. (2019, May 29). 'Gift to the nation': 14 organisations support referendum and reconciliation. *Sydney Morning Herald* [online]. Retrieved November 28, 2019, from www.smh.com.au/national/gift-to-the-nation-14-organisations-support-referendum-and-reconciliation-20190528-p51s2f.html

Public Relations Institute of Australia [PRIA]. (2017). Application for accreditation of tertiary program in public relations and communication. Retrieved March 29, 2018, from www.pria.com.au

Reconciliation Australia. (2017). Welcome to and acknowledgement of country. Retrieved January 12, 2020, from www.reconciliation.org.au/wp-content/uploads/2017/11/Welcome-to-and-Acknowledgement-of-Country.pdf

Reconciliation Australia. (n.d.). Retrieved from www.reconciliation.org.au/

RMIT ABC Factcheck. (2019, November 29). Linda Burney says Australia is the only first world nation with a colonial history that doesn't recognise its first people in its constitution. Is she correct? *ABC News*. Retrieved December 7, 2019, from www.abc.net.au/news/2019-10-10/fact-check3a-is-australia-the-only-first-world-nation-with-a-c/11583706

Roper, J. (2005). Symmetrical communication: Excellent public relations or a strategy for hegemony? *Journal of Public Relations Research, 17*(1), 69–86.

Russell-Mundine, G., & Mundine, G. (2016). Daring to speak the truth: De-constructing and re-constructing reconciliation. *Journal of Indigenous Wellbeing, 1*(1), 83–96.

Shark Island Productions. (2019). *The Final Quarter.*

Shine, R. (2020, June 17). Unpaid fines law reforms prompted by death in custody of Ms Dhu pass WA Parliament. *ABC News*. Retrieved June 18, 2020, from https://www.abc.net.au/news/2020-06-17/wa-unpaid-fines-reforms-pass-wa-parliament-after-ms-dhu-death/12357888

Short, D. (2008). *Reconciliation and colonial power.* Farnham, England: Ashgate Publishing.

Sison, M. (2016). Diversity and inclusion in Australian public relations: Towards a multiple perspectives approach. *Media International Australia, 160*(1), 32–42.

Somerville, I., Purcell, A., & Morrison, F. (2011). Public relations education in a divided society: PR, terrorism and critical pedagogy in post-conflict Northern Ireland. *Public Relations Review, 37*, 548–555.

Spinifex Gum. (2017). 'Ms Dhu'. Retrieved December 1, 2019, from www.youtube.com/watch?v=NEaLIMeUKPc

Surma, A. (2005). *Public and professional writing: Ethics, imagination and rhetoric.* Basingstoke, England: Palgrave Macmillan.

Tutty, J. (2018, July 3). Victorian government's 'powerful' deadly questions campaign takes home Ad of the month for June. *Mumbrella*. Retrieved December 4, 2019, from https://mumbrella.com.au/victorian-governments-powerful-deadly-questions-take-home-ad-of-the-month-for-june-526931

Uluru Statement From the Heart. (2017, May 26). Retrieved December 8, 2019, from www.referendumcouncil.org.au/sites/default/files/2017-05/Uluru_Statement_From_The_Heart_0.PDF

Universities Australia. (2011). *National best practice framework for Indigenous cultural competency in Australian universities.* Retrieved December 1, 2019, from www.universitiesaustralia.edu.au/wp-content/uploads/2019/08/National-Best-Practice-Framework-for-Indigenous-Cultural-Competency-in-Australian-Universities-1.pdf

Universities Australia. (2017). *Indigenous strategy (2017–2020)*. Retrieved December 1, 2019, from www.universitiesaustralia.edu.au/wp-content/uploads/2019/06/Indigenous-Strategy-v16-1.pdf

Vardeman-Winter, J. (2011). Confronting whiteness in public relations campaigns and research with women. *Journal of Public Relations Research, 23*(4), 412–441.

Wahlquist, C. (2015a, November 24). Ms Dhu inquest: Doctors 'would have made a lot more effort' if she was white. *The Guardian*. Retrieved November 21, 2019, from www.theguardian.com/australia-news/2015/nov/24/ms-dhu-death-inquest-doctors-would-have-made-a-lot-more-effort-if-she-was-white

Wahlquist, C. (2015b, November 25). Ms Dhu in 'advanced septic shock' four hours after deemed fit for prison. *Guardian*. Retrieved November 21, 2019, from www.theguardian.com/australia-news/2015/nov/25/ms-dhu-in-advanced-septic-shock-four-hours-after-deemed-fit-for-prison

Wahlquist, C. (2019, June 6). Statue of indigenous AFL star Nicky Winmar pointing at his skin ready to be unveiled. *The Guardian*. Retrieved December 1, 2019, from www.theguardian.com/australia-news/2019/jun/09/statue-of-indigenous-afl-star-nicky-winmar-pointing-at-his-skin-ready-to-be-unveiled

Walters, A., & Longhurst, S. (2017, May 15). *Over-represented and overlooked: The crisis of Aboriginal and Torres Strait Islander women's growing over-imprisonment*. Human Rights Law Centre. Retrieved December 8, 2019, from www.hrlc.org.au/reports/2017/5/18/report-over-represented-and-overlooked-the-crisis-of-aboriginal-and-torres-strait-islander-womens-growing-over-imprisonment

Waymer, D., & Dyson, O. (2011). The journey into an unfamiliar and uncomfortable territory: Exploring the role and approaches of race in PR education. *Journal of Public Relations Research, 23*(4), 458–477.

Waymer, D., & Heath, R. (2016). Critical race and public relations: The case of environmental racism and risk bearer agency. In J. L'Etang, D. McKie, N. Snow, & J. Xifra (Eds.), *The Routledge handbook of critical public relations* (pp. 289–302). Abingdon, England: Routledge.

Weaver, K. (2019). The slow conflation of public relations and activism: Understanding trajectories in public relations theorising. In A. Adi (Ed.), *Protest public relations: Communicating dissent and activism* (pp. 12–28). Abingdon, England: Routledge.

Wolf, K. (2016). Diversity in Australian public relations: An exploration of practitioner perspectives. *Asia Pacific Public Relations Journal, 17*(2). Retrieved November 30, 2019, from https://novaojs.newcastle.edu.au/apprj/index.php/apprj/article/view/66

Wolf, K. (2018). Power struggles: A sociological approach to activist communication. *Public Relations Review, 44*(2), 308–316.

Wolfe, P. (2006). Settler colonialism and the elimination of the native. *Journal of Genocide Research, 8*(4), 387–409.

Woolworths, the Salvation Army and Adam Goodes 'S.T.A.N.D. Together' for natural disaster relief. (2016, November 8). Retrieved November 11, 2019, from www.salvationarmy.org.au/about-us/news-and-stories/media-newsroom/woolworths-the-salvation-army-and-adam-goodes-s-t-a-n-d-together-for-natural-disaster-relief/

Zuckermann, G. (2015). *Engaging – a guide to interacting respectfully and reciprocally with Aboriginal and Torres Strait Islander people, and their arts practices and intellectual property*. Canberra: Government of Australia, Indigenous Culture Support.

8 Environmental protest songs and justice perspectives

Judy Motion

Music is an evocative and communicative mode of popular culture that has long been linked to efforts to transform society. Social change emerges from intense identifications and transient alliances that push against and attempt to dismantle extant social and political boundaries (Jenkins, McPherson, & Shattuc, 2002). By acting as cultural 'flash points' (Motion, 2019) that heighten our concern about social and environmental problems, protest songs function as public relations texts for those who seek to inspire social change and ignite public controversy. This chapter considers the political role that protest music plays in creatively constituting and representing our environmental cosmologies. Although protest music may give rise to the conditions for activism and act as a vehicle for popularising causes, it is an imprecise mechanism for the pursuit of justice and social change. By examining the cultural narratives within music that shape how we think and feel about the future of the planet, our attention is drawn to the particular ways that moments and moods inform and persuade us. The general term 'environmental protest songs' is used in this chapter to categorise and analyse justice-oriented lyrics about nature, even though there is significant variance in content. The commonality lies in feelings of attachment, loss, and mourning that intersect with warnings of apocalyptic threats and dystopian futures. Although often pessimism and negativity prevail, there are also expressions of hope. This chapter opens up a discussion of the role of evocative, emotive communication in transformative public relations by exploring how environmental cosmologies are influenced by and inextricably entangled with popular culture controversies and movements. Transformative public relations may be understood in this context as a contest for social and/or environmental justice that calls into question or seeks to mobilise identities and valuing systems.

As a starting point, this chapter draws upon concepts from environmental humanities – the study of relationships between nature and society – to examine how we conceive of and relate to nature and pursue justice (Rose et al., 2012). Understanding the ways attachments may be formed and how publics identify with and feel about particular entities or issues is a vital aspect of analysing transformative public relations and social change. Here I integrate key concepts of environmental humanities theory – mastery over nature, the nature-culture divide and multispecies relations – with notions of justice, care and respect.

'Mastery over nature' refers to the ways we consider and manage nature as a resource – the assumption is that we can dominate it and control it. The concept of 'nature-culture divide' is based upon the presumption that because we have culture we are in some way superior and that we are therefore separate from nature (Plumwood, 2002). A key dimension of the nature-culture divide is 'human exceptionalism' which refers to the belief that the rules of nature do not apply to humans. The next concept applied here, multispecies relations, describes a mode of undoing the resource-based, exploitative practices we apply to the environment – it adopts an ecological perspective in which all of nature is understood to be interconnected and necessary. Combined, these key concepts call into question traditional thinking about the environment and call for a concerned, caring, engaged practice for interacting with the environment. At the heart of this approach is environmental justice – the pursuit of fairness for the environment. A justice approach not only considers issues of disadvantage (Schlosberg, 2013) but also drills down into the politics of representation – the meaning production and sense-making practices that influence our interactions with the environment. Grove (2015) suggested that we also need to consider attachment to place when thinking through environmental justice issues. Although environmental justice has often been considered from human-centric or human-dominant perspectives that are concerned with the impact of environmental issues on people/society – more recently, environmental justice efforts attempt to think from environment perspectives and speak for nature. The question of who speaks for nature is entangled in issues of governance and power. By looking at the role of music in speaking for the environment I address the following research questions:

How does protest music function as a public relations endeavour?
How is the environment constituted and represented in popular discourse?
What are the implications for understanding public relations as a transformative force?

These questions are explored through a justice lens – the aim is to understand the relationships between protest and public relations in ways that connect with popular culture, environmental attachments and concerns. A number of classic and contemporary, commercially-produced, environmental songs have been selected through an iterative approach, commonly known as snowball sampling, and from online lists of popular environmental songs. Although this approach does offer a modicum of reliability, the intention is to identify the ways the environment is positioned in popular discourse and generate insights and implications for public relations and policy governance rather than to develop a definitive history of environmental protest music. This may mean that some readers' favourite protest songs are not discussed – apologies for any disappointment. Songs sampled range across numerous genres including folk, country, pop, rock, alternative and even thrash metal. Although the last genre was a surprise, on reflection what sounds like furiously fast, percussive-sounding music seems fitting for protest! Further investigation revealed that thrash metal is actually anti-establishment and deals with social issues. This finding calls into question possible assumptions that only certain audiences are interested in environmental issues. The method used for this study is textual analysis – the lyrics, rather than musical composition, are the primary object of analysis. Hutchins and Lester argued that textual analysis is an appropriate methodological technique because 'it is in the realm of representation that the cultural battles over the use-value of the environment are fought' (2006, p. 439). Textual analysis also provides insights into the constitutive aspects of the texts (Fairclough, 1992) offering insights into how the environment is constituted and represented in knowledge. To provide a guiding structure for analysing the songs identified in the iterative sampling approach, a series of common themes were identified and coded. In the following section about the types of environments that are imagined and invoked, the themes include mastering and remaking nature; human exceptionalism and multispecies relations; and apocalyptic futures.

What types of environments are imagined and invoked?

Mastering and remaking nature

Environmental protest songs represent situated, historical contexts. They chronicle questions and debates, illuminate concerns of the times and provide insights into what matters. This section opens with a discussion of protest music from the 1960s, a decade that marked a critical moment in the advancement of the environmental protest movement in western democracies (Longhofer & Schofer, 2010), and critiques of our exploitative relationships with nature. Woody Guthrie's music was a crucial inspiration for sixties folk-inspired protest – and it may be argued that songs such as 'Dustbowl refugees' continue to be relevant in this time of climate change. Famous for writing about social justice issues precipitated by man-made environmental disasters, Guthrie's *Dustbowl Ballads* album about the dust storms, droughts and the Depression of the 1930s was re-issued in the sixties and connected with calls for widespread social change, the civil rights, feminist and nascent environmental movements. His calls for social justice are echoed in songs such as Bob Dylan's 'A hard rain is gonna fall', which expresses a feeling of unease and apprehension about the future and has been interpreted as closely aligned with environmental issues. Also written by Dylan about the same time, the song 'The times they are a changing', has served as a universal protest anthem for railing against injustice and calling for change to be embraced rather than impeded. It is also a declaration of inevitability. The song has been extensively covered by other artists, commercialised and recently some of the lyrics were rewritten by Billy Bragg to highlight the issue of climate change (Reed, 2017). Bragg's version also refers to President Trump's undoing of climate change initiatives, directly addressing Trump's denial of the anthropocenic nature of climate change, and reflects on contemporary social and cultural justice issues (Reed, 2017). These anthemic protest songs have been adopted by diverse movements to popularise activism and the politics of protest. They connect with our anxieties and concerns and reflect prevailing cultural moods. In doing so, they become part of the meaning creation and sense-making processes driving social change – as publics we are offered repertoires for imagining, talking or singing about issues that may, in time, become our own words and feelings – we learn a discourse for talking about justice-related issues.

A classic, catchy little tune remembered from my childhood, the song 'Little boxes', was written by Malvina Reynolds in 1962 and popularised by Pete Seegar. The song points to hillsides lost to urban growth, problems with suburban sameness/uniformity and unsustainable construction materials, describing and satirising them with the term 'ticky tacky'. More broadly, the song undercuts the American dream – calling out failed expectations of prosperity, success and happiness and utopian visions of middle-class lifestyles – it is an appeal to think more deeply about our ways of life. As a child, I thought it a strange song – why would anyone want to live in a little house like a box? As an adult, the song has alternative meanings and generates new sense making. I understand that we need to rethink how we live in urban landscapes and how we create sustainable housing. The Reynolds version of the song was revived and repositioned in popular culture in the mid-2000s as the introductory theme music for the television show, *Weeds*, a story about a single parent who turns to drug dealing to support her family. 'Little boxes' is a lament about the environments that middle-class lifestyles create and maintain. For the millions of homeless and refugees, those little boxes are now an unrealisable dream. The song may no longer only be interpreted as a witty satire of how we are remaking nature with our middle-class aspirations and lifestyles – it points to how issues of social justice are entangled with environmental issues.

A more recent song drawing attention to issues of urban development is Solange's 'Cranes in the sky'. Solange (2017) explained the song reflected upon a time when she was seeking 'peace and refuge' after a break-up:

> I remember looking up and seeing all of these cranes in the sky. They were so heavy and such an eyesore, and not what I identified with peace and refuge. I remember thinking of it as an analogy for my transition – this idea of building up, up, up that was going on in our country at the time, all of this excessive building, and not really dealing with what was in front of us. . . . And, eight years later, it's really interesting that now, here we are again, not seeing what's happening in our country, not wanting to put into perspective all of these ugly things that are staring us in the face.
>
> (Beyoncé, 2017)

'Cranes in the sky' transects pop, soul, ballad genres and laments the ways in which we distract ourselves from important issues and fail to notice what is happening around us. The idea that we are not paying attention, not noticing, is a recurrent theme in environmental protest music. The song is a reminder of the loss we experience as rapid urban growth destroys stillness, silence and space to contemplate and escape. It also draws attention to the ubiquity of ongoing endeavours to achieve mastery over nature – in this instance, colonisation of the sky.

One of the most quintessential and well-known environmental protest songs, 'Big yellow taxi' by Joni Mitchell, is considered a classic environmental protest song and has been extensively covered by many other musicians. For many environmentalists, it has achieved anthemic status. Mitchell explained that she wrote 'Big yellow taxi' on a visit to Hawaii in a 1996 interview with the *Los Angeles Times.*

> I wrote 'Big Yellow Taxi' on my first trip to Hawaii. I took a taxi to the hotel and when I woke up the next morning, I threw back the curtains and saw these beautiful green mountains in the distance. Then, I looked down and there was a parking lot as far as the eye could see, and it broke my heart . . . this blight on paradise. That's when I sat down and wrote the song.
>
> (Hilburn, 1996)

The first verse talks about that experience of seeing natural beauty overridden by the need to cater for tourists and cars. The song denounces urban development and the ways in which we take things for granted and only appreciate them after they have been destroyed. Within the second verse, the lyrics describe how trees are confined and commodified in botanical gardens or what she refers to as 'tree museums'. Mitchell is also concerned about food production and the ways in which we intervene in natural processes with agrichemicals and echoes the concerns voiced in Rachel Carson's *Silent Spring*. The reference to 'the birds and the bees' is prescient and now speaks to contemporary concerns about issues of extinction and bee colony collapse disorder (Suryanarayanan & Kleinman, 2013). The ubiquitous yellow taxi in the chorus is synonymous with separation and loss. This song became so significant because it was representative of the early evolution of the environmental movement that was concerned with widespread use of insecticides and the breakdown of our relationship with nature. In 'The big yellow taxi' lyrics, Mitchell succeeded in voicing concerns about the valuing systems that drive modern society and warning people that some environmental losses may be irreparable. However, the song may also be criticised as harking back to a time that can no longer exist – a nostalgic illusion or delusion about our relationship with nature.

As a counter-point to 'Big yellow taxi', the song 'Nothing but flowers' by Talking Heads imagines what would happen if we did return to the nature that Mitchell laments. The song works on two levels, both imagining a utopian future where nature has reclaimed space and also expressing regret for the loss of modern convenience. Or perhaps it is a meditation on what will happen as nature reclaims the earth? Possibly most telling is an observation that nobody paid attention – it resonates with apathetic responses to climate change. The song concludes with a lament about the loss of culture and convenience, asking not to be stranded in the present because the lifestyle is so strange. It is a song about our ambivalent relationship with modern progress – a love song to junk food, cars and modernity that questions our nostalgic view of nature and asks whether we could actually return to a pristine nature paradise. From this perspective, nature is now so compromised and remade that there may be no turning back.

In a similar way, 'Where do the children play' by the singer originally known as Cat Stevens – now Yusef Islam – highlights our complicated relationship with modernity and pervasive technological influences; colonising the sky and destroying the land. The song questions progress through the chorus – acknowledging progress but asking where children may play. The original video conjured up images of children looking for safe places to play in 'blasted landscapes' (Kirksey, Shapiro, & Brodine, 2013) of war zones, garbage landfills and other ecologically unsafe spaces. In mastering and remaking nature, we have neglected to include spaces for children to play that are not just techno- digital, high-rise, industrial spaces. More recently, in 2017, the group Garbage covered 'Where do the children play' for a fund-raising album *Music to Inspire: Artists United against Human Trafficking*. The aim was to draw awareness to the issue and support the United Nations (n.d.a, n.d.b) efforts to prevent human trafficking. This recent cover of the song extends beyond issues of environmental and social justice into cultural justice. Ross (1998) explained that cultural justice involves 'pursuing justice through cultural means, seeking justice for cultural claims' (p. 2). What this means in practice is that popular culture may be mobilised to defend social or environmental causes or to defend itself. Cultural justice initiatives may be designed 'to voice concerns and destabilise particular valuing systems and practices' (Motion, 2019, p. 730). The participation of Garbage in the United Nations anti-human trafficking project reinforces the universality of the song's concerns for the fate of children.

Some protest songs only attract local attention because they are location or issue specific. 'Damn the dam' was originally an advertising jingle about home insulation, written and sung by John Hanlon, that was adopted by environmental protestors contesting the construction of a hydro-electric dam on Lake Manapouri in New Zealand. The song was awarded New Zealand single of the year in 1973. The song is important because it was used by protestors to create a rallying point for popularising opposition to the ways in which nature was being exploited and remade (Schrader, 2014). The ubiquity/invasion of plastic into our lives and nature features in Radiohead's 'Fake plastic trees' – a critique of both plastic and inauthenticity. The song criticises mass consumption, artificial lives, toxic substances and the wearying efforts of modern life. Listeners are left to wonder what is a natural and authentic lifestyle. Tim Minchin's eco-anthem, 'Canvas bags', instructs us to forego plastic and take canvas bags to the supermarket. Single issue protests may raise awareness, popularise alternatives and result in a single change in behaviour. It is also possible that there is a compounding effect and that the combined influence of a range of popular culture efforts has an impact.

Other protest songs address a broader array of environmental issues. The Pixies song 'Monkey's gone to heaven' is a critique of human assumptions about our place in the universe and our exploitative relationship to the sea, sky and land. The song suggests that dumping sludge and garbage in the ocean, creating a hole in the ozone and scorching land temperatures are all issues created by our alienated relationship with the earth. The song also references numerology and religion. However, protest songs do not always mean what we think they do.

The song title, 'Monkey's gone to heaven' is not, as I assumed, about a nature/culture divide and human alienation from nature – it was actually a place holder phrase before lyrics were developed (Fricke, 1989). A critical insight for protest public relations is that the ways in which we impute our own meanings onto protest songs may either render them meaningless or lend them more value for the environmental movement.

Midnight Oil, an Australian rock band, developed a repertoire of political activist songs that drew attention to environmental issues. On the album *Blue Sky Mine*, a protest song with the same name critiqued the complicated relationship Australia has with the mining industry. Mining in Australia is championed as 'driving prosperity' as a vital contributor to the economic growth and jobs (Minerals Council of Australia, n.d.). The song opens with an understanding that for some, working in the mines is an economic necessity but that it is also a soul destroying job. The song was inspired by the experiences of workers at the Wittenoom asbestos mines who contracted various asbestos-related diseases (Novelli, n.d.). The 'blue' in the song title refers to blue asbestos, and the 'sugar refining company' refers to the Colonial Sugar Refining Company (CSR), the owner of the mines. The song criticises the prioritisation of mining, the fixation with digging up the earth and the disregard for corporate negligence. In the end, Wittenoom was evacuated and lost its status as a town. In Blue Sky Mining, social justice issues are dominant but there is an underlying concern about damage to the environment by air and soil pollution. Plumwood (2002) wrote about the colonisation, not only of people but also land, and the song mourns for the land, the traditional owners and those who suffered working the mine. This song is a significant acknowledgement of the injustices done to Indigenous people and the problems with separation from land and community. Achieving mainstream popular success is challenging for music detailing Indigenous struggles, particularly music by Indigenous musicians. A notable exception was Yothu Yindi, a combined group of Australian indigenous and non-indigenous musicians. 'Treaty' was released by Yothu Yindi in 1991, a song that points to the entangled nature of social and environmental justice and calls for a treaty to safeguard Indigenous lands and rights. The lyrics focused on the broken promises made to Indigenous people and the interconnection of land and people. As concerns with environmental crises escalate, it is critical that there is a greater openness to listening to and addressing land grievances.

In a protest about industrial disaster, the protest song, 'Kodaikanal won't', sung by Sofia Ashraf, draws attention to mercury poisoning from a thermometer factory in Kodaikanal, India by Unilever. The song is rap style and calls upon Unilever to clean up the toxic site. As part of a campaign by workers to seek compensation and reparation, the video clip of the song 'Kodaikanal Won't' went viral, calling upon viewers to sign an online petition (Nath, 2015). The song calls for justice for workers, residents, the river, forest and land. Although Unilever did settle with workers, it has yet to address the environmental issues and so in 2018 an updated version of the song and video, titled 'Kodaikanal still won't', was released, accusing Unilever of environmental racism because it is applying different, lower standards for a clean-up in India. Environmental racism is a combined form of social and environmental injustice that imposes environmental disadvantage and damage on diverse racial communities. These songs express concerns about the unsustainable ways in which humans are exploiting and remaking nature, along with colonising Indigenous peoples. They capture prevailing moods and moments of unease and alarm and call for us to pay attention and care. By reframing how we understand nature, the songs remind us that these issues matter – they act as a public relations form of environmental agenda setting. Some call for action but more often, songs about remaking nature act as markers of injustice by confronting contemporary environmental challenges, such as climate change and global biodiversity loss, rather than offering insights into how to seek justice.

Human exceptionalism and multispecies relations

Adopting a multispecies relations approach means that we need to consider how humans interact with other species – our interconnections and responsibilities – and how to attribute agency beyond humans (Kirksey & Helmreich, 2010). A key question that is explored within multi-species studies is 'how do we co-habit?' The aim is to move outside of a human-centric, human- dominant perspective and consider how we may share and care for all species. A key public relations dimension of multispecies studies would be to offer a voice and to advocate for other species. The 1970s playful, eco-pop song, 'Apeman' by the Kinks, expressed a nostalgic yearning for a simpler way of life. Threats of modern life that included overpopulation, pollution, traffic and nuclear war were countered in the song lyrics by desires to escape city life and seek safety in nature. The song questioned the notion that humans are 'sophisticated', 'educated' and 'civilised' and in doing so, it critiqued human progress and notions of exceptionalism (the idea that humans are the superior species and that culture sets us apart from other beings) by reminding us of our place in the universe and that we are part of nature and descended from apes. The song contended that we are no better than animals in a cage; in fact, we are worse for we capture and imprison animals. 'Apeman', interpreted from a contemporary perspective, encourages concerns about injustice and our excessive way of life.

Like 'Apeman,' the 2018 'Prawn song' by Superorganism is a whimsical cross between psychedelic and Indie pop but offers a commentary on humans from nature – from the perspective of a prawn. The song questions our human way of life and offers a satirical insight into how human endeavours and failures may be viewed from a multispecies perspective – to try and think from another species' perspective is revelatory and suggests humans need radically rethink our relationships with nature (BBC, n.d.). Both 'Apeman' and 'Prawn song' are about our disconnection from nature, poor treatment of other species and a call for a more natural, simple way of living. Simplicity and sense are advocated as a way forward.

'Dead fox' by Courtney Barnett, an Australian singer-songwriter, has a clever reversal of animal-human relations in the animated video clip. Humans, rather than animals, are the roadkill. The song uses the trope of a road journey to tell a story of anxiety over environmental issues that includes organic versus pesticide-contaminated food, big business and supermarkets, road kill, shark culling and eating meat. The song opens with a critique of pesticides in our foods then recalls encounters with road kill on the Hume Highway (between Sydney and Melbourne, Australia). Our cruel culling of sharks is critiqued and contrasted with our obsession with motor vehicles – the song is a provocative tale calling for us to rethink our relationship with other species and the price they pay for our mobility, convenience and lifestyles.

Father John Misty wrote the song, 'Musical comedy', about human exceptionalism – the ways in which humans consider they are special. Misty suggests instead that we are mistaken, nature is in charge and that we are just passing through, that we invent religion and culture but that is not what matters; instead, we need to build communities (see Mosk, 2017). Misty expresses frustration with the human species, with religion, gender inequality, human exceptionalism, politics – a reminder that we are animals, mammals, and we have to decide whether the future is about mutual destruction or support. A key feature of these songs is a reconsiderations of our connections and relationships with nature – they express a 'modest hope' (Kirksey & Helmreich, 2010) that we will rethink our identities and lifestyles.

Apocalyptic futures

Apocalyptic communication is a form of catastrophism that relies on fear appeals for 'opening up or closing down' public engagement (Stirling, 2008) and influencing how we imagine the future. 'Eyes wide open' by Wouter Andre de Backer, known as Gotye, is a song about a dystopian, apocalyptic future. The images accompanying the music video portray a human hybrid – covered in clay searching for water to harvest from a parched landscape. The song predicts our future – humans not listening to warnings, clinging to consumption as a meaningful life, and concludes by likening our way of living to walking the plank with our eyes wide open as we head to an apocalyptic end of humanity. An anthropocenic disaster is foretold with arid landscapes, water scarcity and hybrid/cyborg humans living in dust. Destruction of the planet, Gotye suggests, is inevitable if we fail to make changes. A bleak future for humanity is not a popular theme in music but this song acts as both warning and prediction. The atmosphere evoked in this song is one of anguish and despair. A problem with these types of 'disenchantment' (Hawkins, 2005) lyrics is that although they highlight our disregard for and alienation from nature, they may lead to resentment and environmentalism fatigue. Rather than the 'moralism and despair' generated in apocalyptic or disenchantment rhetoric, Hawkins (2005, p. ix) argued for a type of politics of attentiveness with an emphasis on possibilities for doing things differently.

Anti-nuclear songs conjure images of intractable politics and apocalyptic futures. 'French letter 95' is an Indigenous protest song written and sung by the New Zealand multicultural group Herbs that has included, at various times, Tongan, Samoan, Cook Island and Maori members. Their music combines a

Pacific approach to reggae sound with political messages. French Letter 95 is a protest song about French nuclear testing in the pacific. The backstory to the protests was that the French government had been testing nuclear bombs in Muroroa, a remote Tahitian Island. The New Zealand government was vocal in its opposition to the tests and protests escalated. In 1985 the Greenpeace ship, the *Rainbow Warrior*, had been protesting nuclear testing at Muroroa when it was bombed by the French in the Auckland harbour in New Zealand. 'French letter 95' is an anti-nuclear protest song about the impacts of nuclear testing and, more generally, colonisation. The song summons up images of an idyllic pacific life under a coconut tree that are contrasted with the ocean glow of nuclear tests by 'unwelcome guests' (the French). The value of nuclearity is questioned and labelled 'mis-energy' and the long-term dangers highlighted. The song called for an end to nuclear testing and the French to leave the Pacific. It was an extremely popular reinforcement of New Zealand's anti-nuclear stance and opposition to the secrecy in relation to nuclear testing. It is also, more broadly, representative of the anti-colonisation sentiments of Indigenous peoples who act as guardians, speaking for nature and protesting dispossession of their land and rights (see, for example, Plumwood, 2002).

'Radioactive' by Imagine Dragons uses the powerful imagery of a nuclear disaster to evoke a chaotic world and feelings of despair. However, in an interview, the front man/lead singer and lyricist, Dan Reynolds explained that the song is lyrically about becoming self-empowered, rising above weakness and a personal struggle with depression (3voor12, 2013, https://www.youtube.com/watch?v=Kqxf82n6QZg). He considered it not so much about an apocalypse as a personal expression of an awakening, starting something new. However, the lyrics do serve to conjure up images of nuclearity and remind listeners of the potential of nuclear disaster along with the strong possibilities for action and change. 'Radioactive' has been has been extensively used in various episodes of television series, sports shows and used in the promotional trailer for video game Assassin's Creed III. The music and lyrics are intensely evocative and invoke notions of power, fearlessness and potency – and serve as a reminder that nuclearity is extremely dangerous.

The entangled nature of social and environmental justice issues is a recurrent theme in many protest songs – human fates are entangled with all species and the planet. Although primarily an antiwar song, 'Two tribes' sung by Frankie Goes To Hollywood, is a powerful exploration of the politics of war, nuclear warfare and the problems of our dependence on fossil fuel. REM's 'Orange crush' is another example of the entangled nature of songs protesting for social and environmental justice. The title is ambiguous; although many thought the song was about an orange-flavoured soft drink, the song was actually about Agent Orange, a chemical used by the United States Department of Defense to defoliate the Vietnamese jungle during the Vietnam war. Military personnel who were exposed to it developed cancer years later and some of their children had birth defects. Songs like 'Two tribes' and 'Orange crush' play a significant political role in creating awareness and documenting instances of social and environmental injustice.

These songs point to the loss of control that many experience and call for repair and reparation.

Perhaps the greatest environmental threat, climate change, is interwoven into the song 'Idioteque' by Radiohead, and highlights three crucial climate change themes: apocalyptical threat, excess technology and consumption, and rejection of climate change debates and denial, in dialogue. The apocalyptical theme talks of bunkers, an imminent ice age and fire. The lyrics describe the excess of our tech-nologised way of life in the following way: 'Mobiles squerking, Mobiles chirping, Take the money run . . . everything all of the time'. The reality of the threat and the import of warnings are summarised in the lines, 'We're not scaremongering. This is really happening'. The song claims that it is not trying to conjure a sense of dread – so, instead, we need to consider what protest songs are attempting to achieve'. Are they a mode for circulating alternative truths and offering warnings, or do they contribute to the development of 'civic imagination' (Jenkins, Shres-thova, Gamber-Thompson, Kligler-Vilenchik, & Zimmerman, 2016) in which alternatives, agency and pathways may be imagined along with the creation of empathy? From a public relations perspective, these are generative modes of pro-test that expand knowledge and provoke new ways of understanding. They have an affective impact by raising concern but do not call for or define the actions that could be taken.

Conclusion: implications for public relations

Protest music offers insights into the ways that nature is put into cultural dis-courses and into popular ways of framing environmental issues. Analysis of envi-ronmental protest songs suggests a significant shift in representations of nature. Protest music from the 1960s and 1970s yearned for a pre-modern, unspoiled nature and highlighted 'endangered attachments' (Marres, 2007, p. 776) in order to generate public awareness and concern. Knupp (1981) had argued that protest songs are 'generally negative in their reaction to external circumstances, simplis-tic in their world view, and expressive rather than instrumental in their inten-tion' (p. 377). He also claimed that protest songs are 'generalized, self-interested, solutionless criticisms of the status quo' and that their only purpose is to inspire 'in-group activities' and keep resistance alive (Knupp, 1981, p. 388). The simpler, nostalgic folk songs of the sixties and seventies may have seemed unsophisticated and inwardly-focused but the problem with the type of in-depth textual analysis that Knupp conducted is that often the broader cultural politics are neglected. The music was not only part of youth-oriented, counter-culture critiques – it was commercially produced, successful and very much part of mainstream culture. In contrast to Knupp's claims, Rodnitzky (1999, p. 105) argued that one of the appeals of this protest music was that it had 'meaning and integrity'. Situating the songs of the sixties and seventies within political contexts highlighted concerns about the invisibility of pollutants, fear of technology, separation from nature and, more generally, resistance to the erosion of democratic freedoms. The task of mainstream, commercial protest music, and art more generally, is not so much to suggest solutions instead, it is to inspire a sense of connection to and reflection on political issues and potentially create a sense of social purpose.

More complicated representations of our relationship with the environment and what it means to be human are evident in later environmental protest music. Popular protest music contributes to the development of 'civic imagination' (Jenkins et al., 2016) by questioning human mastery or dominance over the planet, destabilising the boundaries of a nature-culture divide and reimagining multispecies relations. These themes complicate the binaries and boundaries of hegemonic environmental discourses by addressing issues of exploitation and colonisation and opening up justice-oriented modes of thinking. In a time of climate change and mass species extinctions, a careful undoing of human exceptionalism – notions that humans are separate from and entitled to claim mastery over other species – needs to be replaced by care for all species – a revolutionised approach to the rights of nature and multispecies relations.

Protest music is a truncated form of communication, but one of the strengths is that this condensed form allows listeners to also assign their own meanings. It tends to be less didactic and more idiosyncratic, but that may partly reflect the genre that ranges from folk to alternative and thrash metal. In this time of climate change, protest music reflects an apocalyptic, dynamic, prediction of an uncertain, dangerous future. Nature, from this perspective, is damaged, perhaps beyond repair. However, contemporary protest music veers from apocalyptic to sardonic and quirky, allowing some space for hope.

This chapter conceptualises protest music as a mode of transformative public relations. Although, conceptually, transformative public relations takes many forms, it is, ultimately, a communicative attempt to intervene in and change society for the better. It is based on fundamental principles of social and environmental justice that take into account the rights of human and non-human alike and creates space for multiple forms of democratic deliberation and decision making. Thus, an analysis of protest music provides useful insights for NGOs, social movements and activist groups. Protest music re-animates neglected or controversial issues through representations of concerns and commitments to social and environmental change. Popular visions of alternative futures offer hope for a 'transformational ethos' of care (Puig de la Bella Casa, 2011). However, a number of problems that are identified include tensions between competing priorities and environmental amelioration, the challenges of navigating single environmental issues versus tackling climate change and skepticism about whether protest music, celebrity advocacy and popular culture more generally, may meaningfully change our relations with the environment. A further consideration is to contrast the work that is undertaken on a global scale with local musical projects as a way of thinking through the contributions of popular culture and the realisation of social change. Protest music is contextual in that it reflects a certain moment in time. Understanding that moment and its implications for achieving change is critical to successful campaigning. Attentiveness to the cultural politics that surround certain protest songs and the associated justice and social anxieties that are opened up may suggest a range of potential responses to controversial environmental proposals. Particular 'atmospheres' (Critchley, 2017; Stewart, 2011), amalgamations of moods, feelings, conditions, situations, environments and identities, potentially open up a range of entry points for engagement with issues. Richards (2004) argued that politics is interwoven with popular culture and that we seek certain kinds of emotionalised experiences from politics. Protest music, then, offers a vehicle for those emotional experiences that traditional modes of political communication may fail to deliver. Negotiating the affective dimensions of public opinion formation, how various fragments of identity, affect and experience interact, requires the creation of publics or communities with shared concerns. Is protest music powerful enough to create new publics or does it primarily galvanise existing communities and movements? Engagement with protest music may vary from momentary reflection to sustained action. Publics emerge from issues (Leitch & Motion, 2010; Leitch & Neilson, 2004; Marres, 2007) that gain traction and begin to matter. Popular culture, then, may play a vital role in articulating issues and bringing them to public attention – making them matter. Issue articulation, Marres (2007) suggests, is about opening up issues but does not necessarily result in public involvement. So, this chapter has shown that protest music functions very effectively as a form of dissent public relations that may evoke atmospheres, bring issues to public attention, and position them as matters of concern through language and sound. It is less clear whether it is an effective form of protest public relations that mobilises action and influences social and environmental policy change. Within this discussion, the importance of mattering as a vital precursor to change is again evident. Protest music, and by association, public relations efforts on behalf of social and environmental issues, must position such issues as vital concerns to their targeted publics.

References

3voor12. (2013, October 29). *Song stories: Imagine dragons – Radioactive*. Retrieved from https://www.youtube.com/watch?v=Kqxf82n6QZg

BBC. (n.d.). *Superorganism*. Retrieved from www.bbc.co.uk/music/artists/228ae 4f7-2425-4b1f-9d24-78cb9e267651

Beyoncé. (2017, January 10). Solange brings it all full circle with her sister Beyoncé. *Interview Magazine*. Retrieved from www.interviewmagazine.com/music/solange#_

Critchley, A. (2017). Vibrant compositions: Atmospheres of creativity in Sydney, Australia. PhD thesis, UNSW, Sydney Australia.

Fairclough, N. (1992). *Discourse and social change*. Cambridge, MA: Polity Press.

Fricke, D. (1989, June 15). Pixies cast their spell. *Rolling Stone*. Retrieved from https://www.rollingstone.com/music/news/pixies-cast-their-spell-19890615

Groves, C. (2015). The bomb in my backyard, the serpent in my house: Environmental justice, risk, and the colonisation of attachment. *Environmental Politics*, 24(6), 853–873.

Hawkins, G. (2005). *The ethics of waste: How we relate to rubbish*. Lanham, MD: Rowman & Littlefield.

Hilburn, R. (1996). Both sides, later. *Los Angeles Times*. Retrieved from www.latimes.com/archives/la-xpm-1996-12-08-ca-6804-story.html

Hutchins, B., & Lester, L. (2006). Environmental protest and tap-dancing with the media in the information age. *Media, Culture and Society, 28*(3), 433–451.

Jenkins, H., McPherson, T., & Shattuc, J. (2002). *Hop on pop: The politics and pleasure of popular culture.* Durham, NC: Duke University Press.

Jenkins, H., Shresthova, S., Gamber-Thompson, L., Kligler-Vilenchik, N., & Zimmerman, A. (2016). *By any media necessary: The new youth activism.* New York, NY: New York University Press.

Kirksey, S. E., & Helmreich, S. (2010). The emergence of multispecies ethnography. *Cultural Anthropology, 25*(4), 545–576.

Kirksey, S. E., Shapiro, N., & Brodine, M. (2013). Hope in blasted landscapes. *Social Science Information, 52*(2), 228–256.

Knupp, R. E. (1981). A time for every purpose under heaven: Rhetorical dimensions of protest music. *Southern Speech Communication Journal, 46*(4), 377–389.

Leitch, S., & Motion, J. (2010). Publics and public relations: Effecting change. In R. Heath (Ed.), *The Sage handbook of public relations* (pp. 99–110). Thousand Oaks, CA: Sage.

Leitch, S., & Neilson, D. (2004). Bringing publics into public relations: New theoretical frameworks for practice. In R. Heath (Ed.), *Handbook of public relations.* Thousand Oaks, CA: Sage.

Longhofer, W., & Schofer, E. (2010). National and global origins of environmental association. *American Sociological Review, 75*(4), 505–533.

Marres, N. (2007). The issues deserve more credit: Pragmatist contributions to the study of public involvement in controversy. *Social Studies of Science, 37*(5), 759–780.

Minerals Council of Australia. (n.d.). Driving prosperity. Retrieved August 30, 2019, from https://minerals.org.au/driving-prosperity

Mosk, M. (2017, April 17). Understanding the importance of Father John Misty's 'pure comedy'. *Atwood Magazine.* Retrieved from https://atwoodmagazine.com/pure-comedy-father-john-misty-review/

Motion, J. (2019). Undoing art and oil: An environmental tale of sponsorship, cultural justice and climate change controversy. *Environmental Politics, 28*(4), 727–746.

Nath, P. K. (2015, August 5). How the Kodaikanal video went viral. *The Hindu.* Retrieved from https://www.thehindu.com/news/national/tamil-nadu/how-the-kodaikanal-wont-video-went-viral/article7500019.ece

Novelli, J. (n.d.). Song place: Wittenoom Australia. Blue sky mine by midnight oil. *Song Facts.* Retrieved from www.songfacts.com/place/wittenoom-australia/blue-sky-mine

Plumwood, V. (2002). Decolonising relationships with nature. *PAN: Philosophy Activism Nature, 2*, 7–30.

Puig de la Bellacasa, M. (2011). Matters of care in technoscience: Assembling neglected things. *Social Studies of Science, 41*(1), 85–106.

Reed, R. (2017, January 25). Hear Billy Bragg reimagine Bob Dylan anthem as Trump protest. *Rolling Stone.* Retrieved from www.rollingstone.com/music/music-news/hear-billy-bragg-reimagine-bob-dylan-anthem-as-trump-protest-110498/

Richards, B. (2004). The emotional deficit in political communication. *Political Communication, 21*(3), 339–352.

Rodnitzky, J. L. (1999). The sixties between the microgrooves: Using folk and protest music to understand American history, 1963–1973. *Popular Music and Society, 23*(4), 105–122.

Rose, D. B., van Dooren, T., Chrulew, M., Cooke, S., Kearnes, M., & O'Gorman, E. (2012). Thinking through the environment, unsettling the humanities. *Environmental Humanities, 1*(1), 1–5.

Ross, A. (1998). *Real love: In pursuit of cultural justice*. London, England: Routledge.

Schlosberg, D. (2013). Theorising environmental justice: The expanding sphere of a discourse. *Environmental Politics, 22*(1), 37–55.

Schrader, B. (2014, October 22). Arts and social engagement – criticising society. *Te Ara – the Encyclopedia of New Zealand*. Retrieved from www.TeAra.govt.nz/en/music/45288/damn-the-dam

Stewart, K. (2011). Atmospheric attunements. *Environment and Planning D: Society and Space, 29*(3), 445–453.

Stirling, A. (2008). 'Opening up' and 'closing down': Power, participation and pluralism in the social appraisal of technology. *Science, Technology & Human Values, 33*(2), 262–294.

Suryanarayanan, S., & Kleinman, D. L. (2013). Be(e) coming experts: The controversy over insecticides in the honey bee colony collapse disorder. *Social Studies of Science, 43*(2), 215–240.

United Nations. (n.d.a). The United Nations voluntary trust fund for victims of human trafficking. Retrieved from https://www.unodc.org/unodc/human-trafficking-fund.html

United Nations. (n.d.b). Music to inspire the fight against human trafficking. Retrieved from http://www.unodc.org/documents/human-trafficking/Human-Trafficking-Fund/Final_UN_-_Music_To_Inspire_Deck.pdf

9 *Cassolada*

Communication, protest and the 2017 Catalan Indy Ref

Kate Fitch

Introduction

While writing this book, I spent a month as a visiting scholar at a public university in Barcelona. That month was an extraordinary time to visit Catalonia[1] in that I arrived two days before the Catalan independence referendum on 1 October 2017, which had been declared illegal by the Spanish government, and Catalonia declared independence from Spain as I was queuing to check in at the airport to depart four weeks later. It was not originally my intention to write about my experience there. However, on reflection, for a scholar interested in communication and media and writing a book about the role of public relations in contemporary culture and social change, it is difficult to ignore the widespread protests over police violence and censorship linked to the referendum during my visit. My first day at the university, the day immediately following the referendum, included a stop-work protest and on the second day, the university was closed due to a general strike. The evenings were punctuated by *cassolada*, the sound of collective protest through the banging of pots and pans. For my Catalan friends and colleagues, this was a disruptive and emotionally challenging period and that disruption and instability continued long after I left. This chapter offers a reflexive account of my observations and experiences of living and working in Barcelona in October 2017. Its focus is on the communicative acts of protesters and their capacity to organise through networked media.

Investigating the significance of protest and resistance in relation to the Catalan independence referendum in 2017 challenges corporatist understandings of public relations and enables reflection on the complex links between activism and public relations. In particular, sociocultural and critical perspectives consider whether activism can be thought of as a form of public relations, or whether the two should not be conflated (Weaver, 2019). In her historical investigation of the suffragette movement, O'Brien concludes that the 'history of activist and protest PR has largely been written out of the history of the profession' (2019, p. 60). There is in fact a long history of discussing activism in relation to public relations, dating back to the 1980s and 1990s (see for example, Crable & Vibbert, 1985; L. Grunig, 1992; Heath, 1997). However, these perspectives tend to frame activism as a challenge for organisations and as an issue that had to be managed rather than seeing activism in terms of public relations activity. In an extreme example of how this framing plays out in practice, Canadian anti-activist, Ross Irvine, who conducted workshops in Australia at the invitation of the Institute of Public Affairs and the Public Relations Institute of Australia in 2005, sought to mitigate the work of activists through issues management, declaring 'public relations is war' and viewing terrorist, criminal and activist as interchangeable terms (Wilson, 2005, p. 1). Other scholars have advocated for public relations professionals to be organisational activists by representing community concerns and acting as the organisation's moral compass (Berger & Reber, 2005; Holtzhausen, 2012; Holtzhausen & Voto, 2002).

However, it is only in the last decade or so that public relations scholars have begun to consider how activism, as persuasive and purposive communication conducted outside of corporate institutions and engaged in social change, might allow us to rethink public relations. As Weaver notes, 'contestation and transgression do not fit well with normative models of ideal PR practice' (2019, p. 22). Adi (2019) calls for greater attention to protest and dissent, and a more nuanced understanding of both these particular forms of activism and the use of communication strategies and tactics by protestors and dissenters. Dissent PR is focused on ideas and aims to promote 'new thinking' in national or public life (Adi & Moloney, 2012, p. 103). Building on this understanding, Moloney and McKie define dissent PR as 'the dissemination of ideas, commentaries and policies through PR techniques in order to change current, dominant thinking in private or public life' (2016, p. 157). In contrast, protest PR is a form of communication that 'persuades via occupations, demonstrations, strikes, public speaking and other forms of non-violent and violent protests in order to implement those ideas, behaviours and policies into law and other forms of executive action' (Adi & Moloney, 2012, p. 104). Other protest PR techniques might include 'marches, rallies, stunts, strikes, boycotts and lawsuits to create influence on policy makers' (Moloney & McKie, 2016, p. 157). This distinction suggests that dissent PR is strategic in terms of the overarching themes and narrative and protest PR is a tactical implementation designed to show dissent to the dominant social or political narrative, and that protest PR results from dissent PR (Adi, 2019; Adi & Moloney, 2012). In recent years, public relations scholars have begun to consider the significance of protest from perspectives other than organisational issues management; for example, scholars have investigated anti-corruption protests in Romania (Crișan, 2019); the 2013 Gezi Park protests in Turkey (Göncü, Saka, & Sayan, 2019); and the Occupy movement (Adi & Moloney, 2012; Adi, 2015), as well as the history of protest PR and its relationship with social change (O'Brien, 2019; Russell & Lamme, 2017). Göncü et al. (2019) found that even relatively spontaneous protests employed communication strategies and tactics effectively, combining events such as demonstrations with digital media activity to culminate in an effective and coherent overarching strategy despite the diverse political perspectives of participants.

My aim in this chapter is to consider the significance of protest PR and dissent PR in relation to the protests in Barcelona following the Catalan independence referendum and the events of October 2017. I draw on my observations and impressions and make links with the relevant scholarly literature, in order to make sense of my experiences and to understand how activism and protest may inform theorising about public relations. These impressions are informed by my access to (primarily English language) news and other media, my experiences working in a Catalan university, and in the context of chance conversations with people in the streets. I acknowledge that focusing on what communication means in this context is disruptive for traditional conceptualisations of public relations and its strong association with the corporate sector (Weaver, 2019). I consider the protests, demonstrations and other acts of persuasive communication I witnessed over that month in terms of both dissent and protest PR.

The chapter is structured in six sections. In this section, I discuss recent scholarship on protest PR and dissent PR. In the next section, I outline my approach in this chapter for reflecting on my experiences in Catalonia in October 2017. I then describe and reflect on the communication, protests and actions I witnessed immediately prior to and in the weeks after the Catalan independence referendum held on 1 October 2017. These protests began in September in response to Spain's attempts to shut down the referendum, and escalated following the referendum in response to the violent actions of police at polling stations (Catalonia Independence Referendum, 2017). In the fourth section, I discuss some of the events, notably the #FreeTweety and *cassolada* protest actions, I witnessed, drawing on literature on activism and networked protests. In the fifth section, I consider the challenges for understanding 'truth' in a polarised media environment, with censorship through the shutting down of internet domains and legal threats against media outlets, and in an era of misinformation. Finally, I consider the significance of the discussion in this chapter for the themes of this book: the role of public relations in social change and the significance of activism and protest for conceptualising public relations.

Investigating protest and dissent

In Catalonia, independence debates are 'grounded on competing visions of nationhood' as unionist parties maintain Spanish sovereignty whereas Catalan independence supporters argue Catalonia is a nation entitled to self-determination (Cetrà, Casanas-Adam, & Tàrrega, 2018, p. 128). Opposition to Spain is fuelled in part by the brutal suppression of Catalan identity under Franco's dictatorship (Guibernau, 2013a). There is well-established scholarship on Catalonia's status as a 'stateless nation' (Serrano, 2013) and the extensive promotional work, including strategic communication, public diplomacy, public relations and nation branding, that maintains a distinct Catalan identity nationally and internationally and enables the Generalitat, the Catalan-state based government to operate as a quasi-nation-state (Garcia, 2013; Johnson & Cester, 2015; Vela & Xifra, 2015; Xifra, 2008; Xifra & McKie, 2012). L'Etang (2009) identified the ways in which nations, including stateless nations, engage in public relations as a form of diplomacy embracing media relations and advocacy. I am not in this chapter attempting to enter into debates about political legitimacy, but rather, to understand how public relations strategies and techniques were harnessed to protest against the actions of the Spanish state in response to the Catalan independence referendum. Protestors were not all supporters of independence for Catalonia.

The referendum was concerned with whether Catalonia should be an independent country. The legitimacy of the Catalan-government referendum was disputed by Spain, who had suspended Catalan referendum law. As the Spanish government had declared the referendum unconstitutional, police were instructed to prevent the referendum. The constitutional challenges to the referendum alongside legal and other threats to prevent the promotion of the referendum, included confiscation of referendum materials, shutting down websites, apps and internet domains, raids on media outlets, legal threats against media outlets that accepted referendum-related advertising, and preventing the use of public buildings as polling stations (Catalonia Referendum, 2017; Della Porta, O'Connor, Portos, & Subirats Ribas, 2017a; Tàrrega, 2017).

Despite attempts by Spain to disrupt the referendum, approximately 2.3 million people did vote; 90% of them voted yes. In fact, this number only represents 42% of the electorate, who remain deeply divided on the issue of Catalan independence (Burgen, 2017). On the day of the referendum, images of police violence against unarmed citizens at polling stations were shared widely via social media and through Catalan and international media outlets. The response of international leaders was to condemn the violence; Angela Merkel allegedly telephoned Spanish president Rajoy on the day to call for it to cease immediately (Merkel calls Rajoy, 2017; Rogers, 2017). The Catalan independence referendum was a major political crisis for Spain and one that threatened European unity. In the face of these challenges, a contested communication campaign involving governments, civil society organisations, and activists played out in a dynamic media environment where it was difficult to fully understand the competing narratives and agendas.

My response to the events that I witnessed over the weekend of, and in the weeks after, the referendum is to write an auto-ethnographic chapter that attempts to make sense of my experiences in Catalonia in October 2017. I draw on notes and journal entries I made and visual documentation I recorded during my visit, along with contemporaneous news stories. I make links with the relevant scholarly literature, in order to make sense of these experiences and to understand activism and protest for theorising about public relations. I insert extracts from my reflective journal in italics to share some of these impressions. These impressions are informed by my access to news and other media, my experiences working in a Catalan university, and in the context of happenstance conversations with people in the streets and other public places. I did not conduct formal interviews and I am not drawing on direct quotations. These conversations were often politically motivated and initiated by people keen to explain their positions. For example, one young woman approached my partner and I in a square as we emerged from a metro station on our first full day to see a small number of pro-Madrid supporters gathering. 'Do you understand what is going on?' she asked on hearing us speak English. A university student, she had spent the previous night sleeping in a local school as part of a widespread occupation of schools to be used as polling stations the following day (Schools Open, 2017). Every conversation I had with people was polite and respectful, and they expressed a range of views about Catalan independence.

Catalan Indy Ref #10

I look back over my photos of posters and stencils, snapped in the street on my first day to try and document my first 24 hours and the lead up to the referendum. Everywhere were flyers urging people to vote. These were in multiple languages: Arabic, English, Spanish and Catalan. Poblenou Vota Si *[Poblenou votes yes].* Democracia! Si Tú No vas ellos ganan *[Democracy Now! If you don't go (to vote), they win]. This last one featured blank faces with a gag like slash across the mouth.*

'1-Oct Votarem' [We are voting 1 October] was stencilled onto roads, pavements and walls and A4 sized posters covered buildings and walls, many printed on home printers in response to the confiscation by police of referendum materials. The multiple languages reminded me that Guibernau (2013b) argues Catalan nationalism can be cosmopolitan and inclusive. For example, recent migrants, as 'new Catalans', were invited to speak at a pro-independence rally two days before the referendum (Mason, 2017). Della Porta et al. argue the linking of claims for Catalan independence with social justice, by including citizens with migrant backgrounds, enabled 'innovative framing' and greater mobilisation (2017a, p. 165).

Police were ordered to prevent public buildings, often schools, being used as polling stations. Schools were occupied by families and local communities to keep them open and maintain access for the referendum. Many school communities organised activities using coded messages on social media (Catalonia Referendum, 2017). Posters promoted activities at local schools for Friday and Saturday night to justify the 'sleepovers': *Festa Inici de Crus!* [orientation week party] including barbeques, football games, open air cinema and bands. One poster advertised a concert, *Cantada de benvinguda al nou dia* [sing along to welcome the new day] at 5 a.m. on the day of the referendum at a primary school to celebrate 'world music day'. In fact, at 5 a.m. the school was locked up like a fortress with people outside in the dark and in heavy rain prepared to defend it. I walked between three local polling stations, two schools and a medical centre, spending some time at each before the polls opened at 9 a.m.

I witnessed the euphoria that came with both the coming together of communities to occupy and defend local schools to be used as polling stations, the gathering outside those schools in heavy rain and the dark, and in some instances, singing and chanting, the clapping and joy when the polls opened and the cheering when people, particularly elderly people, emerged after voting. Votarem, votarem *[we are voting]* they chanted. They sang Catalan songs, including the anthem, Els Segadors.

Each local station had a camera person, filming continuously. I wondered if this was to document any trouble. Members of Mossos,[2] the Catalan police force, were outside some of the local polling stations but I saw no intervention. At one station, two members of Mossos stood against a wall checking their phones and occasionally going to a local café to buy coffee. Mid-morning I returned to my rented flat. I learnt of police violence at some polling stations through social media and a large convoy of Policia Nacional vehicles drove past the flat with their sirens and lights on. I raced back to the nearest polling station.

The joy was understandably lost as people heard about the violence at some polling stations and more and more people gathered at the polling stations to defend them. By late morning at one local station, a medical centre in Poblenou, the crowd stood with their backs to the entry, arms folded, in lines, four or more deep. It was clearly a defensive position and the tension was palpable. That night, the Catalan television news – after reporting on the horror of the day – closed with historic footage of exiled Catalan cellist Pau Casals playing El Cant des Ocells *[Song of the Birds] at the United Nations.*[3]

One woman later told me she spent the following day in tears in response to the stress and fearfulness of spending that day at a polling station, waiting for the Spanish national police after hearing about attacks on voters at other stations. I was well aware from among the people I spoke to that first weekend – in bars, cafes, squares – that not everyone wanted independence. Some had planned to vote no, spoil their ballot papers, or abstain. But, the heavy-handed actions of Rajoy's government leading up to the independence referendum – for example, declaring it illegal, arresting government officers and closing Catalan government internet domains – resulted in some of these people occupying schools in the two nights before the election and defending the right to vote. After witnessing the violence via social media and on Catalan television news, one person told me on the night of the referendum that regardless of the result, 'Spain has lost'.

Activism and networked protests

Technology played a significant role in communications around the Catalan independence referendum in that it facilitated rapid communication to organise protests, such as the general strike on Tuesday 3 October to protest against police violence at the referendum. Della Porta et al. describe the critical role grassroots protest played in relation to the Catalan independence movement in recent years and specifically in relation to the independence referendum:

> In the wake of the hard-line actions taken by the Spanish authorities which prevented the Catalan government from logistically preparing for the vote, the organisational burden was taken up by ordinary citizens. People were organised through local 'Comitès de Defensa del Referendum' (Referendum Defence Committees) that coordinated through Twitter, WhatsApp and Telegram.
>
> . . .
>
> They occupied polling stations – preventing them from being sealed by the police the Friday before the referendum. Farmers' tractors were used in

hundreds of polling stations as protective barriers. A judicial order led to the removal of the official webpage (referendum.cat), which had provided people with information about the referendum: thereafter, individual citizens started launching replica webpages under new domains, emerging as fast as the authorities could remove them.

(Della Porta et al., 2017a)

Activists were well aware of the need for security in the alternative arrangements being made as one reporter describes retrospectively the care with which grassroots supporters communicated and strategised:

Communication among the volunteers prepared to hide voting slips and ballot boxes was conducted with extreme caution and careful planning. No information was passed on by phone or even in a WhatsApp message. Thousands of individuals downloaded the messaging apps Telegram and Signal, which are more secure, although most of the instructions were relayed in person. Even when information was passed on face to face, those involved turned off their cell phones, in case they were bugged.

(Tedó, 2017)

Technology afforded rapid organisation of protests such as stop-work protests at many workplaces the day after and a general strike two days after the referendum. The euphoria of mass protest that Tufekci (2017) described was something that I witnessed outside the Policia Nacional headquarters in one of the main avenues in Barcelona.

Two days after the referendum, following the general strike, I found myself outside the national police headquarters in Via Laetana. The streets were blocked off, blue lights were flashing, and the crowd was chanting and pointing at the police building. The atmosphere was electric. The chants included 'these streets will always be ours' and, my personal favourite, 'this building is going to be a library'.

The library chant aimed at the building housing Policia Nacional is significant (*Catalan News*, 2017). Libraries often feature in networked protests as they symbolise participatory methods of organising and the social exchange of ideas and knowledge above state authoritarianism (Tufekci, 2017, pp. 90–91).

The day after the general strike, I spoke to staff in a local café. They told me how they had left the protests, fearful that agitators were deliberately trying to provoke their group in a violent confrontation. And they described how when someone had tried to burn a Spanish flag, many protestors stepped in, concerned about how such imagery would look on social media with the potential for it to be widely distributed: 'How will that look online? It will go viral. That's not the image we want.' The consistent narrative for Catalan secessionists was non-violence and civil disobedience: *Som gent de pau* [We are people of peace] (Mackey, 2017). The strike also attracted protesters against the police violence on the day of the referendum who did not support Catalan independence (Marsden, 2017).

Given the state-imposed restrictions on formal communication networks, internet domains and media reporting, which I discuss in the following section, the role of social media in enabling connections was significant (Castells, 2015). I discuss here two examples of protest that illustrate how social media platforms enabled a cartoon character and the banging of pots and pans to become important symbolic acts of protest and resistance. The Looney Tunes cartoon character Tweety Pie became an unexpected protest symbol for Catalan independence (Ferraris, 2017; Orihuela & Mayes, 2017). Tweety Pie was painted on the side of a cruise ship for marketing purposes; unfortunately for Times Warner, that ship was moored in Barcelona port to accommodate some of the 5,000 Spanish police (both Guardia Civil and Policia Nacional) brought into the region ahead of the referendum. The hashtag #FreePiolin (Tweety Pie is known as Piolin in Spain) began to trend on Twitter; protestors wore Tweety Pie masks at demonstrations; graffiti and referendum posters featured Tweety Pie; and an activist dressed as Tweety Pie frequented St Jaume square to discuss Catalan independence with tourists. While Warner Brothers was not happy their trademarked character had come to symbolise Catalan independence and requested the ship's owners take immediate action, in reality there was little they could do given the #FreePiolin or #FreeTweety movement appeared to be somewhat organic. In a similar fashion, penguins became symbolic of government censorship in Turkey, when CNN Turkey showed a documentary about penguins as CNN International broadcast live images of protestors clashing with police in Gezi Park (Tufekci, 2017).

One of the strongest memories of my stay in Barcelona is the nightly sound of the *cassolada*, a collective protest using pots and pans that continued throughout the month of October. The *cassolada* was reported to begin on 20 September in response to the Guardia Civil raiding Catalan government offices, arresting officials and confiscating ballot papers, and organised through social media (Della Porta et al., 2017a; Generalized cassolada, 2017). It usually started at 10 p.m. and lasted for approximately 15 minutes, but sometimes it started earlier in immediate response, for example, to a televised speech from the king or the prime minister, or other events. In the high-density suburbs of Barcelona, the sound echoed in all directions. At one occupied school the night before the referendum, where there were few available pots and pans, families rattled keys and banged fences with sticks. There are even mobile apps, developed in Latin America where the banging of pots is also a popular form of protest, that recreate the sound, in case you are away from home at the time of the *cassolada* (Bruguera, 2017). *Cassolada* was declared the Catalan 'neologism' of 2017 (its original meaning was eating food cooked in *cassola* or casserole pots) (Catalans choose cassolada, 2018).

Media, internet and censorship

On the day of the independence referendum, I returned to my rented flat mid-morning. I was still jetlagged and had been up since 5 a.m. to join locals heading through the rain and the dark to defend polling stations. I turned on the television to watch the news of this historic day. And I perused social media.

At that point, any complacency I had about witnessing the birth of a nation ended. Something bad is happening, I said, staring with disbelief at footage of police beating people at polling stations shared via Twitter. I changed news stations and could find nothing about the referendum on Spanish television news. Nothing.

I used the #1O, #1Oct and #CatalanReferendum hashtags to find information on Twitter about the referendum. As a regular visitor to Barcelona since 2010, I already followed a number of Catalan organisations and independence activists, sources that I trusted. Yet, watching Spanish television news, I could find no reference to the images and eyewitness accounts being shared online. Similarly, Tufekci described seeking breaking news coverage of protests in Turkey: 'I kept refreshing all the news channels . . . refresh, change channel. Nothing. Nothing. Nothing'. said one interviewee, mirroring my words (2017, p. 37). My partner, a broadcast journalist, realised before me that Spanish television was unlikely to report on either the referendum or police violence at the referendum and we switched to Catalan public broadcasters, who did. I had little confidence in unbiased reporting from that point on. The Spanish public broadcaster TVE showed very little of the violence, or indeed the referendum itself, and this editorial decision was later condemned by its own staff based in Catalonia (Hedgecoe, 2017).

The Spanish media environment is a polarised, pluralist media system, which means that media outlets are closely aligned with particular political parties and ideological positions; in particular, the issue of Catalan independence is a highly mediatised conflict (Dekavalla & Montagut, 2018; Gagnon, Montagut, & Moragas-Fernández, 2019). Tàrrega (in Cetrà et al., 2018) argues media outlets became key social actors in the contradictory and diametrically opposed positions of competing national projects: the Spanish unionist parties versus the Catalan independence groups. Despite the absence of a formal Vote No campaign, Tàrrega maintains there was a 'pseudo campaign' by anti-independence parties with media releases, social media posts, and campaign-like events, which they stated were designed 'to unmask the lies of the independence movement' (Partido Popular, 2017, cited in Cetrà et al., 2018, p. 137). The resulting news stories in Spanish unionist media challenged the veracity of images of police violence, calling them 'fake news', with an overriding perception that pro-independence media were highly manipulative (Cetrà et al., 2018). Yet, all media in Spain adopt certain political positions in relation to Catalan secession. In the words of political scientist, Oriol Bartomeus: 'the editorial battle over Catalonia is particularly fierce' (cited in Hedgecoe, 2017). This polarisation, where news outlets became key players in relation to debates on Catalan independence, served Spanish readers poorly:

Suspicion of *El Pais* has left much of Spain and Spanish readers without a place to read even modestly neutral coverage of the complex Catalan crisis. Elsewhere in Spain's media landscape, deep partisan lines between outlets have made coverage of the Catalan events often unrecognizably different from one end of a newsstand to another. Local Catalan public broadcaster TV3 has come into criticism for being too secessionist, Madrid national channel TVE for sometimes shrilly unionist stories and famously raucous political talk segments.

(Herman, 2017)

One news site compared the front pages of different Spanish papers the day after the referendum, observing diverse reporting 'either with a focus on police brutality against a people trying to exercise a democratic right, or by blaming Catalans for stirring up trouble' (Govan, 2017). In contrast, international news coverage on the same day reported on the police violence, with widespread images of police in riot gear attacking unarmed civilians (Spain's Day of Shame, 2017). Other commentators found that the reporting of the general strike on 3 October demonstrated the deeply divided polarisation in Spain and the ways in which it was exacerbated by the media (Hedgecoe, 2017).

The Spanish government recognised the media as powerful players in the Catalan independence movement and therefore sought to use legal and judicial means to curtail media reporting on the referendum. Communication platforms and media institutions were considered to be under attack even before I arrived in Barcelona, with reports of raids on newspaper offices, legal restrictions on the promotion and reporting of the Catalan independence referendum, and the shutting down of internet domains and apps (Spain's Guardia Civil, 2017; Tàrrega, 2017). According to Tàrrega (2017), more than 140 websites were closed in the lead up to the referendum. In September 2017, media outlets were warned about possible criminal charges for promoting, or even reporting on, the independence referendum (Cetrà et al., 2018) and, following the High Court of Justice of Catalonia's decision, news editors were ordered to 'refrain from publishing, by any means, all propaganda or advertising related to the referendum on 1 October' (Spanish police enters HQ, 2017). These warnings had significant effects as some media outlets no longer accepted campaign advertising.

In the weeks prior to the referendum, the Guardia Civil confiscated 9.6 million ballot papers, froze financial assets and/or closely monitored payments of the Catalan government, the Generalitat, and threatened legal action against the organisers of the referendum (Della Porta et al., 2017a; Spanish government announces seizure, 2017). Guardia Civil officers raided Catalan government offices and arrested officials (Della Porta et al., 2017a; Spanish police arrest, 2017). Their heavy handed approach, which also included seizing campaign literature and referendum posters from multiple print works, and, as noted above, threatening legal action against journalists and news outlets, has been condemned by inter- national organisations, including the United Nations (Jones, Burgen, & Rankin, 2017; Spanish police arrest, 2017; Spanish police enters HQ, 2017). The attempts to shut down discussion about the referendum led to a judicial order to shut down the Catalan government website, Referendum.cat (Della Porta et al., 2017a). The response of the Catalan government was swift. Catalan president, Carles Puigdemont, tweeted a link to a cloned website and asked followers to amplify the information (Badcock, 2017a). Ballot papers were shared online and people were able to print these at home.

Misinformation and fake news circulated widely on social media, fuelling anxiety and polarising the debate over events on the day of the Catalan referendum. Maldito Bulo, a fact checking website, tried to highlight the 'fake news' being shared, particularly the use of images from unrelated events (Erickson, 2017). Examples of fake news included pictures of broken fingers and people injured in a 2012 miners' strike rather than at polling stations, and stories of a police death and a paralysed child. Lesaca (2017) analysed social media posts shared in relation to the Catalan referendum and found that one significant source was a Russian media conglomerate. Of the top 100 accounts to share links, 84% were almost certainly digital bots (Lesaca, 2017). However, the extent to which Russia was involved in misinformation campaigns in relation to the referendum is contested, with some arguing it was exaggerated or pointing to a large bot army disseminating an anti-Catalan narrative (Palmer, 2017; Rolandi, 2018). In evidence presented to British Parliament, the founder of Transparency Toolkit stated that the *El Pais* journalists had misanalysed data and overstated the influence of Russian bots; McGrath (2018) noted that there was a need for greater scrutiny of the data and understanding of allegations of fake news.

Public relations and resistance

The Catalan independence referendum took place against competing conceptualisations of national identity and needs to be understood in terms of not only Catalan and Spanish history but in the context of growing global tensions, competing nationalisms and political separatist movements (see Johnson & Cester, 2015). That is, the broader context for strategic communication around national identity and the Catalans' appeals to Europe, reinforced by years of public diplomacy, informed appeals for support from Europe, support that was not forthcoming (Birnbaum, 2017; Vela & Xifra, 2015). The 'imagined community' of the Catalan nation significantly informed campaigns and movements for independence (Della Porta, O'Connor, Portos, & Subirats Ribas, 2017b). Further, the long history of Catalan oppression, including under the Spanish dictator, Franco, informed ongoing communication strategies and meaning making in response to certain events. For example, the comparison of Puigdemont's fate to that of former Catalan president Lluis Companys, who was executed on Franco's orders in 1940, was highly inflammatory (PP Official Compares, 2017; Stothard, 2017).

In Barcelona, I witnessed the heady and conflicted torment of multiple communications in a fast-moving and dynamic situation. I never lost sight of the impact on the people for whom this mattered – the tension as people constantly refreshed news feeds and attempted to continue their everyday lives during such political turmoil. The communications from different civil society organisations, from Catalan government institutions, local community 'defence committees', various social institutions and student organisations point to the strategic communications necessary for social change. It was difficult to know which sources to trust, whether news outlets, influencers, or government communiques. The difficulties in understanding the events were compounded not just by the speed of these events but by the competing perspectives, the speed of information, and questions of trust, given traditional media outlets and government sources offered ideologically driven perspectives that presented highly divergent accounts and frames of events.

The response to Spanish intervention in the capacity of the Catalan government to hold the referendum, and reports of police violence on the day of the referendum and later the arrest of civil society leaders as well as democratically elected government members highlights the role of grassroots as well as more formally constituted organisations in communication and resistance. According to Cetrà (in Cetrà et al., 2018), police violence at the referendum not only enabled effective collective resistance and mobilised support for Catalan autonomy but 'the Spanish government's strategy proved both repressive and ineffective, and the Catalan government gained significant political capital and control of the narrative' (p. 129). The Catalan government developed a consistent narrative that framed communications: the independent referendum was a social justice issue supported by the people, the long history of oppression by the Spanish state (with particular reference to the Franco era) and the wily Catalans, just like Tweety Pie, were always one step ahead of their oppressors (see, for example, Badcock, 2017a; Campbell, 2017; Ferraris, 2017). There were countless news stories illustrating or reinforcing this narrative: how the Spanish government was outwitted by storing ballot boxes in Elna (a Catalan town in France) and the subsequent distribution of election materials by 'students, workers, OAPs, grandparents, parents and people on the dole . . . working in conjunction with the Catalan government' (Tedó, 2017); how Catalan farmers 'tricked' Spanish police by threatening to close the border with France on the day of the general strike and then trapping them on the border by using tractors to block the road back to Barcelona (Khan, 2017); and how the Catalan government was always ahead of the Spanish with back-up plans for ballot boxes, websites, and election material (Badcock, 2017a, 2017b).

Following the referendum, the rector of the university I was visiting issued a statement condemning the police violence. Indeed, all Catalan universities issued a joint statement condemning the violence and referring to the role of the university in upholding a democratic society. Over the course of the month, there was increasing concern about the growing suppression of the media by the Spanish government who had threatened to assert direct control over Catalan public broadcasters with the Spanish government approval of measures in Article 155, which included direct intervention in Catalan media institutions. In response, along with 130 other communication and media scholars, I signed a statement to express concern on what we perceived to be 'one of the biggest attacks to Catalan democratic institutions'. That statement was issued on 26 October in Catalan, Spanish and English, and expressed support for the Catalan Audiovisual Media Corporation and the Catalan News Agency.[4] The communication deans from

Catalan universities issued a similar statement, arguing against the intervention of the Spanish government to control Catalan broadcasters, based on the application of Article 155 of the Spanish constitution:

> We consider that the intervention of the State powers on Televisió de Catalunya, Catalunya Ràdio and the Catalan News Agency would be an attack on freedom of expression, would violate the right of citizens to receive truthful information (Article 20 of the Constitution) and, ultimately, would be to the detriment of democracy and the fundamental rights of the people.[5]

For an academic more used to the neoliberal, market orientation of my former Australian university concerned with reputation management and market attractiveness, these were extraordinary events to witness and to participate in. I was appalled by the actions of the Spanish government, first around censorship and suppression, and later by the violence inflicted on citizens entitled to vote. Yet most of what I understood was mediated through traditional and social media, in an environment where rumours and misinformation raised significant concerns around trust in a polarised media environment with conflicting accounts and perspectives.

Conclusion

One of the aims of this book is to understand the complex links between culture and public relations. Reflecting on my experiences and observations in relation to the Catalan referendum in 2017 allows me to consider the ways in which communication and media are entwined in the dynamic construction of Catalan identity and the complex social networks that play into those representations, as well as the ways in which activists and non-state actors contested challenges to the Catalan government's attempts to hold the referendum. To do so challenges corporatist understandings of public relations and enables some reflection over persuasive communication techniques and their use by protestors and dissenters (Moloney & McKie, 2016). Studying protest PR reflects a particular worldview that 'privileges societal justice and social impact over organisational reputation' (Adi, 2019, p. 49; see also Demetrious, 2013; L'Etang, 2016).

If activist public relations – including protest PR and dissent PR – strategies are built on shared political and social goals (McKie & Xifra, 2016), then how did these apply in relation to the Catalan referendum? The initial goals were clearly in support of Catalan autonomy, and the strategies harnessed a narrative built around Catalan identity and the history of Spanish oppression. The actions of the Spanish police – raiding printers and government offices, shutting down internet domains, and threatening media outlets with legal action – culminated in violence on the day of the referendum and ultimately reinforced the narrative of historical and ongoing Spanish oppression and mobilised even non-supporters of Catalan independence. Although Catalan independence movements are often considered the domain of elite groups (Barrio & Rodríguez-Teruel, 2017), the challenge to the legitimacy of the referendum led to considerable grassroots organisation around the referendum and in subsequent protests (Della Porta et al., 2017b). Technology afforded opportunities for networked protests and activists used purposive, persuasive communication to foster collective resistance against the Spanish government through acts of dissent PR.

This chapter has shown how Catalan independence supporters, including civil society groups, political parties, government representatives as well as ordinary citizens, developed a number of strategies that turned on themes encompassing non-violence, Catalan national identity, Spanish oppression, collective action and social justice. The heavy-handed tactics of Spain, including violent attempts to prevent people voting, only served to reinforce and highlight this oppression and to frame it within an historical narrative of continuing Spanish oppression. A Spanish communication scholar said to me the following year that Catalonia was very good at propaganda and that Spain had failed to tell their story. Certainly, Catalan protestors and dissenters were effective at protest PR in terms of constructing a clear and consistent narrative. Rallies, strikes, demonstrations, were organised at short notice in order to demonstrate both solidarity and support for their issues and concerns. In this way, Catalans effectively highlighted the repressive tactics of the Spanish government; the police violence on the day of the referendum was widely condemned internationally. However, at the time of completing this book, Catalan independence seems unlikely in the immediate future. The then-Spanish president, Rajoy enacted Article 155 in response to the declaration of independence on 27 October 2017, sacking Catalan leader Puigdemont and the Catalan government and imposing direct rule on Catalonia. Five elected members of the Catalan government and two leaders of civil society organisations, Òmnium Cultural and the ANC, Jordi Cuixart and Jordi Sànchez, have been convicted of sedition and sentenced to between nine and thirteen years in jail, and another five including former Catalan president Puigdemont, remain in exile (Gea, 2019; Violent Clashes, 2019). In October 2019, Spain reissued European arrest warrants for Puigdemont and other ministers who remain abroad. Scholars view the independence referendum on 1 October 2017 as a pivotal point in the conflict with Spain, and one that has escalated confrontation between Spain and Catalan governments and changed the political landscape (Gagnon et al., 2019). The conflict is ongoing.

In this chapter, I have attempted to move beyond identifying or defining communication around the ill-fated referendum as public relations or wholly in terms of public relations strategies and tactics but instead to consider what the activities that I have identified as protest PR and dissent PR mean in terms of changing ideas and public discourse around particular issues. In this case, that issue related to Catalan independence, built on a strategic narrative of social justice, Catalan national identity, and Spanish oppression. Communication played a significant role in constructing, amplifying, demonstrating and reinforcing that narrative, and enabled protestors and dissenters to contribute to public and political debate about Catalan independence. As Weaver argues, 'public relations could be completely disrupted and re-imagined . . . in the context of its use by actual *active publics'* (2019, p. 25). Indeed, communication, facilitated through social platforms, enabled the construction of Catalan identity that underpinned the claim for independence (protest PR) and facilitated acts of collective resistance that helped those publics become active (dissent PR).

Notes

1 I use Catalonia in this chapter. Catalunya is the Catalan name.
2 The Mossos d'Esquadra is the Catalan regional police force. Their apparent refusal to prevent the referendum led to the Mossos police chief, Josep Lluis Trapero, being removed in late October 2017 when the Spanish government invoked Article 155 of the Spanish Constitution (Diez & Mateo, 2017). They are distinct from the Spanish police forces, Policia Nacional and Guardia Civil.
3 A traditional Catalan carol made famous by Pau Casals, a Catalan cellist exiled in 1939. He began every concert playing an instrumental version and it is deeply symbolic of Catalonia. Casals played it at the UN in 1971 where he said it was a song about peace (Raymont, 1971).
4 '131 researchers sign a statement rejecting the intervention of the CCMA and the CAN, to reject intervention of the Spanish government in Catalan public media' was released on 26 October 2017.
5 Comunicat de les facultats amb etudis de Comunicació de Catalunya [Communication of the faculties with studies of Communication of Catalonia] was released on 23 October 2017.

References

Adi, A. (2015). Occupy PR: An analysis of online media communications of occupy Wall Street and occupy London. *Public Relations Review, 41*(4), 508–514.

Adi, A. (Ed.). (2019). *Protest public relations: Communicating dissent and activism.* Abingdon, England: Routledge.

Adi, A., & Moloney, K. (2012). The importance of scale in occupy movement protests: A case study of a local occupy protest as a tool of communication through public relations and social media. *Revista Internaional de Relaciones Publicas, 4*(2), 97–122.

Badcock, J. (2017a, September 15). Spain plays cat and mouse as Catalonia vote looms. *BBC.* Retrieved from www.bbc.com/news/world-europe-41268845

Badcock, J. (2017b, September 27). Catalan referendum: Spain battling to halt the vote. *BBC.* Retrieved from www.bbc.com/news/world-europe-41398627

Barrio, A., & Rodríguez-Teruel, J. (2017). Reducing the gap between leaders and voters? Elite polarization, outbidding competition, and the rise of secessionism in Catalonia. *Ethnic and Racial Studies, 40*(10), 1776–1794.

Berger, B., & Reber, B. (2005). Framing analysis of activist rhetoric: How the Sierra club succeeds or fails at creating salient messages. *Public Relations Review, 31*(2), 185–195.

Birnbaum, M. (2017, November 1). Catalan separatists counted on support from the E.U. but they got the cold shoulder. *Washington Post.* Retrieved from www.washingtonpost.com/world/europe/catalan-separatists-counted-on-support-from-the-eu-but-they-got-the-cold-shoulder/2017/11/01/62df9380-be6b-11e7-9294-705f80164f6e_story.html

Bruguera, L. (2017, October 20). The 3.0 alternative to the saucepan. *El Punt Avui*. Retrieved from www.elpuntavui.cat/politica/article/17-politica/1263694-l-alternativa-3-0-a-la-cassolada.html

Burgen, S. (2017, October 3). Thousands protest and strike over Catalonia referendum violence. *The Guardian*. Retrieved from www.theguardian.com/world/2017/oct/03/catalonia-holds-general-strike-protest-referendum-violence

Campbell, Z. (2017, October 13). How Catalonia pulled off its independence vote from Spain using 'pizza' code words and secret schemes. *The Intercept*. Retrieved from https://theintercept.com/2017/10/12/catalonia-referendum-independence-secret-vote-spain/

Castells, M. (2015). *Networks of outrage and hope: Social movements in the Internet age* (2nd ed.). Cambridge, England: Polity Press.

Catalan News. (2017, October 4). 'This building will become a library,' people chant in front of Spanish headquarters in Barcelona. #3Oct [Tweet].

The Catalans choose 'cassolada' as neologism of 2017. (2018, January 8). *El Periódico* Retrieved from www.elperiodico.com/es/sociedad/20180108/cassolada-elegido-neologismo-catalan-del-2017-6537754

Catalonia independence referendum: Spanish police seize ballot boxes, hundreds injured as voters cast votes. (2017, October 2). *ABC*. Retrieved from www.abc.net.au/news/2017-10-01/spanish-police-seize-ballot-boxes-in-catalan-referendum/9005680

Catalonia referendum: Tractors roll into Barcelona to support vote. (2017, September 29). *BBC*. Retrieved from www.bbc.com/news/world-europe-41439787

Cetrà, D., Casanas-Adam, E., & Tàrrega, M. (2018). The 2017 Catalan independence referendum: A symposium. *Scottish Affairs*, *21*(1), 126–143.

Crable, R., & Vibbert, S. (1985). Managing issues and influencing public policy. *Public Relations Review*, *11*(2), 3–16.

Crişan, C. (2019). Romania's protests: From stakeholders in waiting to activists becoming PR practitioners. In A. Adi (Ed.), *Protest public relations: Communicating dissent and activism* (pp. 185–204). Abingdon, England: Routledge.

Dekavalla, M., & Montagut, M. (2018). Constructing issues in the media through metaphoric frame networks. *Discourse, Context & Media*, *26*, 74–81.

Della Porta, D., O'Connor, F., Portos, M., & Subirats Ribas, A. (2017a, October 5). 'The streets will always be ours' – Catalonia, a referendum from below. *Open Democracy*. Retrieved from www.opendemocracy.net/can-europe-make-it/donatella-della-porta-francis-oconnor-martin-portos-anna-subirats-ribas/streets-w

Della Porta, D., O'Connor, F., Portos, M., & Subirats Ribas, A. (2017b). *Social movements and referendums from below: Direct democracy in the neoliberal crisis*. Bristol, England: Policy Press.

Demetrious, K. (2013). *Public relations, activism, and social change: Speaking up*. London, England: Routledge.

Diez, A., & Mateo, J. (2017, October 28). Spanish PM removes Catalan regional premier from post, calls December 21 polls. *El Pais* [online]. Retrieved from https://elpais.com/elpais/2017/10/28/inenglish/1509171087_827308.html

Erickson, A. (2017, October 17). How fake news helped shape the Catalonia independence vote. *Washington Post*. Retrieved from www.washingtonpost.com/news/worldviews/wp/2017/10/19/how-fake-news-helped-shape-the-catalonia-independence-vote/?noredirect=on&utm_term=.399781ac0443

Ferraris, R. (2017, September 30). How Tweety Pie became unlikely symbol of Catalan nationalism. *The National*. Retrieved from www.thenational.ae/world/europe/how-tweety-pie-became-unlikely-symbol-of-catalan-nationalism-1.662986

Gagnon, A.-G., Montagut, M., & Moragas-Fernández, C. M. (2019). Discourses, actors and citizens in the communicative construction of conflicts: The Catalan case. *Catalan Journal of Communication & Cultural Studies, 11*(2), 161–169.

Garcia, C. (2013). Strategic communication applied to nation building in Spain: The experience of the Catalan region. *Public Relations Review, 39*(5), 558–562.

Gea, A. (2019, October 14). Spain jails Catalonia separatist leaders for their role in failed bid for independence. *ABC News*. Retrieved from https://mobile.abc.net.au/news/2019-10-14/spain-jails-leaders-of-catalan-secession-bid-for-independence/11601772

Generalized cassolada against the offensive today. (2017, September 20). *El Punt Avui*. Retrieved from www.elpuntavui.cat/societat/article/5-societat/1243759-cassolada-generalitzada-contra-l-ofensiva-d-avui.html

Göncü, B., Saka, E., & Sayan, A. (2019). Reading Gezi Park protests through the lens of protest PR. In A. Adi (Ed.), *Protest public relations: Communicating dissent and activism* (pp. 150–169). Abingdon, England: Routledge.

Govan, F. (2017). Spanish press review: From repression to the 'treachery' of Catalan police. *The Local*. Retrieved from www.thelocal.es/20171002/spanish-press-review-from-police-brutality-to-the-treachery-of-the-catalans

Grunig, L. (1992). Activism: How it limits the effectiveness of organizations and how excellent public relations departments respond. In J. Grunig (Ed.), *Excellence in public relations and communication management* (pp. 503–530). Hillsdale, NJ: Lawrence Erlbaum Associates.

Guibernau, M. (2013a). Secessionism in Catalonia: After democracy. *Ethnopolitics, 12*(4), 368–393.

Guibernau, M. (2013b). Nationalism versus cosmopolitanism: A comparative approach. *Journal of Catalan Intellectual History, 5*, 13–34.

Heath, R. (1997). *Strategic issues management: Organizations and public policy*. Thousand Oaks, CA: Sage.

Hedgecoe, G. (2017, October 6). Catalonian media reflect polarised Spanish society. *BBC*. Retrieved from www.bbc.com/news/world-europe-41517569

Herman, M. (2017, October 27). Spain's most famous paper stumbles amid Catalonia independence crisis. *Columbia Journalism Review*. Retrieved from www.cjr.org/business_of_news/catalonia-independence-el-pais-spain.php

Holtzhausen, D. (2012). *Public relations as activism: Postmodern approaches to theory and practice*. New York, NY: Routledge.

Holtzhausen, D., & Voto, R. (2002). Resistance from the margins: The postmodern public relations practitioner as organizational activist. *Journal of Public Relations Research, 14*(1), 57–84.

Johnson, M., & Cester, X. (2015). Communicating Catalan culture in a global society. *Public Relations Review, 41*, 809–815.

Jones, S., Burgen, S., & Rankin, J. (2017, September 28). UN rights experts criticise Spanish efforts to block Catalan vote. *The Guardian*. Retrieved October 31, 2017, from www.theguardian.com/world/2017/sep/28/un-rightsexperts-criticise-spanish-efforts-to-block-catalan-vote

Khan, S. (2017, October 12). Catalan farmers trick Spanish police and trap them in field to stop them disrupting general strike. *The Independent*. Retrieved from www.independent.co.uk/news/world/europe/catalan-independence-spanish-police-referendum-general-strike-trick-a7997701.html

Lesaca, X. (2017, November 22). Why did Russian social media swarm the digital conversation about Catalan independence? *Washington Post.* Retrieved from www.washingtonpost.com/news/monkey-cage/wp/2017/11/22/why-did-russian-social-media-swarm-the-digital-conversation-about-catalan-independence/?utm_term=.2f3511b78ab9

L'Etang, J. (2009). Public relations and diplomacy in a globalized world: An issue of public communication. *American Behavioral Scientist, 53*(4), 607–626.

L'Etang, J. (2016). Public relations, activism and social movements: Critical perspectives. *Public Relations Inquiry, 5*(3), 207–211.

Mackey, R. (2017, October 4). Massive protests in Catalonia as general strike is observed. *The Intercept.* Retrieved from https://theintercept.com/2017/10/03/massive-protests-catalonia-general-strike-observed/

Marsden, S. (2017, October 3). Catalan referendum: Thousands strike and take to the streets to protest against police violence. *The Independent.* Retrieved from www.independent.co.uk/news/world/europe/catalan-referendum-general-strike-barcelona-protests-a7981716.html

Mason, P. (2017, October 3). 'We are with you Catalunya' – the revolt in Spain is bigger than flags and language. *The Guardian.* Retrieved from www.theguardian.com/commentisfree/2017/oct/02/catalans-independence-revolt-spain-independence-flags

McGrath, M. (2018, March). Written evidence submitted by M C McGrath. Retrieved from http://data.parliament.uk/writtenevidence/committeeevidence.svc/evidencedocument/digital-culture-media-and-sport-committee/fake-news/written/80989.html

McKie, D., & Xifra, J. (2016). Expanding critical space: Public intellectuals, public relations and an 'outsider' contribution. In J. L'Etang, D. McKie, N. Snow, & J. Xifra (Eds.), *The Routledge handbook of critical public relations* (pp. 349–359). Abingdon, England: Routledge.

Merkel calls Rajoy asking for explanations, other European leaders start to comment (2017, October 1). *El Nacional.* Retrieved from www.elnacional.cat/en/news/merkel-calls-rajoy-explanations-catalan-referendum_197541_102.html

Moloney, K., & McKie, D. (2016). Changes to be encouraged: Radical turns in PR theorisation and small-step evolutions in PR practice. In J. L'Etang, D. McKie, N. Snow, & J. Xifra (Eds.), *The Routledge handbook of critical public relations* (pp. 151–161). Abingdon, England: Routledge.

O'Brien, M. (2019). Activists as pioneers in PR: Historical frameworks and the suffragette movement. In A. Adi (Ed.), *Protest public relations: Communicating dissent and activism* (pp. 44–64). Abingdon, England: Routledge.

Orihuela, R., & Mayes, J. (2017, September 28). Tweety Pie gets caught up in spat over Catalonia referendum. *Bloomberg.* Retrieved from www.bloomberg.com/news/articles/2017-09-27/tweety-pie-gets-caught-up-in-spat-over-catalonia-referendum

Palmer, E. (2017, November 17). Spain Catalonia: Did Russian 'fake news' stir things up? *BBC.* Retrieved from www.bbc.com/news/world-europe-41981539

PP official compares Puigdemont to executed leader. (2017, October 9). *Catalan News.* Retrieved from www.catalannews.com/politics/item/pp-official-compares-puigdemont-to-executed-leader

Raymont, H. (1971). Casals is acclaimed in concert at U.N. *New York Times*. Retrieved from www.nytimes.com/1971/10/25/archives/casals-is-acclaimed-in-concert-at-un-casals-conducting-hymn-at-un.html

Rogers, J. (2017, October 1). Catalonia referendum: Merkel demands answers from Rajoy over police actions. *Express*. Retrieved from www.express.co.uk/news/world/861102/Catalonia-referendum-independence-Angela-Merkel-Mariano-Rajoy-Guardia-Civil

Rolandi, A. (2018, April 20). Report refutes Spanish claims of Catalan 'fake news'. *Catalan News*. Retrieved from www.catalannews.com/society-science/item/report-refutes-spanish-claims-of-catalan-fake-news

Russell, K., & Lamme, M. (2017). Public relations history through women's eyes. *Media Report to Women, 45*(4), 5, 23.

Schools open all over Catalonia to prevent police from sealing them off. (2017, September 30). *Ara*. Retrieved from www.ara.cat/en/Schools-Catalonia-prevent-police-sealing_0_1879012347.html

Serrano, I. (2013). Just a matter of identity? Support for independence in Catalonia. *Regional and Federal Studies, 23*(5), 523–545.

Spain's day of shame: How the world reacts to Catalonia crisis. (2017, October 2). *The Local*. Retrieved from www.thelocal.es/20171002/catalonia-crisis-how-the-world-reacts

Spain's Guardia Civil shuts down ANC's website, the platform opens another in under two hours. (2017, September 27). *Ara*. Retrieved from www.ara.cat/en/Spains-Guardia-Civil-ANCs-platform_0_1877212356.html

Spanish government announces seizure of 100,000 1-O posters. (2017, September 16). *Ara*. Retrieved from www.ara.cat/en/Spanish-government-announces-seizure-posters_0_1870613119.html

Spanish police arrest Catalan officials in attempt to halt illegal independence referendum. (2017, September 20). *ABC*. Retrieved from www.abc.net.au/news/2017-09-20/spanish-police-arrest-catalan-officials-to-halt-referendum/8966006

Spanish police enters HQ of several Catalan newspapers. (2017, September 16). *Ara*. Retrieved from www.ara.cat/en/Spanish-HQ-several-Catalan-newspapers_0_1870613118.html

Stothard, M. (2017, October 10). Madrid warns of jail risk for Catalan leader. *Financial Times*. Retrieved from www.ft.com/content/ae1fca4c-acd0-11e7-aab9-abaa44b1e130

Tàrrega, M. (2017, September 30). Spain's disregard for Catalan press freedom is setting a dangerous precedent. *The Conversation*. Retrieved from https://theconversation.com/spains-disregard-for-catalan-press-freedom-is-setting-a-dangerous-precedent-84922

Tedó, X. (2017, October 3). How the Catalan referendum was hatched in Elna. *Ara*. Retrieved from www.ara.cat/en/How-Catalan-referendum-hatched-Elna_0_1880811970.html

Tufekci, Z. (2017). *Twitter and tear gas: The power and fragility of networked protest*. New Haven, CT: Yale University Press.

Vela, J., & Xifra, J. (2015). International representation strategies for stateless nations: The case of Catalonia's cultural diplomacy. *Place Branding and Public Diplomacy, 11*(1), 83–96.

Violent clashes erupt as Spanish court jails Catalonia leaders. (2019, October 14). *BBC News*. Retrieved from www.bbc.com/news/world-europe-49974289

Weaver, K. (2019). The slow conflation of public relations and activism: Understanding trajectories in public relations theorising. In A. Adi (Ed.), *Protest public relations: Communicating dissent and activism* (pp. 12–28). Abingdon, England: Routledge.

Wilson, K. (2005, September). Activists: How to beat them at their own game. *The Australia Institute, 44*, 1–3.

Xifra, J. (2008). Soccer, civil religion, and public relations: Devotional – promotional communication and Barcelona football club. *Public Relations Review, 34*(2), 192–198.

Xifra, J., & McKie, D. (2012). From realpolitik to noopolitik: The public relations of (stateless) nations in an information age. *Public Relations Review, 38*, 819–824.

10 Critical reflections

Kate Fitch and Judy Motion

Introduction

As we were almost ready to submit our book to the publisher, a video and then a hashtag, #TooStrongForYouKaren, began trending in Australia. The video showed a white couple, Rob and Karen, challenging their Indigenous neighbours about their Indigenous identity and Karen tugging at the Aboriginal flag they were flying on their car. The Indigenous father videoed some of the interaction and at one point said 'it's too strong for you Karen' as she failed to remove the flag from the car sitting in his own driveway. The reaction online was swift. The white couple and their places of employment in Mildura, Australia were quickly identified and shared via social media. Rob was a franchisee for two McDonald's stores. Boycotts of those stores were quickly organised and a sit-in arranged for the Mildura store the next day. Poor, but some rather witty, food reviews were posted by 'customers' of those stores and memes and remixes of Karen pulling at the flag quickly emerged online. Within hours, someone had cut the video of Karen into a genuine McDonald's advertisement about supporting armed forces and the nation's flag bearers. Within two days, Indigenous rapper, Adam Briggs had mixed a short video featuring Karen and the flag, drawing on his song performed as part of a duo act: A.B. Original's 'January 26' about Australia Day (often referred to as Invasion Day or Survival Day by Indigenous Australians) but including the spoken words 'Too Strong for You Karen'. The daughter of the couple who were racially abused then made t-shirts featuring the hashtag to sell (she was a t-shirt designer). The local Member of Parliament was interviewed and condemned racism. On Sunday morning, McDonald's Director of Corporate Relations issued a short statement to the media, confirming Rob's franchisee relationship with McDonald's had ended.

We include this event because it encapsulates many of the themes around social justice and popular culture in our book, and the ways in which popular culture affords opportunities for creative resistance and social change. It also highlights the public relations work at play, through communicative activity by individuals and activists, by elected members of parliament and other prominent figures, by Indigenous organisations and government departments, and finally by McDonald's in their need to respond to public concerns. The #TooStrongForYouKaren example illustrates public discourse around race emerging in creative ways, using song, video, memes, food reviews and t-shirts as well as via social media and more traditional media, which serve to highlight a serious social justice issue. For activists, popular culture is an important site for producing new meanings, a vision for the future and a place to build communities. We therefore investigated the ways in which a more community-driven conceptualisation of public relations can be harnessed in social change.

We make visible in this book different dimensions of public relations work in popular culture and social change in order to conceptualise the positive social and environmental justice work public relations can do. Social change often evolves from community spaces and organising; it also emerges from social movements, which are collective, purposive and strategic. The work undertaken in these spaces not only influences popular culture but also transforms our understandings of how public relations may be deployed to meaningfully engage publics. But the ways public relations is deployed to do good work, to make issues matter, is under-researched and under-theorised.

This book has therefore addressed a significant gap in the literature by exploring the entanglement of public relations and popular culture and the potential of public relations to be harnessed in support of social justice and bring about rights-based social change. *Popular Culture and Social Change* opens up critical scholarship on public relations to explore alternative and eclectic communicative cultures. Public relations' meaning making, mattering and sometimes pleasure making is neglected in more linear and strategic framing of public relations that attempt to evaluate and measure campaign success through pre-determined objectives and key performance indicators. Addressing concerns about the negativity of critical public relations (see Vardeman-Winter, 2016), this book proposes a more optimistic conceptualisation of public relations as a resource for progressive social change in order to better understand the (often subterranean) societal impacts and cultural influence of public relations activity. It concludes that public relations creates popular cultures that are deeply compromised and commercialised, but, at the same time, can be harnessed to advocate for social change in supporting, reproducing, challenging or resisting the status quo.

This chapter is structured in three sections. This first section identifies the significance of expanding understandings of public relations and its relationship with popular culture and social change. The second section discusses the diverse chapter contributions that range across music, fashion, rebellion, fortune telling, and social movements to explore the ways public relations influences the production of popular culture and, how alternative, often community-driven conceptualisations of public relations work, can be harnessed for social change and in pursuit of social justice. The final section presents a theoretical framework to address the critical questions we raised in Chapter 1, in order to understand how a reconceptualised understanding of public relations advances social, cultural and environmental justice.

Chapter contributions

Given our interest is in the ways in which public relations is entangled with our everyday lives, many of our chapters engaged with contemporary cultural trends: from zombies and influencers to fashion and forecasting. Our chapters identified and engaged with aspects of culture in everyday life because we wanted to explore both the embeddedness of public relations in culture and its multiple and complicated engagements with culture. We also wanted to investigate agency in engaging and resisting such public relations activity and how everyday experiences can be critical spaces for social transformation. For this reason, we have included auto-ethnographic chapters reflecting on our own experiences and engagement with public relations and with communicative resistance across very different spheres.

In the opening chapter, we established the role public relations plays in popular culture through meaning making. Our interest in popular culture is the ways its concern with the everyday and its entanglement with consumption and production also offers potential for creative resistance and social transformation. We argued that studying the intersection of public relations and popular culture enables a stronger understanding of power and public relations in contemporary culture.

In Chapter 2, we theorised the ways public relations normalises power relations by identifying how public relations activity routinely seeks to socialise our everyday lives. This public relations activity also raises questions for us around agency, particularly in relation to consumption, and the ways we become 'willing vehicles of power' (Foucault, 1980). Free agency may be an illusion, given these choices are in fact made from limited options inflected by public relations; however, a range of agentic possibilities were identified including embodied force; contingent preferences; civility; and justice-oriented, rights-based systems of decision making. Although discourses of public relations may attempt to frame many aspects of our lives, the concept of communicative rights was introduced as a potential counterbalance and set of guidelines for how public relations may perform within popular culture.

In Chapter 3, we observed that much public relations work in creating trends is in fact mundane and mimetic. The creation of trends has little to do with social justice and environmental issues but instead mimics already recognisable phenomena to leverage and monetise popularity. Rather than forecasting future trends, public relations here borrows from popular culture in ways that are mimetic and imitative and closes down opportunities for agency and genuine social change. Alternative discourses of positivity were identified as moments that open up possibilities for reconfiguring popular culture and, more generally, society.

In Chapter 4, we theorised the links between neoliberalism and public relations, noting that public relations inserts neoliberal values into the everyday. This is an important aspect of the 'hidden work' of public relations. Using the cultural trope of the zombie, we investigated how the zombie is an apt metaphor for understanding public relations as an industry and as an occupational practice. Public relations work is founded on promoting commercial interests even as it inserts empty, 'democratic' rhetoric around engagement and empowerment of publics into the everyday.

In Chapter 5, we theorised how power is inscribed in social practices and institutional norms, illustrated through the aesthetic labour required of female public relations practitioners to stay on trend and be cool. While the representations in this chapter are of practitioners who work primarily in consumer and lifestyle consultancy sectors, they nevertheless illustrate how the body is a 'variable boundary' (Butler, 2008) for cultural and political signification. We found that the commodification of the mediated practitioner body is closely linked with entrepreneurship and employability.

In Chapter 6, we continued with the theme of body and dress, by investigating mattering and fashion, and the ways in which fashion choices by prominent women can be powerful statements. That is, particular messages are advanced through aesthetic choices. For example, Melania Trump's failure to successfully engage with the popular is often linked with her dress choices, whereas Michelle Obama's fashion selection often elevated or opened up possibilities for change. Mattering is positioned as a critical concept for understanding how public relations efforts may drive positive social change.

In Chapter 7, we explored the important role public relations might play in reconciliation, and therefore offer an alternative conceptualisation of public relations where it plays a prominent and positive role in social justice and social change. In seeking a more transformative public relations in this book, one concerned with social justice, we embrace the opportunities to persuade, transform and resist. That is, we are interested in the ways in which public relations, as work performed by individuals as well as by organisations, can intervene in existing power relations and knowledge structures in positive ways.

In Chapter 8, our investigation of environmental protest songs explored how they offer both a mode for circulating alternative truths and perspectives and contribute to the development of civic imagination (Jenkins, Shresthova, Gamber-Thompson, Kligler-Vilenchik, & Zimmerman, 2016). From a public relations perspective, we treat these songs as generative modes of protests that expand understanding and knowledge. They are affective, in that they draw attention to concerns and suggest ways that issues come to matter. The analysis also provides insights into how a careful undoing of human exceptionalism – our attempts to place ourselves outside of and master nature – is necessary for developing equitable multispecies relations and addressing climate change.

In Chapter 9, we developed understandings of activist public relations, specifically using the concepts of protest PR and dissent PR, drawing on the work of Adi (2019) and Moloney and McKie (2016). We considered the ways these forms of public relations enabled protestors and dissenters to contribute to public and political debate about Catalan independence. The framing of Catalan national identity as a social justice issue was amplified through communication efforts, various forms of collective resistance and public diplomacy and enabled publics to become active publics.

In this concluding chapter, we summarise the major contributions of the book. We present a theoretical framework on public relations, popular culture and social change that builds on key themes that emerged from these chapters.

Theorising public relations, popular culture and social change

The main contribution of this book is to offer a cultural analysis of public relations in our everyday lives and of its potential for promoting social critique and justice. In exploring the complicated relationship between popular culture and social change, and the intermediary role that public relations plays in traversing political, professional, cultural and civic boundaries to support, reproduce or challenge the status quo, we found tension between popular and promotional cultures. Public relations is transformative in that it creates publics and opportunities for engagement but it tends to do so in line with a neoliberal logic (Cronin, 2018).

We subtitled this book 'the hidden work of public relations' because we wanted to expose subterranean aspects of public relations work. We began this book with thinking about how public relations work oscillates between visibility and invisibility, and how it is often conceptualised in terms of the 'behind the scenes' and manipulative aspects of professional practice. However, we concluded that the significant impact of public relations, in terms of framing public discourse and meaning making, was more insidious. Davis's (2013) description of public relations as a Trojan horse is apt. Although the democratising framing of public relations as engagement and dialogue appears to offer representation and agency, it, as Cronin (2018) argues, inflects the everyday with market discourse and neoliberal language. However, public relations can also be employed to resist dominant narratives and meanings, and engage with culture to offer forms of creative resistance. This activity is significant but not always obvious.

We played with ideas of boundary riding as a mode of enquiry to allow us to navigate the complex entanglement between public relations, popular culture and social change. We wanted to make the sociocultural impact of public relations work more visible and found that this impact extends beyond serving organisational interests in terms of addressing business goals. Public relations activity informs meaning making and identity construction in multiple, contradictory ways. Our endeavour to consider the ways public relations is transformative and can bring about social change concerned with human rights and social and environmental justice demanded an approach that allowed us to open up traditional ways of thinking around public relations and to conceptualise how it might be harnessed by activists and others interested in social change.

We argue that public relations is deployed to play a double game within popular culture – neoliberal agendas are advanced that undermine progressive social change while, simultaneously, cultural forms of social critique are promoted to advocate for social, cultural and environmental justice. Popular culture is thus a contested and compromised space with competing agendas. Investigating public relations interventions in popular culture offers an ideal opportunity to think through the complexities of various pursuits of social and cultural authority, integrity and justice, discern multiple ways in which the dominance of, for example, sexism, racism and anti-environmentalism may be undermined, and understand how the importance and value of our everyday experiences may be reasserted within popular culture.

In this book, we have engaged with understandings of public relations that are playful, creative and culturally resonant. We put resistance and playfulness at the centre of things, by taking elements of popular culture and using them to think through contemporary issues concerning the various roles of public relations. Chapter 4 used zombies to consider the ways in which public relations work often remains in the shadows; it allows us to excavate traditional boundaries for, and mainstream ways of thinking about, public relations. Chapter 8 identified the playful satires in protest music that highlight our comical assumptions about ourselves and our relations with nature. This playfulness is an important contribution and constitutes a form of creative resistance. We have documented some of this resistance in relation to real protests. For example, we noted the ludic qualities in the Catalan independence protests in Chapter 9. The absurd use of a trademarked cartoon character, Tweety Pie, known for its wiliness and adaptability in outwitting its foe, became a symbol for the Catalan independence narrative around pushing back and outwitting the Spanish police force. This playfulness brings a dynamic and transgressive dimension to communicating to persuade and transform.

Studying the relationship between popular culture, public relations and social change makes a significant contribution to understanding how social and cultural practices take shape and the potential for transformation. As a vehicle for social change, public relations traverses boundaries to support, reproduce, challenge or resist the status quo and help establish the conditions for social change. Dominant discourses can be undone by narrating alternative discourses and perspectives and undermining boundaries of thinking determined in part by public relations work. Researching community-driven and participatory forms of public relations therefore enables a better understanding of how public relations might be harnessed to challenge existing knowledge and power structures in order to bring about positive social change and social justice.

Conclusion

This book contributes new understandings to public relations and its role in society. It builds on critical scholarship on public relations, and the ways public relations is bound up with power and knowledge, to investigate its involvement in popular culture and social change. This chapter discussed three key ideas. First, we conceptualise public relations as communicative activity that engages with meaning making, and recognise that this activity is not the exclusive domain of corporate and government sectors. Rather, we identify the contradictory ways public relations engages with popular culture in terms of a double game: commodifying culture to promote organisational self-interest, inflecting culture with neoliberal and promotional discourse, and drawing on culture to offer – and construct – alternative narratives and meanings. We view public relations practitioners as cultural intermediaries, whose promotional work uses popular culture as a resource, and recognise meanings are co-created, challenged and reappropriated in promotional work (Davis, 2013; Edwards, 2018). Second, we argue that activists, artists, community and civic groups use public relations to render visible, popularise and influence issues of concern. They draw on popular culture to represent and frame issues in alternative discourses, to reconfigure relationships and to undertake affective work. That is, public relations can contribute to social change and be employed to promote social justice. Third, popular culture offers a creative, critical and transformative space for exploring transgression and resistance and therefore an important space for exploring power and the role of public relations in contemporary culture. The work undertaken in these spaces not only influences popular culture but it also transforms our understandings of how public relations may be deployed to meaningfully engage with publics and how active publics use public relations to bring about social change.

References

Adi, A. (Ed.). (2019). *Protest public relations: Communicating dissent and activism.* Abingdon, England: Routledge.

Butler, J. (2008). *Gender trouble: Feminism and the subversion of identity.* Abingdon, England: Routledge.

Cronin, A. M. (2018). *Public relations capitalism: Promotional culture, publics and commercial democracy.* Cham, Switzerland: Palgrave Macmillan.

Davis, A. (2013). *Promotional cultures.* Cambridge, England: Polity Press.

Edwards, L. (2018). *Understanding public relations: Theory, culture and society.* London, England: Sage.

Foucault, M. (1980). *Power/knowledge: Selected interviews & other writings 1972–1977 by Michel Foucault.* New York, NY: Pantheon.

Jenkins, H., Shresthova, S., Gamber-Thompson, L., Kligler-Vilenchik, N., & Zimmerman, A. (2016). *By any media necessary: The new youth activism.* New York, NY: New York University Press.

Moloney, K., & McKie, D. (2016). Changes to be encouraged: Radical turns in PR theorisation and small-step evolutions in PR practice. In J. L'Etang, D. McKie, N. Snow, & J. Xifra (Eds.), *The Routledge handbook of critical public relations* (pp. 151–161). Abingdon, England: Routledge.

Vardeman-Winter, J. (2016). 'Critical public relations is so critical!' Objections, counterobjections, and practical applications to critical-cultural public relations work. In J. L'Etang, D. McKie, N. Snow, & J. Xifra (Eds.), *The Routledge handbook of critical public relations* (pp. 185–199). Abingdon, England: Routledge.

Index

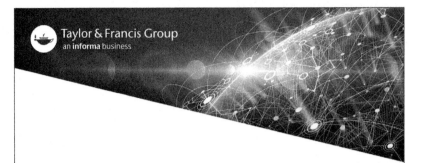

Printed in the United States
By Bookmasters